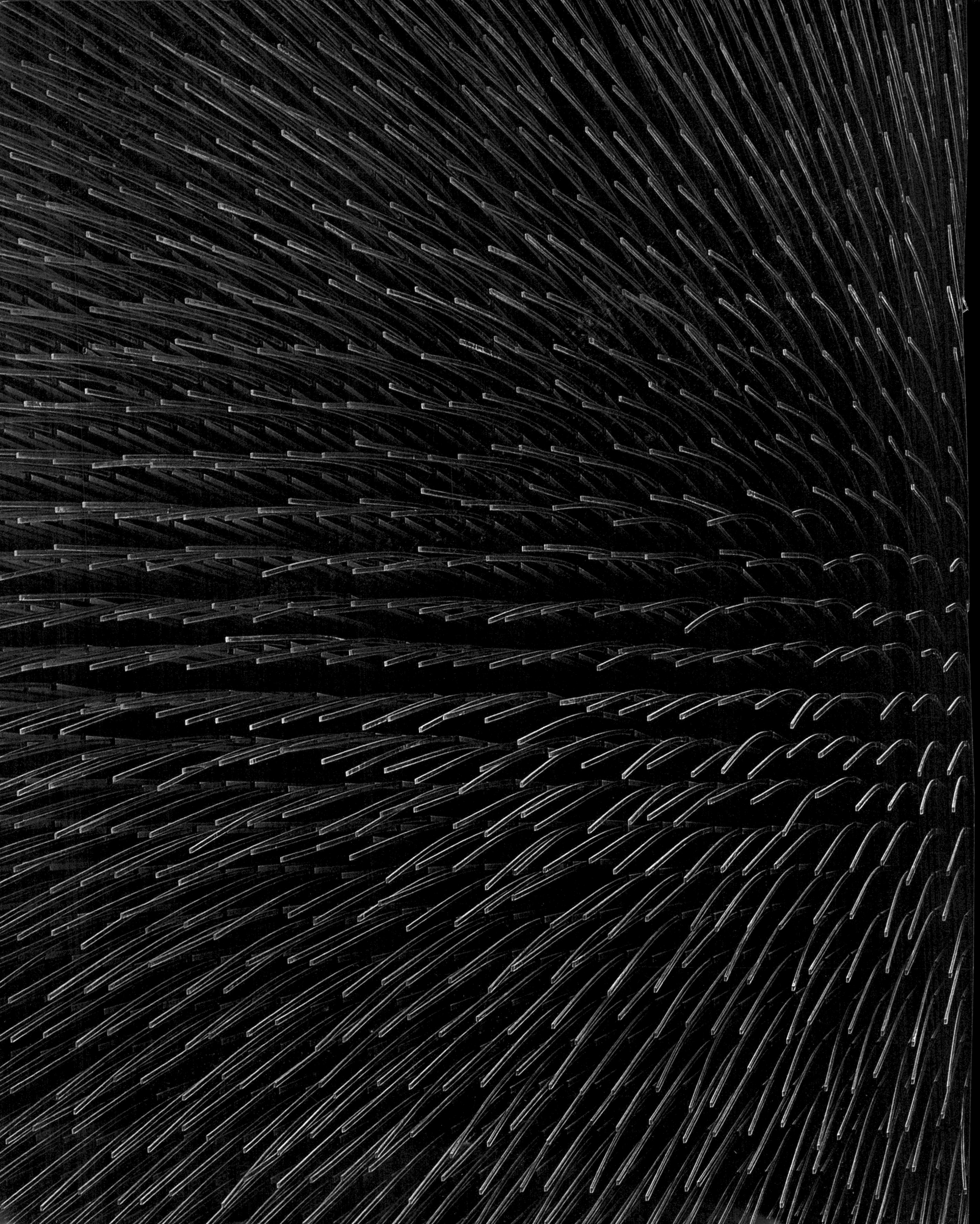

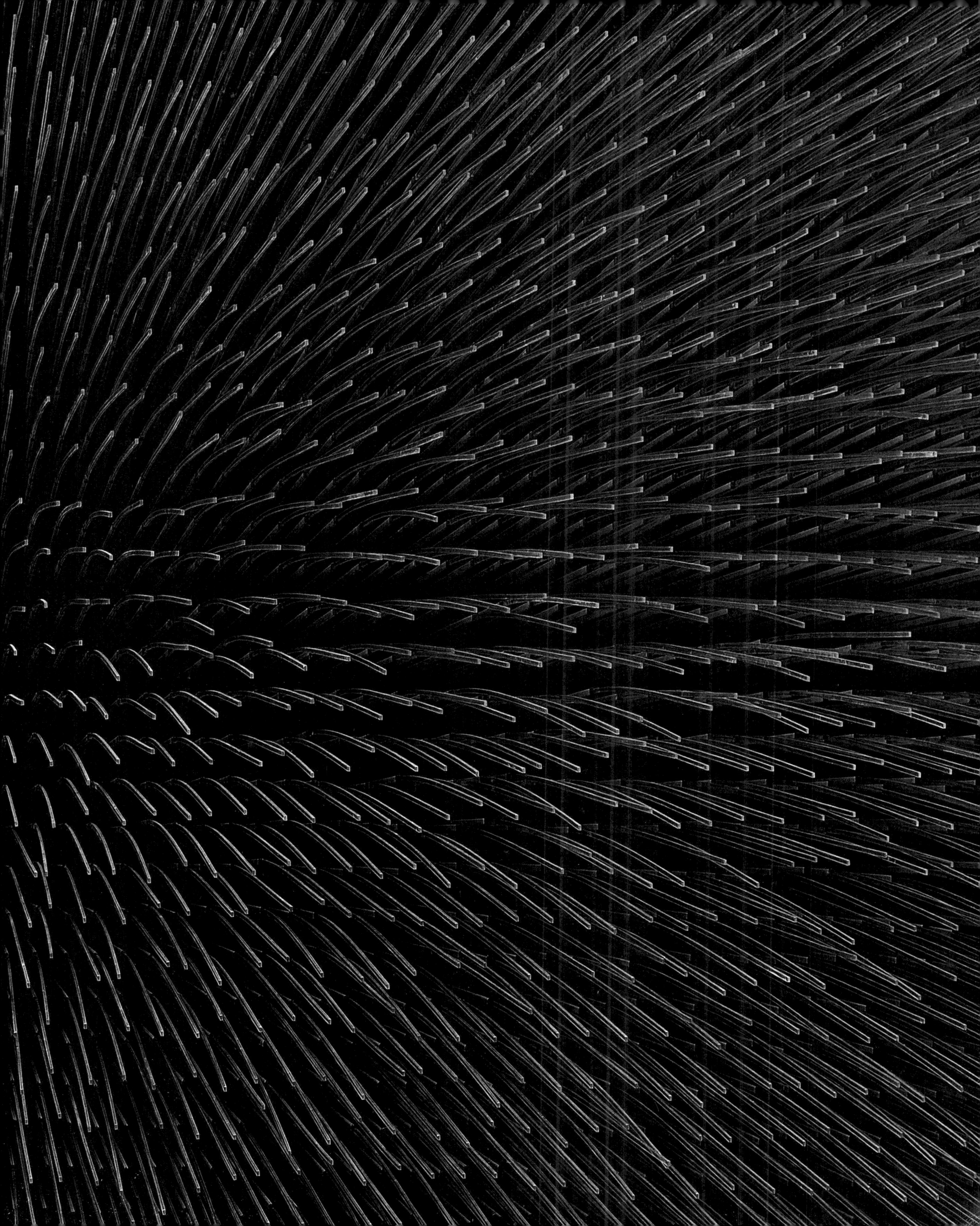

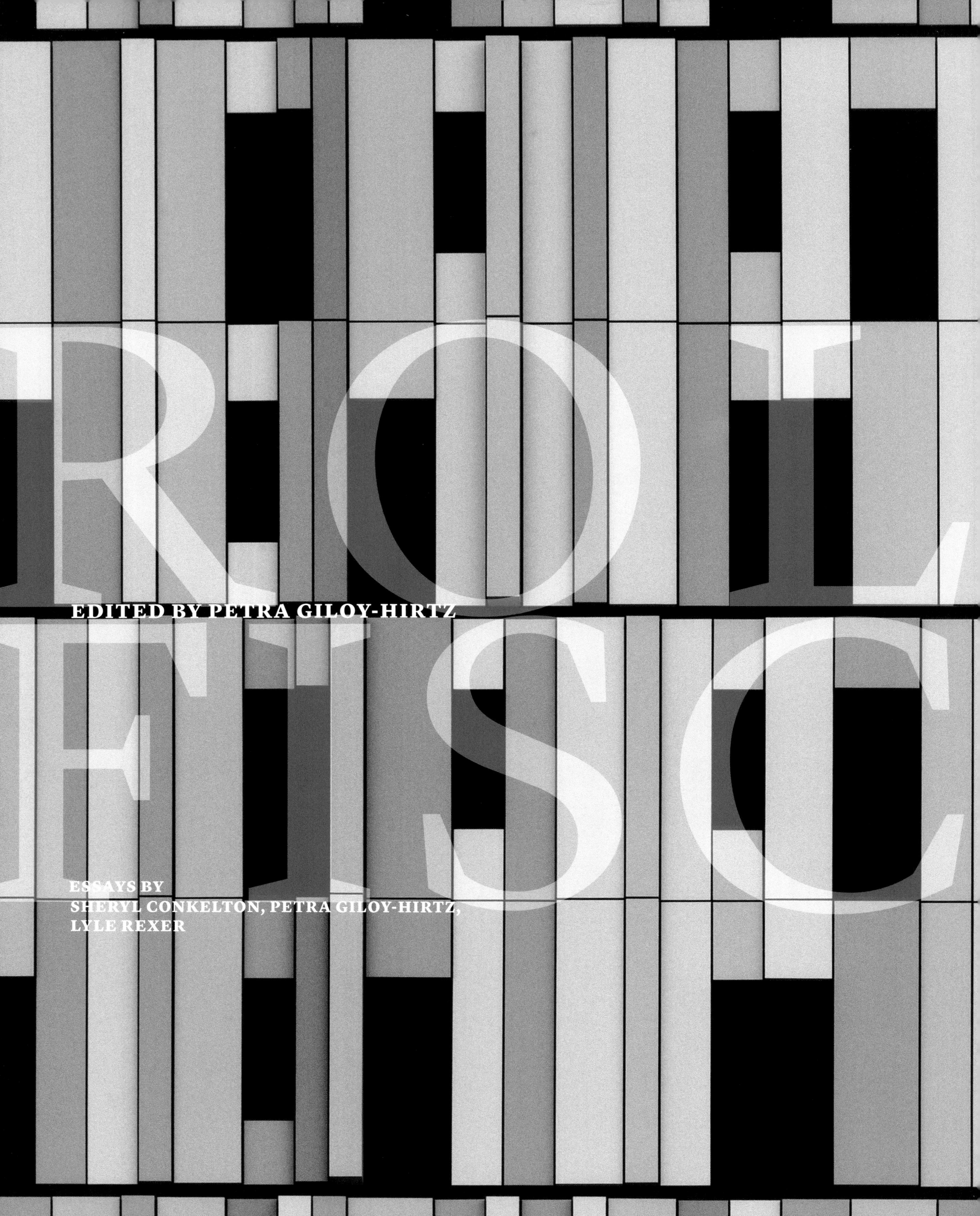
EDITED BY PETRA GILOY-HIRTZ
ESSAYS BY
SHERYL CONKELTON, PETRA GILOY-HIRTZ,
LYLE REXER

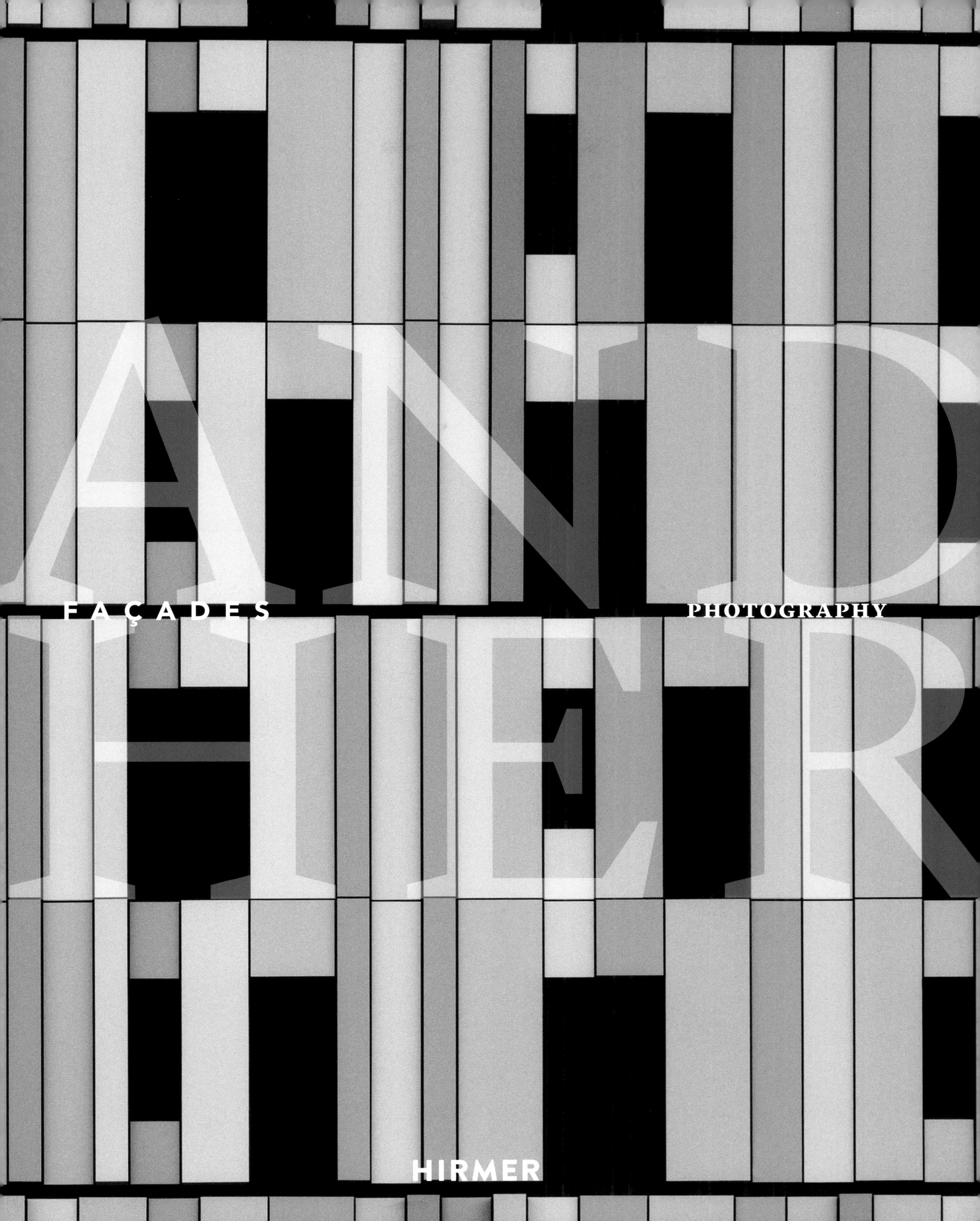
FAÇADES
PHOTOGRAPHY
HIRMER

A VOCABULARY OF URBAN SURFACES
ROLAND FISCHER'S UNIVERSAL SYMBOLS OF A NEW ORDER

Petra Giloy-Hirtz is a curator and author. Her recent publications and exhibitions include *Julian Schnabel: Polaroids*, The Hague Museum of Photography (2011); *David Lynch: The Factory Photographs*, The Photographers' Gallery, London (2014); *Dennis Hopper: The Lost Album*, Royal Academy of Arts, London (2014). She lives in Munich.

PETRA GILOY-HIRTZ

ICONOGRAPHY OF THE METROPOLIS

Lines, grids, rhombuses; circle, rectangle, and square; color fields characterized by strict reduction and highly aesthetic: an inventory of forms and structures. Photographs resembling painting. Rather than invented and constructed by a creative mind, they are found in cities and captured by camera. They are portraits: countenances of the urban environment, surfaces of buildings. Since the 1990s, Roland Fischer has photographed the façades of banks, corporations, and museums in the metropolises of the world. The images, a series of about a hundred façades, add up to a compendium of contemporary architecture, to a visual grammar of abstract forms. The face of new urbanity is transformed in images, similar to abstract paintings, replete with art-historical references. They tell of the way the world has changed, of a new global paradigm where money, technology, people, and goods flow unchecked across borders. Its aesthetic appearance is not rooted in the specific socio-cultural context; indeed, the iconography of signs is independent of geography, be it in Beijing, Tokyo, Shanghai, New York, Hong Kong, Melbourne, Osaka, Boston, Brasilia, Los Angeles, Paris, São Paulo, Singapore, Dallas, Madrid, Washington, Chicago, Toronto, Chongqing, or Montreal. The "image repertoire of a city," its "categories of representation"[1] are homogenized supra-nationally.

1 Richard Sennett, *Flesh and Stone. The Body and the City in Western Civilization* (New York: Norton, 1994), 366.

PHOTOGRAPHY AFTER *DOCUMENTARY REALISM*

Roland Fischer's interest in architecture is not conceptually different from his interest in the human face. Just as his *Nuns and Monks*, the *Los Angeles Portraits*, the *Collective Portraits of Soldiers*, *Workers*, *Farmers* and *Students* and the *Pilgrims* are not portraits in a traditional sense, the *Façades* do not continue the tradition of documentary photography. Fischer has always been interested not so much in "representation as in the image," in abstraction.[2] In his series of cathedrals, for instance, he superimposes the exterior walls of a structure on its interior, so as to penetrate the shell and reveal the inside. Or he simultaneously combines, in a Cubist manner, views of secular modern spaces and structures photographed from various standpoints as in the *New Architectures* series. From a distance, his tableau of 1,050 individual photographs of pilgrims in Santiago de Compostela appears abstract like a pattern on a façade.

2 Roland Fischer, "Interview with Agar Ledo," in *Roland Fischer, Camino* (exh. cat., Centro Galego de Arte Contemporánea, Santiago de Compostela / Diözesanmuseum Freising, 2003/04), 53.

Roland Fischer already photographed urban surfaces when he was still living in Los Angeles, yet only in the metropolises of China did a conceptual project grow out of his interest in high-rise façades. "I was able to encapsulate two key aspects of the medium of photography here: the fact that each and every pixel of a photograph is always connected to reality, and the independent appearance of a photograph as an image without reference. From a distance one could perceive these photographs quasi as Color Field paintings, at the same time however they remain a 'classic' picture of an object that can be seen somewhere. In the photographic image both aspects are interwoven and each detail has a dual meaning."[3] On the wall the photographs—technically perfect C-prints on acrylic measuring 180 by 125 centimeters, unframed and reflecting the light—appear like objects.

3 Fischer, 54f.

GLOBAL MASKS OF THE URBAN

What can photography do? What stories does it tell? How can its imagery be read? What statements does it make about the state of the world? When Fischer's works show façades, they reduce the buildings to their surfaces, to design, décor, ornament. They present the skin that protects and hides the interior—the technology, the function and the people working or living inside—from the public. They do not show dwellings or the human dimension. Their specificity lies in absolute reduction: neither sky nor earth nor any environment serves to frame a subject or provide a backdrop. Rather, the subjects are isolated from any context and transformed into abstract images—each time a section standing for the whole, a *pars pro toto*, each time different and yet strangely standardized, be it an industrial corporation, a bank, a hotel, a university, a prison, the headquarters of a labor union, a city hall, or a luxury store. The specific subject, place, and time are only indicated by the title of the work.

These "façades" appear like commentaries on power, appropriation, and assimilation. With the global dissemination of capital and technology the architecture of the city has changed. That is, not just through an "International Style" that developed from a desire to overcome the individual, the local, the national. Interiors seal themselves off—"fortress architecture"[4]—behind impenetrable façades.

4 Michael Hardt and Antonio Negri, *Empire* (Cambridge: Harvard University Press, 2000), 337.

GEOMETRY AND INTERPRETATIVE MODELS

Roland Fischer unfurls a wealth of images in the photographs of his *Façades* series—a compendium of symmetries, similarities, and differences. Where do those forms come from and what is behind them? Their affinity to painting is obvious in their allusions to Mondrian, Frank Stella, Peter Halley, and many others. Yet their origins lie well before European Modernism: under certain conditions of civilization and in different periods geometric forms exist—often they are archaic patterns of other cultures—that refer to the spiritual, the magical or the symbolic.[5] *Patterns That Connect*,[6] the global linkage of universal signs and symbols, points to the trove of images in collective memory that art and architecture draw on and that they, in turn, add to.

5 Jürgen Adam, *Magiciennes de la laine. Marokkanische Teppiche und die Malerei des 20. Jahrhunderts* (exh. cat., Pinakothek der Moderne: Munich, 2013), 16.

6 To quote the title of a study by American art historian Carl Schuster, *Patterns That Connect: Social Symbolism in Ancient & Tribal Art* (New York: Harry N. Abrams, 1996).

In the 20th century, order, proportion, and balance were charged with transcendental significance. Today that "geometric mystification" has given way to other associations, such as the structural homology of geometric forms and a geometrization of social space. Inspired by the ideas of the French Structuralists—ideas that also resonate in Roland Fischer's work[7]—American painter Peter Halley describes in his essay "The Deployment of the Geometric" the transformation of the landscape, society and thought through geometry as regimentation. He sees his own painting as pictures of prisons, cells, and walls.[8] Geometry as a reference to an interconnected world. And the human aspect? In ***Flesh and Stone***, his study on the body and the city, Richard Sennett explains that "order means lack of contact."[9]

Underlying the surface of Roland Fischer's *Façades* are thus deeper layers of meaning. Either way, "what pictures want" is our attention, our "scopic drive."[10] May the viewer find aesthetic pleasure and be amazed by the fascinating visual diversity while perambulating through this volume.

7 See Roland Augustin, "Roland Fischers photographisches Werk und der Strukturalismus," in *Roland Fischer, New Photography 1984–2012* (exh. cat., Saarland Museum: Saarbrücken, 2012), 19–23.

8 Peter Halley, "The Deployment of the Geometric," in *Peter Halley, Collected Essays, 1981–1987* (Culver City [CA]: Lapis Press, 1988), 127–130.

9 Sennett, 21.

10 W.J.T. Mitchell, *What Do Pictures Want. The Lives and Loves of Images* (Chicago: University of Chicago Press, 2005), 72.

ROLAND FISCHER'S FAÇADES: ARCHITECTURE'S CLOSED LANGUAGE

Lyle Rexer is a critic, curator, and lecturer. The author of many books and articles on photography, he is a core faculty member of the School of Visual Arts in New York. He lives and works in Brooklyn.

To perceive the distance between the divine and the human, it is enough to compare these crude wavering symbols which my fallible hand scrawls on the cover of a book, with the organic letters inside: punctual, delicate, perfectly black, inimitably symmetrical.

— Jorge Luis Borges, *The Library of Babel*

Many years ago in New York there was a restaurant whose walls were papered with large black-and-white aerial photographs of many of the major cities of the world: New York, Paris, London, Buenos Aires, Rio, Mexico City, Caracas, Chicago, Los Angeles. Every time I visited I would examine this topography of urban expansion with intense fascination and growing despair, for the cities inspired in me a sense of grandeur but also a more unsettling recognition that they were all the same, that the forms of experience they embodied were fundamentally similar, shaped by identical developments and permitting none of the variations that language, climate, history, and physical geography once promoted. The modern city was the herald of global capitalism, radically homogenizing desire and marginalizing difference.

The phenomenon has expanded and intensified in a world burdened by its own growth. The survival of human beings has become unimaginable under any other system, but also, probably, impossible under this one. Hong Kong, Beijing, Guangzhou, Dubai represent additions to the global map of modern architecture without its originating myths.

The contemporary city is forged not as the members of the Bauhaus imagined it could be, as a design challenge adumbrating social renovation, but as the expression of economic rules, relations, and technological applications. The result is the same in all places: rather than the designed entities of Chandigarh and Brasilia, the entrepreneurial expansion of Shanghai, a different form of rationalization, the chance outcome of local but universally consistent decisions. In practice, the contemporary city has proven to be less unitary in form due to levels of economic inequality unimaginable to the progressive imagination: Luanda, Mexico City, New Orleans, the transborder megalopolis of the Bight of Benin.

Architecture is implicated as the form-giving process of this hyper-rationalized but unpurposed urbanism, imposing a global visual Esperanto. In this description, the efforts of individual architects, however radical their dissents or visionary their gestures, appear as centrifugal events that mark the periphery of much larger constellations, the way poetic expressions mark the border between the vast instrumental uses of language and idiosyncratic nonutilitarian ones. As he has with the genre of the portrait, photographer Roland Fischer has brought the analysis of a formal "language," in this case of modern architecture, to a terminal point.

Historically photography grew up with the appearance of modern architecture, that is, the replacement of imperial styles (and vernacular practices) by reproducible, scalable, decontextualized industrial formats. Photography's initial role was twofold: to memorialize and archive the obsolete past and to promote if not celebrate the forms and activities of the emergent metropolitan world. Photography was the only possible mode for both roles. First and foremost, its reductive two-dimensionality and black-and-white tonality emphasized the formal regularities and repetitions of the new forms. Second, its reproducibility guaranteed the proliferation of archives for a variety of administrative uses. Finally, as many critics have pointed out, its monocular perspective emphasized (or reinscribed) the rationalized geometry of utilitarian control that would make possible more efficient and productive urban settings.

Beginning in the 1970s, photographers, artists, theorists, and architects themselves began to analyze these developments and subject them to sophisticated visual and linguistic critiques. From Bernd and Hilla Becher's formal catalogues of defunct industrial structures through the "New Topographics" of American photographers, the neutrality and large-format detail of work by graduates of the Düsseldorf Art Academy, up through the digital dystopias of Beate Gütschow, a host of contemporary works have highlighted the connection between formal language and architecture as an ideological instrument. Fischer has explored this connection at its root.

His strategy is simple but its implications are far-reaching. The broad question Fischer appears to be asking is: in what sense do the generalized forms of architecture encountered repeatedly in urban settings around the world constitute a language, that is, a system of communication that operates according to rules subscribed to by its users but is independent of any specific content or situation and not subject to interventions by individual agents? To frame this investigation, Fischer has followed a basic insight of Surrealism (and of American photographers of the 1920s to 1960s) in decontextualizing his subjects, radically cropping the in-camera view to emphasize formal properties and reduce anecdotal information. A photographer such as Aaron Siskind or Minor White would have pursued such an approach in order to open up psychological, linguistic/poetic, and spiritual associations for the viewer. The photograph would form a bridge between subjectivities, a bridge whose traffic was initiated and largely controlled by the artist.

Fischer, on the other hand, emphasizes graphic form and pattern in order to reduce associations. He does not seek to fashion a sign-less, nondenotative concrete photography, along the lines of Gottfried Jäger's work (and that of many younger photographers). He has no interest in purifying his images or returning to a prelinguistic, prereferential Garden of Eden. Instead he seeks to focus undivided attention on the visual subject. Only slight temporal traces appear in the telltale shadows that mark some façades, and evidence of artistic subjectivity is limited to a few slightly angled points of view. Otherwise the views are direct and rigorously flat, isolated from any background information. Because pattern dominates, it is impossible to place the façades materially, historically, or geographically. They have no authors, periods, or locations (except as indicated by titles). Fischer's subject is not the building or the structure but the surface appearance only, and not the entire surface but a part, enough to identify a *motif*. The images give no indication of the size of the façades, and the photos themselves further obfuscate any original scale by the flexibility of their presentation: they could be printed literally any size (just as the buildings themselves could be any size). Freed (nearly) from any responsibility to account for their subjects, the images hover at the point of pure abstraction, displaying phoneme-like elements in systems of organized repetition.

The path Fischer has pursued in portraiture sheds light on the goals of his façades. In that genre he has experimented with both large-format single images and massive grids called *Collective Portraits*. More important, however, has been the photographic treatment of the subjects themselves. In choosing monks and nuns for a series from the 1980s, he renewed discussion of the idea that photographic portraits could provide access to the interiority of the sitter or for that matter lead to any conclusions about anything beyond appearances, on the other side of the picture. The photographs had a remarkable impact, especially on critics such as the American Michael Fried, precisely because they refused to decide the question one way or another. His mostly elderly figures in their religious habits bear the lines of age on their faces, the topography of apparent experience, but no life events or mental states can be inferred from the surfaces. Viewers can speculate on the individual decisions that led these people to join their orders; but sealed by their vocation their lives are enigmas that hide in plain sight.

Begun a decade later, the series of pool portraits shot in Los Angeles and later in China offered far less of their subjects, less even than the deadpan portraits of Thomas Ruff and Thomas Struth. Fischer immersed the subjects in water up to their shoulders and posed them devoid of emotion and shorn of identifying accoutrements. If one intention of the Düsseldorf School was to grant the subjects autonomy from the photographer's (and the audience's) projections, Fischer pushed past that political position to liberate their appearances from any pre-existing conditions of reality. Especially with the *Chinese Pool Portraits*, there is so little about which to speculate that we are thrown back on the elements of the face, or rather the elements of faciality, of photographic facial appearance already minimized (to Western eyes at least) by the selection of young, unblemished Asian "façades." The slight variations in pose seemed to constitute a kind of lexicon or inventory of attitudes without corresponding emotions.

The overall effect of Fischer's portraits is to revise the concept of the photographic sign and to reconstitute the viewer's relation to the object. As Julia Kristeva suggests about abstract painting, Fischer's portraits elaborate a signifying process that analyzes the components of what was originally given as the foundation of representation. Or, put another way, the portraits thematize aspects of photography that conventions of the image had made invisible. They pave the way for the rigor of the façades.

Buildings as actualities can only be inferred from their façades, which function as synecdoches, parts that hint at the larger wholes. But the larger wholes are simple multiplications of design elements and demand our attention not merely as formal objects but as elements of communication. A strict linguistic approach is less useful here than a semiotic one. What and how do the façades communicate in these photographs? First of all they present a code, but strictly limited. They indicate industrial forms of construction based on precise and consistent repetition, and these forms can be applied across a wide range of cultural and geographic settings—Le Corbusier's Modulor. The patterns are individual but not in any sense local or vernacular. Closely related to the idea of repetition is their non-organic, geometric structure. There is no way to measure them against a human scale through the evidence of handwork or spontaneity, or for that matter through gestures of individual architectural style or material ("that's a Gehry"; "that's a Hadid"). Nor do they recall the patterning of medieval Christian and Muslim decoration, whose goal was to lead the eye toward infinity. If infinity is celebrated in today's forms, it is the infinity of an expanding network of financial institutions capable of raising such structures almost overnight. Fischer's achievement here is to show us in essence the dominance and continuity of modern architectural practice. At the same time, the reduction of the façades to their design properties reveals once again the cognate visual practices of concrete art from diverse positions over the last eight decades, from the Constructivism of Mondrian to the *fisicromia* of Carlos Cruz-Diez, the Neo-Concretism of Lygia Clark, and the Op art of Bridget Riley, to the typographic paintings of Tauba Auerbach, among others. Taken together they seem mere illustrations of Johannes Itten's Basic Course in design at the Bauhaus. Fischer's images echo them all.

Modern architecture—corporate commercial and civic architecture—has absorbed and recycled these positions to produce aesthetic gestures devoid of spiritual ambitions. They delimit a space for the aesthetic in architecture (and society) that is purely visual. The common fantasy of previous avant-garde movements in art and design was the belief that abstraction in whatever form was a means and measure of liberation. Aesthetic/artistic movements could divorce themselves from or transform economic forces, and in the process of remaking consciousness, remake social relations.

This turning away from obdurate (class-based) reality in favor of aesthetic theory has been endlessly criticized, but Fischer, like Gerhard Richter, underscores what the world looks like on the other side of abstraction. With Richter's recent stripe "paintings" (and with those of Wade Guyton in the United States), the entire history of modern painting's various ambitions comes to a close in the purging of any possibility of content-related gesture. These are large design objects that exist to occupy a specific economic role and physical place within collections of like objects, similar to a currency that is printed in different colors but is stored in bank vaults and spent in the same old way.

Similarly, Fischer's façades imply that what occurs inside the contemporary office building has no perspicuous relation to the patterns presented on the outside except that in some sense both are abstract, the former dealing with data management and capital flows, the later with the "flow" of design through the circuits of urban expansion and consumption. Again, this has nothing to do with whether the individual buildings might be perceived as beautiful, inspiring, necessary, or even transformative in a limited sense. The *Façades* series (ideally Fischer would multiply them to near infinity) communicates the message of their own ubiquity, interchangeability, and replaceability. They form a perfected language, infinitely diverse in its vocabulary but limited in its syntax. They reflect a perfected present without a past, the end of history without an apocalypse.

FAÇADES

Sheryl Conkelton is a curator, writer, and educator currently living in Houston.

Roland Fischer's series *Façades* presents very abstracted images of building façades. Stripped of contingencies of shadow and movement, tightly cropped to eliminate any specification of location or other connection to subject, and reduced to geometric formations, they appear resistant to interpretation. Their subjects are revealed only in their titles: *Suntory, Tokyo*; *Museum, Munich*; *nab, Melbourne*; *Uniqlo, Osaka*; *Wells Fargo, Dallas*; *Holiday Inn, São Paolo*; *Iglesias, Mexico City*; *High School, Utrecht*—a roster of corporations and institutions from around the globe. In the familiar territory of specifying language, a landscape of globalized culture becomes legible, and the vast, taut surfaces emerge as multivalent references to the abstract and obscured dynamics of late capitalism.

The shallow and repetitive character of the *Façades* images draws attention to the function of the "façades" of the series' title: the designs of these buildings take advantage of abstraction's now-commonplace genericism to offer signs of modernity that are apparently unprovocative and empty of meaning. They obscure the activities of the nominal institutional subjects behind them. The presentation of the façades renders sleek surfaces resistant to penetration or any kind of differentiation, and vision slides along their surfaces, suggesting the expedition of capital's undifferentiated commodity. As examples of neoliberal capitalist production they materialize the displacement of "the space of places with a space of flows."[1]

1 The phrase belongs to Manuel Castells. See Manuel Castells, *The Information Age: Economy, Society and Culture* (Malden, MA: Blackwell, 1996).

This reading is apt and intentional, but the appearance of these abstract designs also enables a differently sited reference to earlier abstractions, specifically those of modern art movements such as Constructivism, Suprematism, and Neoplasticism. In this project, Fischer continues to expand on an interest that has informed his major photographic series: an inquiry into the nature and function of art, and, particularly in *Façades*, its place in a contemporary society in which a number of dynamics have profoundly altered the ways in which photographs—images of all kinds—are created, distributed, and received.

Fischer's practice has consistently engaged the large-scale image and typological structures, and his work shares some characteristics with that of Thomas Struth, Andreas Gursky, and Candida Höfer. Their images display an apparent pictorial objectivity that invites scrutiny and restrains it at the same time, holding viewers at the surface and deflecting attention from the ostensible subjects to an array of conceptual operations. Their works have been subsequently theorized through several critical iterations: as a new kind of objectivity, anti-aesthetic and disinterested; as media-critical spectacle; and as "tableaux" designed to create confrontation; and their position has been historicized as a nodal point for conceptual photography.

Fischer's projects, although they have some visual and conceptual similarities, are distinguished from them through the deployment of certain strategic contradictions. In three series Fischer has fashioned a peculiar and contrarian hybridity by combining typological study with otherworldly imagery. The subjects of *Nuns and Monks* (1984–86) are people who have chosen to join a contemplative order—whose strongly held beliefs are reflected in their choice to inhabit a religious interiority—not anonymous individuals or a cast of types. In *Los Angeles Portraits* (1989–93), the blue water background isolates but is not neutral or inactive; its deep color and aleatory effects provide ambiguous depth and sometimes subtle movement, giving the pictures unexplained, quiet life. In *Chinese Pool Portraits* (2007), the blue water is utilized again, and in this series most of the women look away from the viewer, self-absorbed or distracted by something outside the container of the picture. Or, when they do gaze straight out, they look past the presumed viewer, not confronting but simply being. Instead of presenting disinterested, blank faces to be projected upon, the images of all of these series are somehow gently activated, and gesture towards or literally present some kind of spirit-infused or metaphysical state.

Collective Portraits (1997–2005), a project Fischer developed while he was in China, is different from these early series in conception and effect, initially seeming to refer back to typological and archival concerns. The works present different types of people categorized by the work or activity they engage: students, farmers, soldiers, pilgrims, workers. In each piece hundreds of individual portraits are aggregated into vast gridded arrays. These come the closest to typological manipulation, with their strict alignment, the elimination of most differentiating detail through careful cropping, and their tight focus on the operation of comparison. Their sheer numbers invoke the archive, with its immense resource for meaning-making and potential for multiple interpretations. Yet the *Collective Portraits* also produce effects that exceed expectations of the typology, using huge scale to evoke physical response on the part of the viewer. The arrays, with the presentation of their virtually impossible-to-quantify mass, conjure a sublime effect, one that punctures neutrality and interrupts pure intellectual operation.

In these different series Fischer used strategies and marshaled elements of conceptual practices to explore aspects of the photographic—its indexical status, its archival capacities, its serial extensions—but also experimented with affect. Each series presents elements that elicit some strongly felt if not somatic experience, a dissonance that disturbs exclusively conceptual readings that might preclude metaphorical function. The projects engage an idea of the aesthetic, not as an expression of the beautiful, which these pictures often are, but to articulate an expansive idea of art's symbolic function and production of meaning.

Continuing this exploration, the series *Façades* (1997–2014) also constructs a complex field of inquiry into aesthetic function, employing the subject of Modernist abstraction not simply as a recuperative project but as a

Brechtian gesture that opens up a productive exchange between past and present. Utilizing the process of abstraction, its potential for metaphor, and its historical position, Fischer generates a multivalent discourse about the possibility of art's agency within a neoliberal culture that has foreclosed its independence. The procedures of that capitalism depend on the continuous abstraction of finance to displace products and labor with financial speculation. *Façades* in literal terms represents neoliberal capitalism's co-option of modern art as a disguise. The series also gestures toward its own historically complex position within neoliberalism with its multiple operations of abstraction: the formal device of modern art and its specific historical reference to aspirations of transcendence; the process of defamiliarization that takes place in the operation of representation; a social procedure that recodes objects and which photography can be seen to produce alongside the abstraction of financial capital.[2]

Significantly, the *Façades* photographs are not themselves abstractions. They are depictions of subjects that have been carefully framed and structured to appear nonrepresentational. With this operation Fischer points to the nature of photography as an abstracting procedure, the transformation of three-dimensional subject into two-dimensional image. He compounds this effect by revealing very little depth, or excluding it altogether from the

2 A far more nuanced presentation of the deployment of abstraction has been made by Mark Godfrey. See Mark Godfrey, "Response to George Baker: Photography and Abstraction," in Alex Klein, ed., *Words without Pictures* (Los Angeles: Los Angeles County Museum of Art, 2009), 285–87.

photographs; this obscures the actual subjects and emphasizes their flatness. Many of the pictured surfaces are virtually identical to their material matrix, creating confusion and anxiety about them as objects and their meaning, an effect Fischer takes full of advantage of in a related series, *Groups of Five* (1997–2014).[3] The large size of the *Façades* images allows the abstract patterning to accrue as a visual field and also, ironically, to defuse the spectacularity of its scale. Instead, the repetitive rhythm of the geometric patterns generates compositional movement, creating visual play rather than information.

3 This series (unfinished but projected to be about twenty works in total) consists of groups of five images, much smaller in size than the *Façades* images. There is less indication of depth in each image, and the comparisons that arise from their serial arrangement enable them to be easily read as geometric abstractions, which further emphasizes the relationship to painted abstraction.

Abstraction is an operation in *Façades*, but it is also a subject that is interrogated in Fischer's constructions. His flattened and reductive images make reference to the historical moment of early modern art. Modern artists' development of a nonobjective art was informed by a variety of anti-materialist and spiritual doctrines. Their new visual languages rejected imitation of the visible world; they were, instead, intended to function as sign systems with metaphoric possibilities that would engage the ineffable and produce a new sublime. Fischer's mimicry of abstract motifs and compositions is an experimental construction of reference, one that deliberately aligns his project with the earlier artists' inventions. This suggests an interest in their motivations, and his evocation of them is a strategy to introduce and insert the conditions of abstraction's genesis.

In a statement about *New Architectures*, a project that he began while working on *Façades*, Fischer remarked that its multiple-exposure images were transformations of "spaces/structures in a sort of cubist tradition... the result is, in a way, like a 'third' reality."[4] Cubism's multiple viewpoints, working as a metaphor, might indicate an unfixed or unreal position, an otherworldly perspective. Fischer achieves this in the *New Architectures*, generating overlapping planes that make visual reference to the multiplied perspectives of Cubism. In *Façades* he develops something different in his implication of disparate historical moments: the picturing of abstraction becomes a way to refer to those early modern movements and to allude to the values that were invested in their ideal and idealistic forms. The *Façades* images activate a conversation among their institutional subjects and their neoliberal conditions with those of their modern counterparts; various functions of abstraction appear and disappear as subjectivities shift and meanings are continuously replaced.

4 Roland Fischer, Artist Statement, "new architectures," 2009. http://www.rolandfischer.com/wp-content/uploads/2012/10/statementnewarchs.pdf. Accessed July 1, 2014.

The allusion to the invention of abstraction also references its earlier moment of representational crisis and the profound shift in forms and in expectations of artistic function. Abstraction constituted a radical break with traditional representation and a turn away from the pictorial. The operation of abstraction expanded the conceptual repertoire of aesthetic forms; in addition to representations of realities and the explication of their potential meanings, art might provide its own unique experience, prompting intellectual and somatic responses. It proposed art as an exemplary realm, independent of the world and capable of providing unique experiences that could both affect and exceed the conditions of social existence.

The *Façades* series occupies a similar moment of crisis and reflects anxiety about the function and status of art as meaningful production. Neo-liberal capitalism is informed by the idea of market exchange as society's fundamental dynamic, an ethic that directs all production.[5] Under neoliberalism, absorption into market conditions strips art of its independent critical status and its historical agency; art is merely one commodity indistinguishable from others. The digital forms that enable such a system produce a web of media that erases the differences and separations among art, documentation, text, photography, video, and animation. Untethered from its original purpose, the value of any object is not determined by intention or by its circumstances as real or virtual production but by its availability and capacity for utility at any moment: then art circulates as all images do. Aesthetics are devalued as a special instrument, and art is no longer a plausible other.[6]

Fischer activates several strategies to engage these conditions. There are numerous elisions and confrontations of abstraction and depiction or representation in *Façades*, playfully employed to complicate the material and theoretical operations of his subject and medium. As digitally produced

5 This is drastically reduced from the description of neoliberalism developed by David Harvey. See David Harvey, *A Brief History of Neoliberalism* (New York: Oxford University Press, 2005).

6 Nicholas Brown, "The Work of Art in the Age of Its Real Subsumption under Capital," 2012. http://nonsite.org/editorial/the-work-of-art-in-the-age-of-its-real-subsumption-under-capital. Accessed June 14, 2014.

images,[7] the photographs are both post-media objects and pictures of neoliberal institutions that contain them. Fischer has exploited photography's process of excerpting and flattening to create compositions that render his images' appearance more abstract, yet this also makes more apparent their modern art referents. As images they are not abstractions themselves but point to abstraction as a subject, implicating both its metaphorical function and its historical moment. That moment was precipitated, according to some theoretical accounts, by photography's capacity to represent reality more accurately than painted realism. The *Façades* images refer to this historical situation at the same time as they enact their own, and the alternation of abstraction and representation is iterated across their subtle variations. In some images the picture plane is identical to the surface being photographed, obliterating the difference between subject and object. In others the camera was tilted to a slight degree, allowing depth and creating a sense of space that draws attention back to their photographic status. Fischer uses photography, an abstracting medium, to represent abstraction, and, ironically, through that act of depiction, he also achieves its opposite.

Fischer makes use of the oppositional actions of abstraction and representation in another way. Images generate all types of possibilities: metonym, metaphor; a moment and its infinite extension; the circumstances of their own generation and of a parallel situation in the real world; attachment

7 The *Façades* images were made with film cameras until 2007 when Fischer switched to digital cameras. All of the prints are digital prints, that is, printed from digital files.

to a subject or a referent as well as complete detachment. They operate as the façades of institutions do—covering, disguising, redirecting—and also critique these operations. As images, photographs do these things, and arguably also present a material difference, as objects, with a surface quality distinct from that of other media, and a capacity, material and conceptual, to produce sensation unlike painting or language. Fischer is interested in the problem of photography's difference, in its "either and" potential; and in each of his projects he has engaged some contradiction that suggests this aspect of real or bare life: the constant exchange of opposites, the "cascade of antinomies" that must be resolved, or at least accommodated, in everyday life.[8] Fischer generates a palpable sense of irreducibility and ambiguity and amplifies it by constructing *Façades* as a continuous exchange between representation and abstraction.

These dynamics and their shifting among multivalent possibilities infuse *Façades* with a sense of liveliness and even agency. Different from Fischer's earlier series with their frisson of contradiction between seeming objectivity and the subtle gestures towards the symbolic, it is one that creates manifold affect. *Façades* extends beyond the resistance embedded in the act of exposing a neoliberal strategy, and its deployment of multiple inquiries suggests a dynamic subjectivity, one alluded to in the references to modern abstraction and asserted in the movement among registers of meaning proposed by the *Façades* project.

8 Fischer quoted this phrase by Peter Wollen, the film critic, concerned with film's particular aesthetics and capacity to function as a system of signs, in an interview with the author, August 2, 2014.

A number of theorists have recently proposed that the appropriative activities that generate meaning-making in the neoliberal regime of affective economies constitute a new kind of subjectivity and individual agency. Fischer's *Façades* engages those theoretical positions with the reintroduction of modern abstraction and its positions, inserting them among what Fredric Jameson has called "the less palpable abstractions of the image or the logo, which operate with something of the autonomy of values of present-day finance capital."[9] Among them is the possibility of photographic function inscribed, not only on the level of depiction or information, but in the critical position generated in its alternating operations of symbolic meaning and real affect. In *Façades* Fischer constructs a productive conversation between historical moments and opens up a vigorous and activating interchange among positions and subjectivities.

9 Fredric Jameson, "The End of Temporality," in *Critical Inquiry* 29, no. 4 (summer 2003), 703.

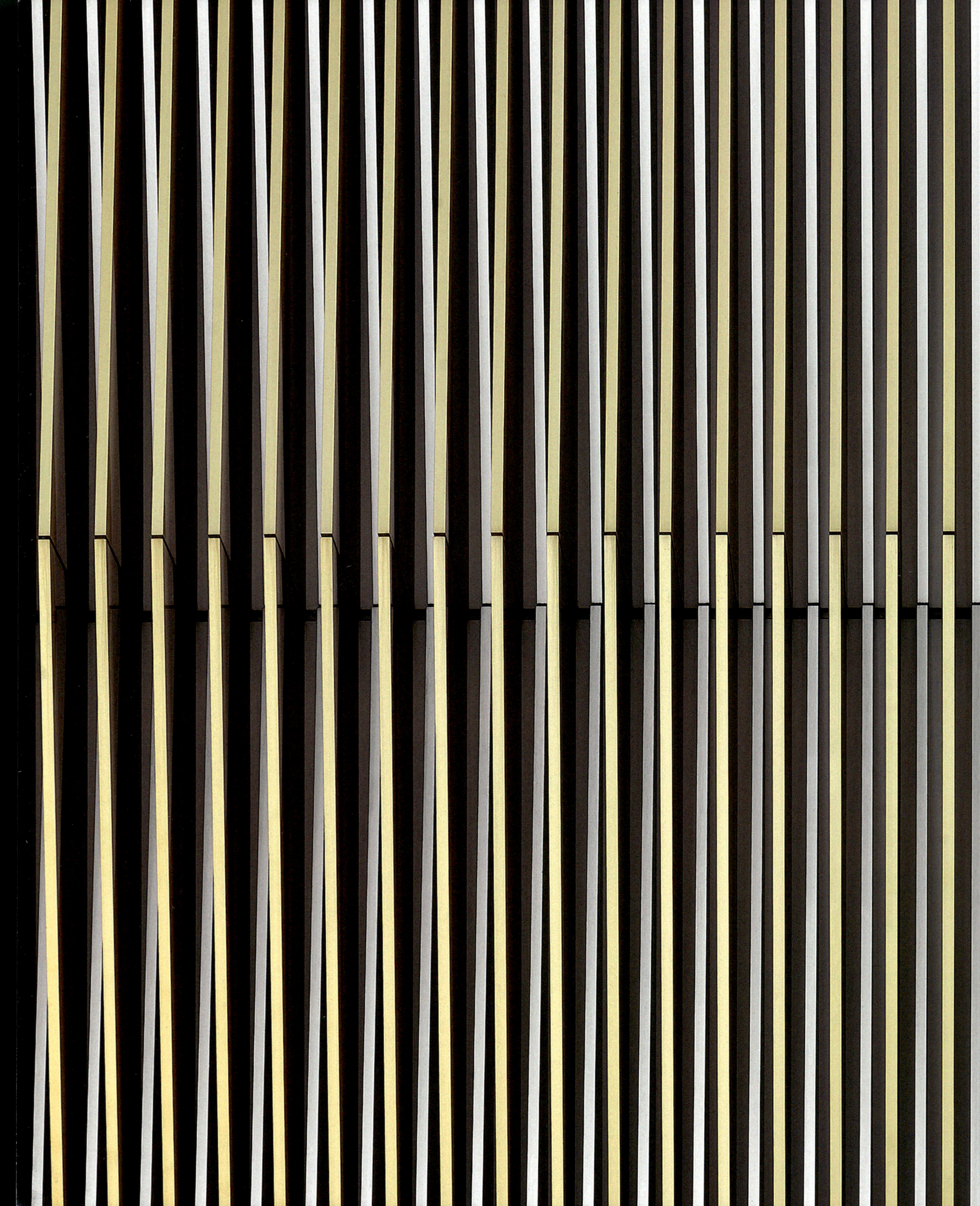

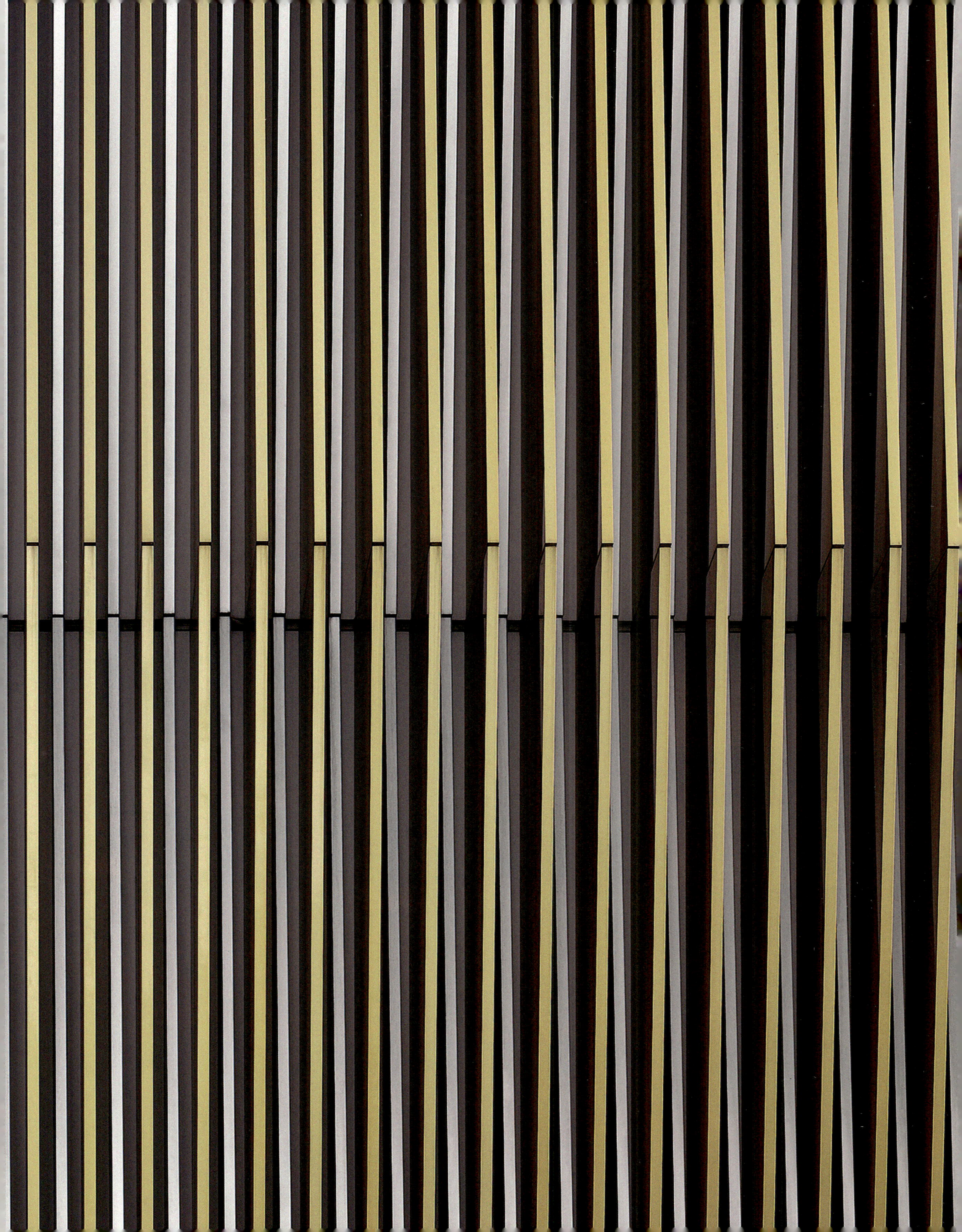

WTC
NEW YORK
1999

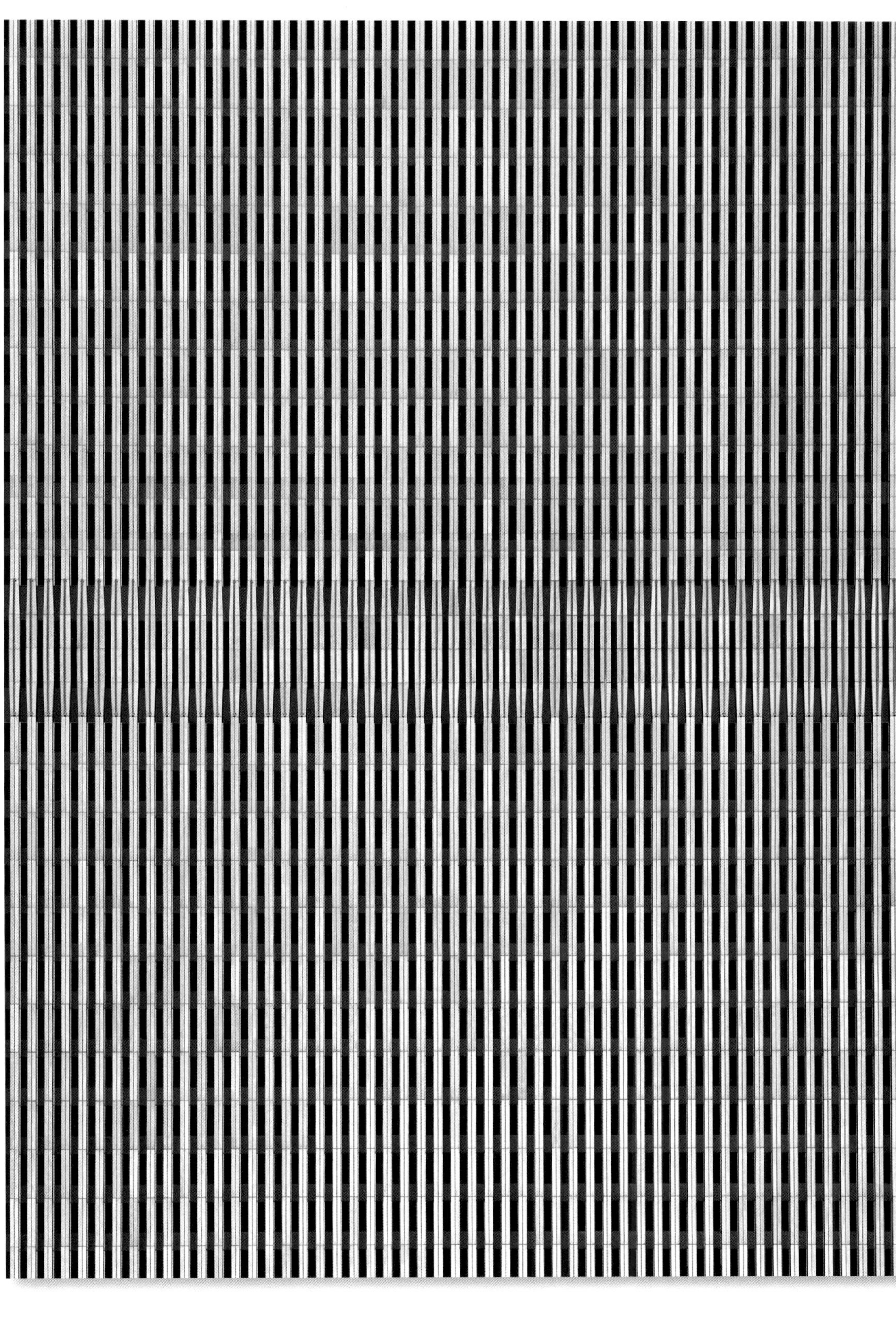

YUANTONG
BEIJING
2010

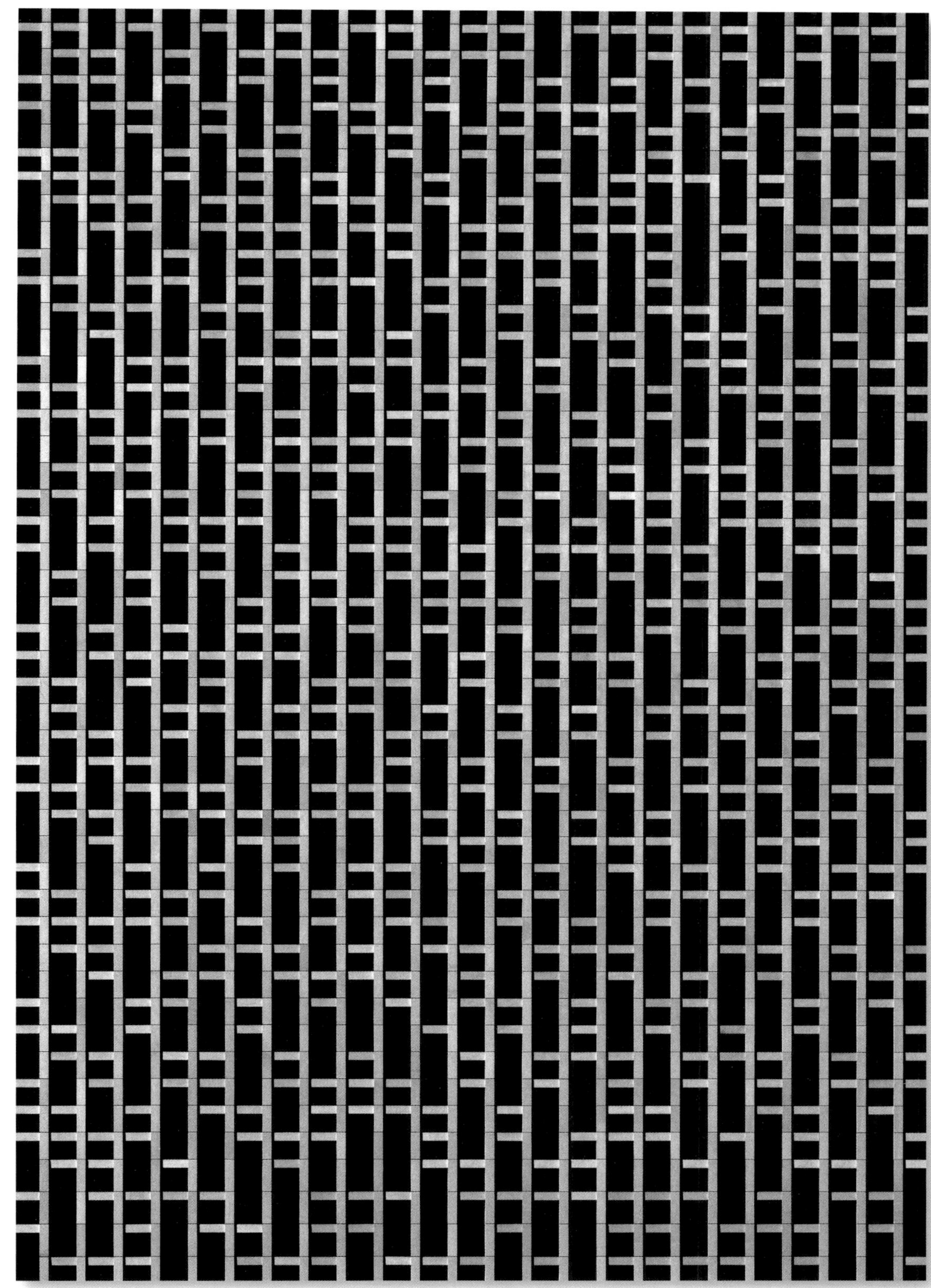

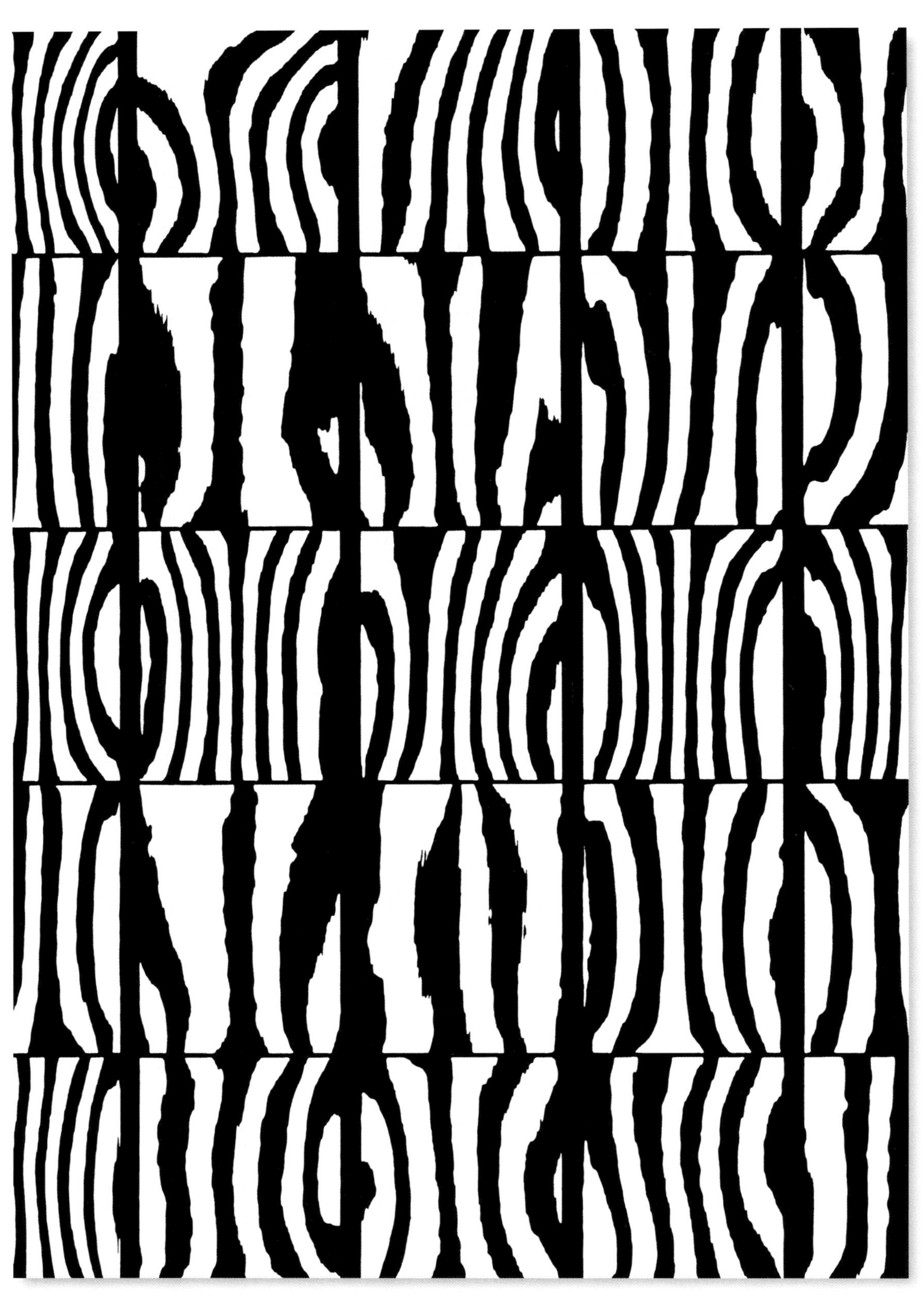

SOUTHWEST
HOUSTON
2002

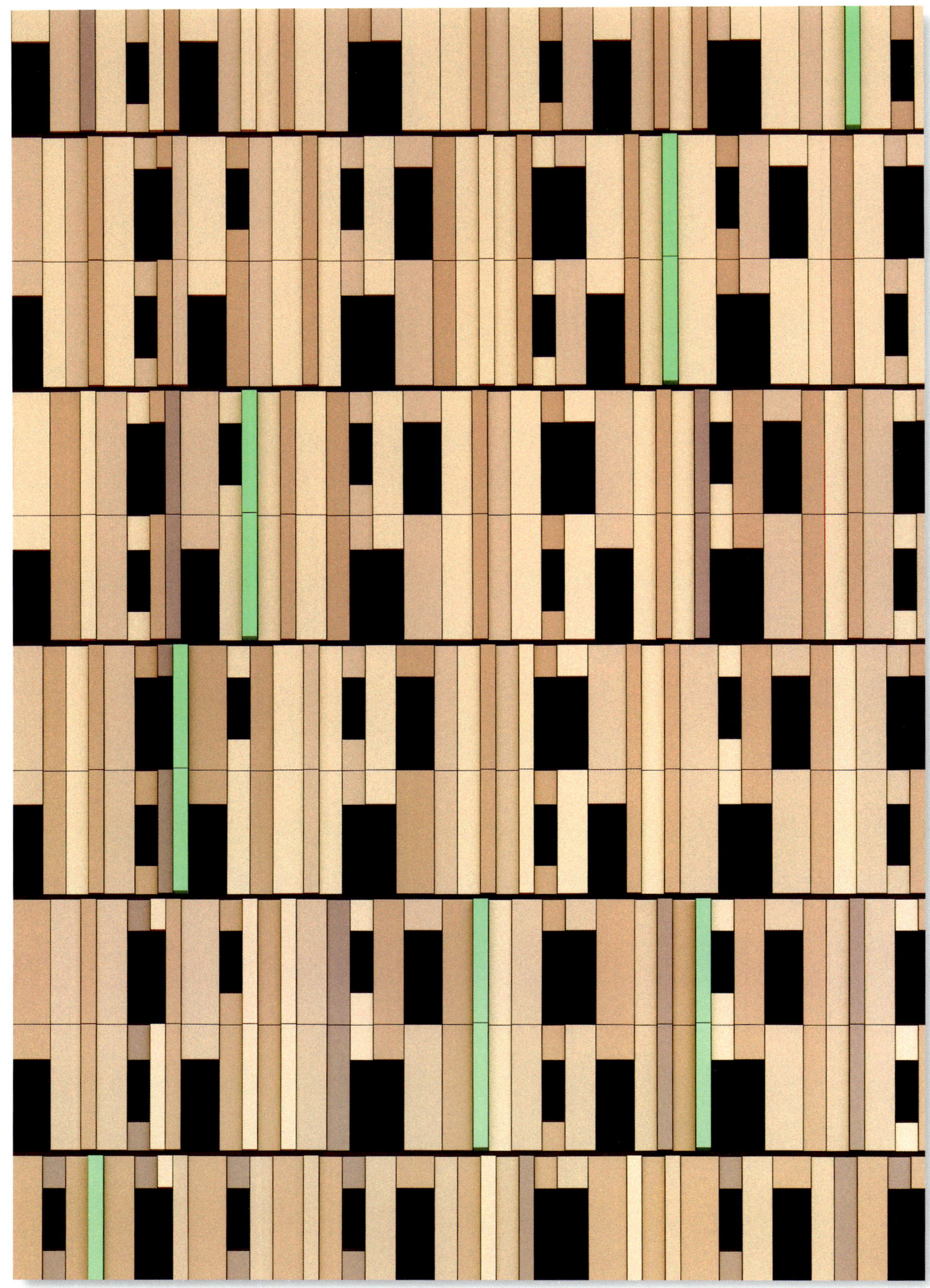

HUNTINGTON AVE
BOSTON
2013

> CCC
COPENHAGEN
2014

> HIGHSCHOOL #2
UTRECHT
2014

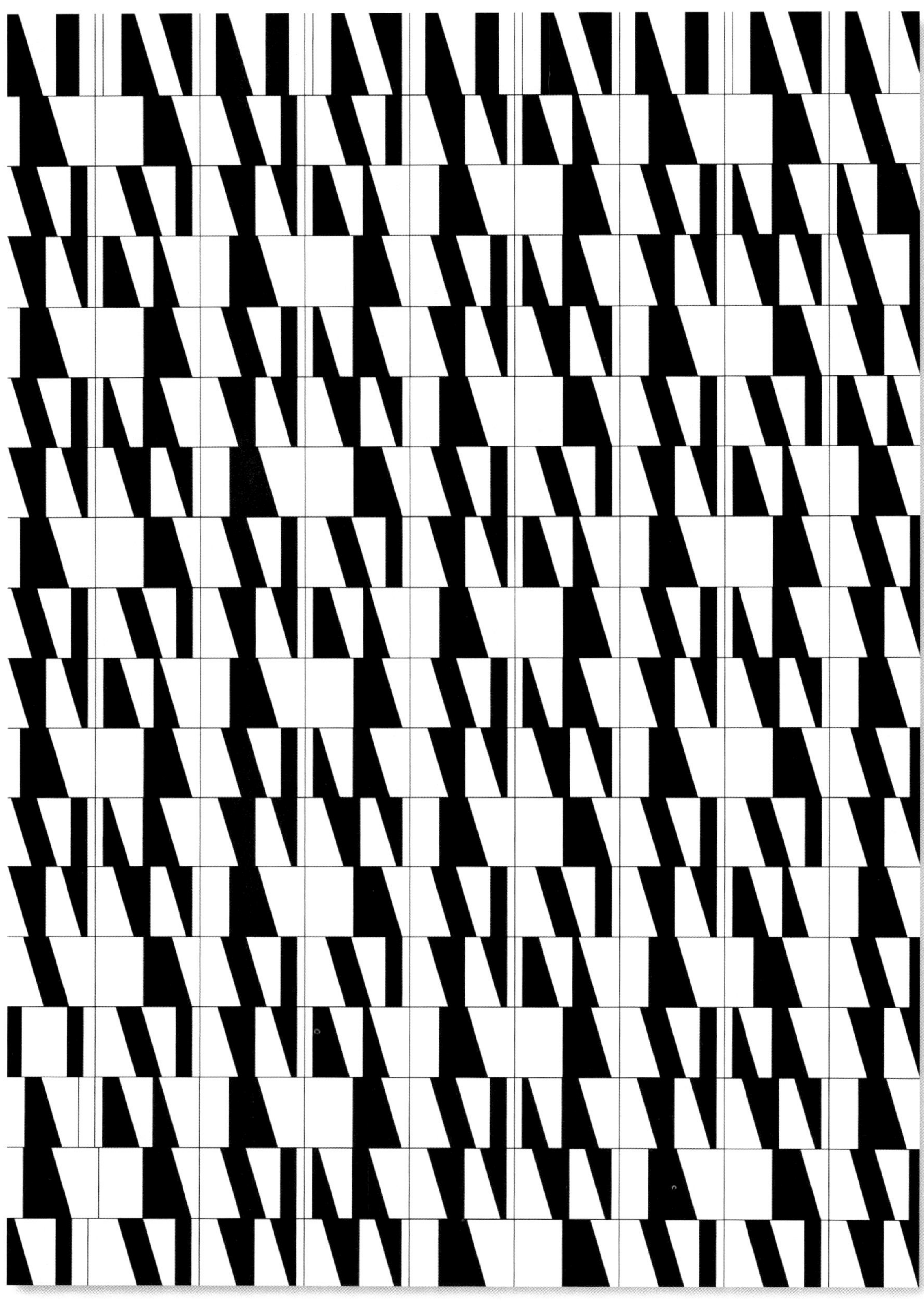

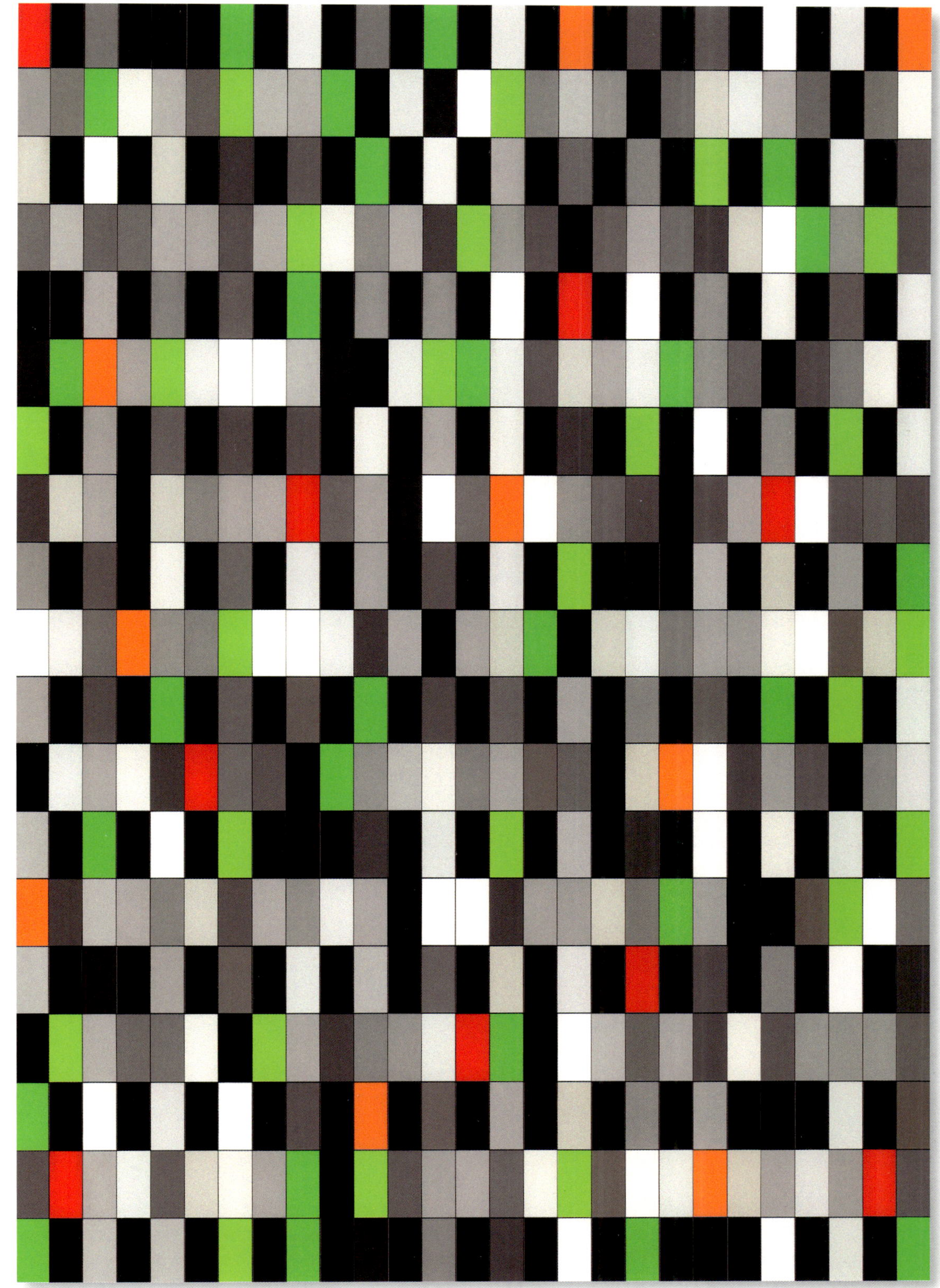

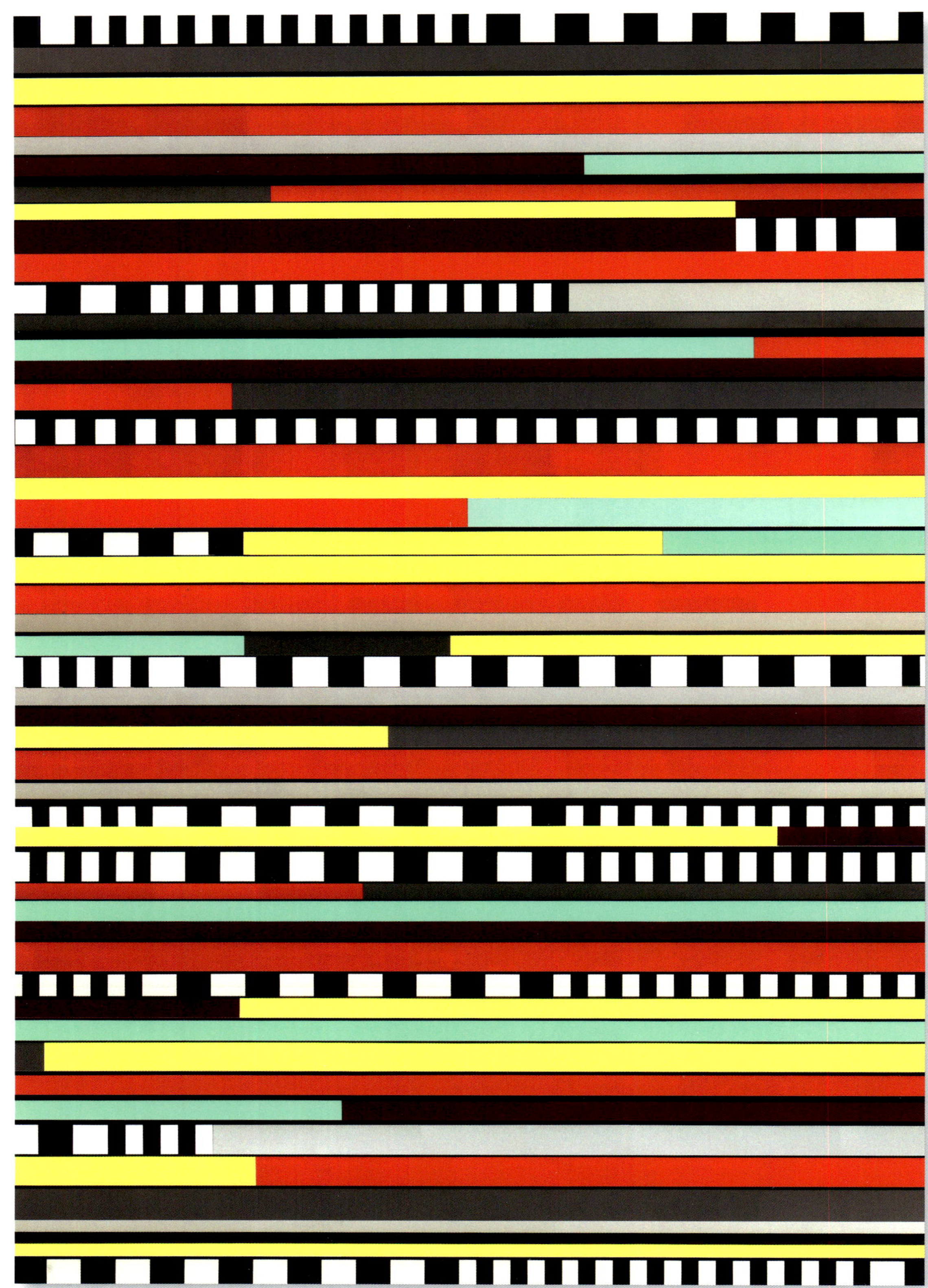

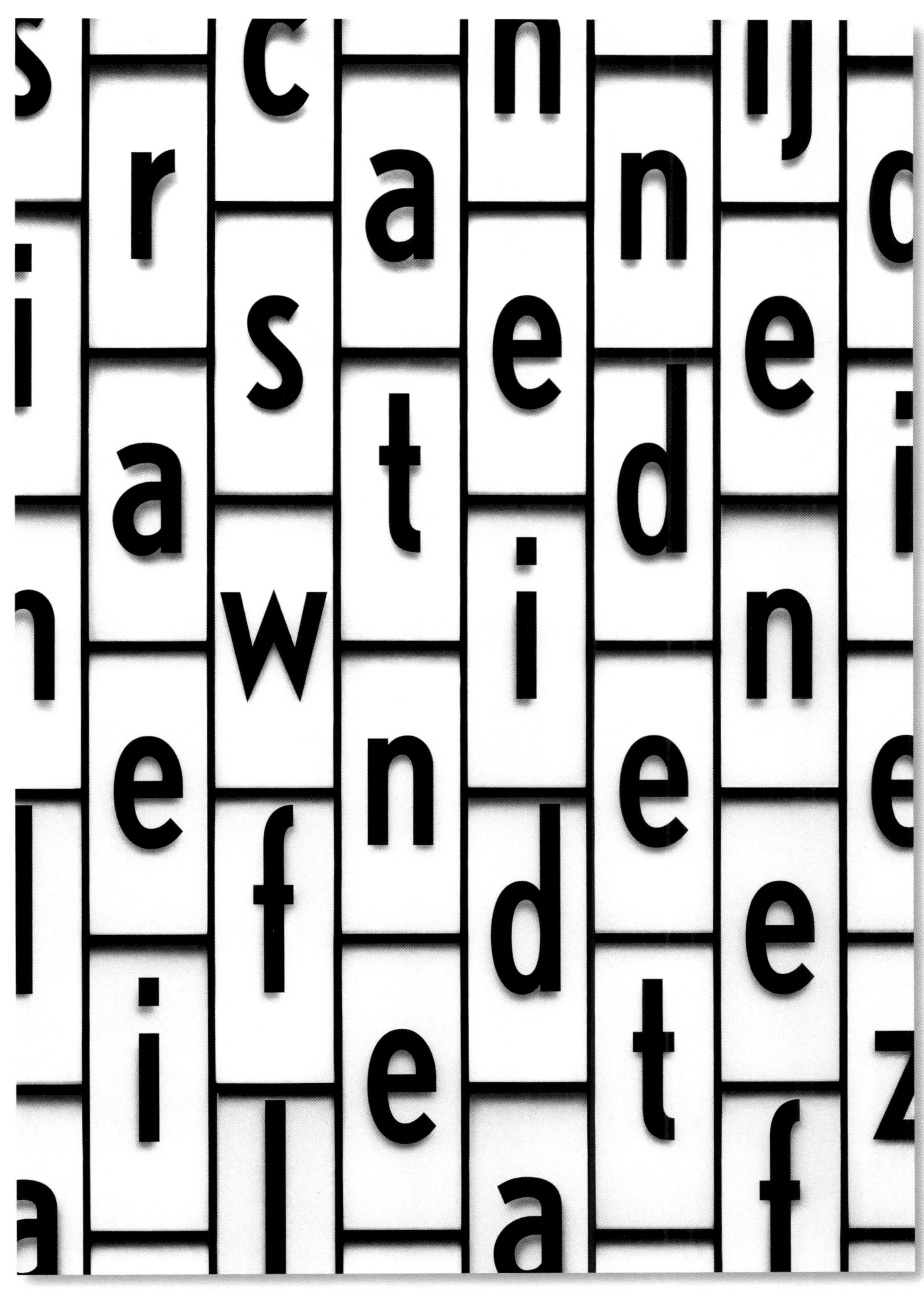

< HIGHSCHOOL
UTRECHT
2013

< SEE WIN
EDE
2013

NAB
MELBOURNE
2011

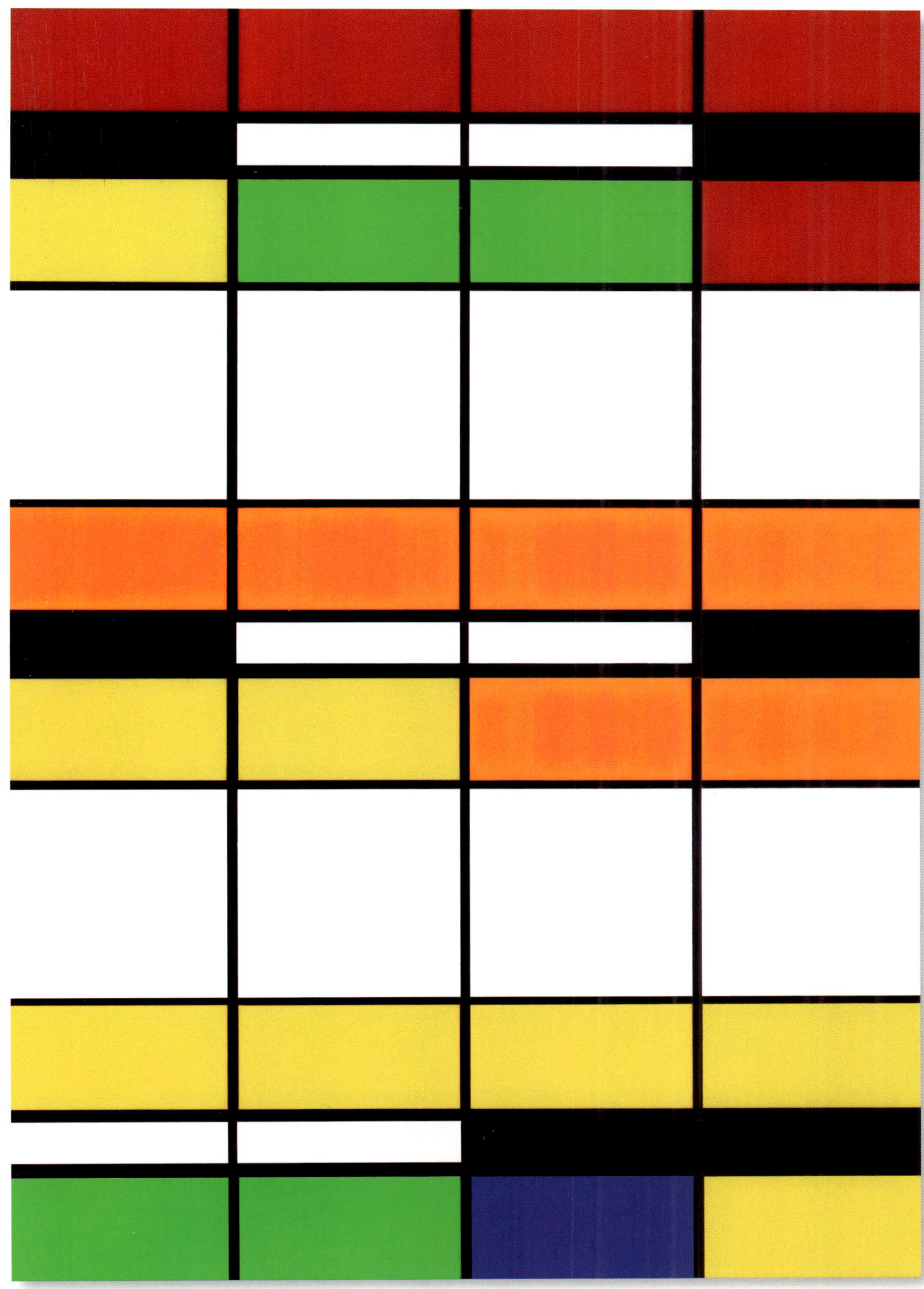

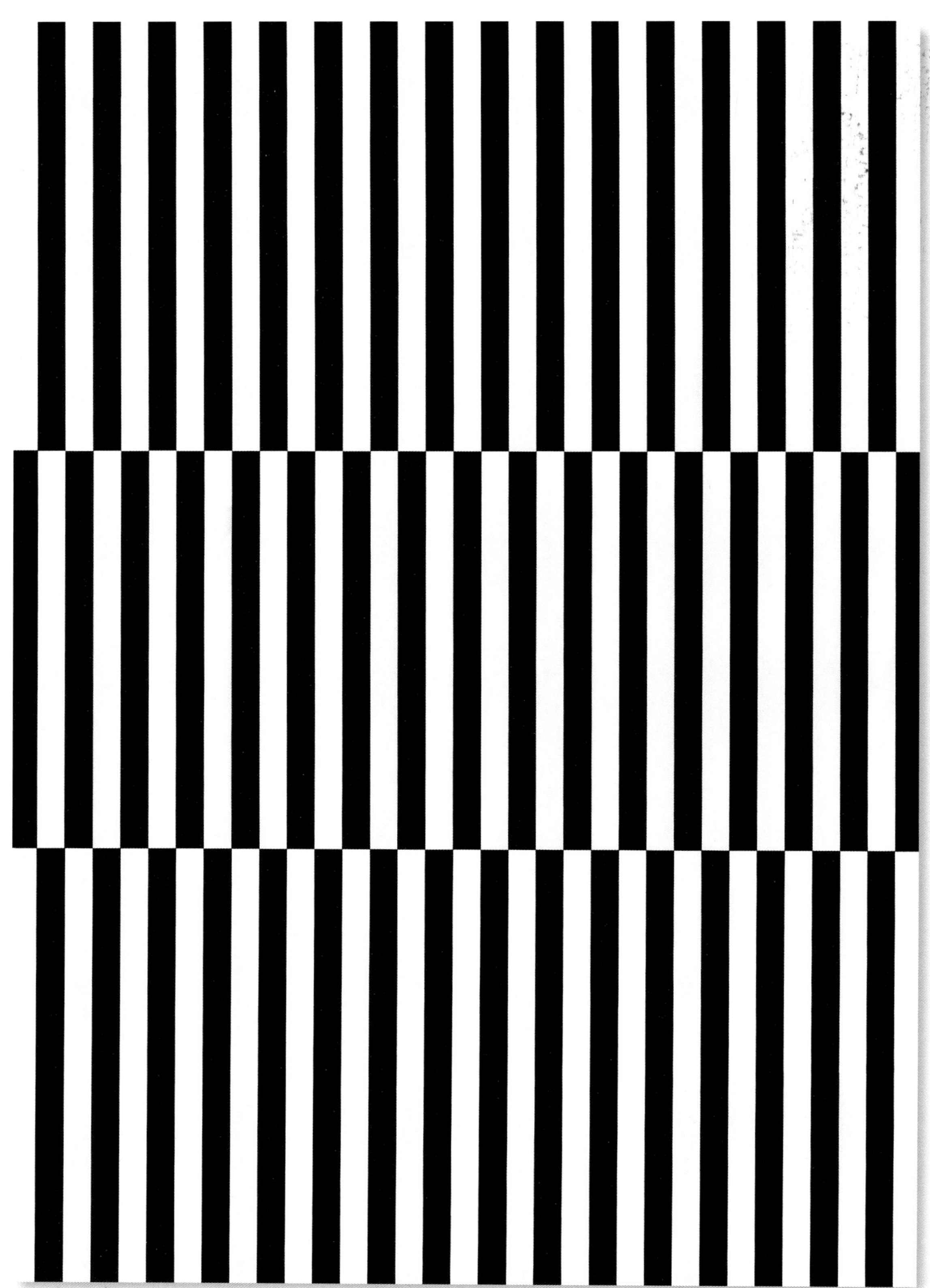

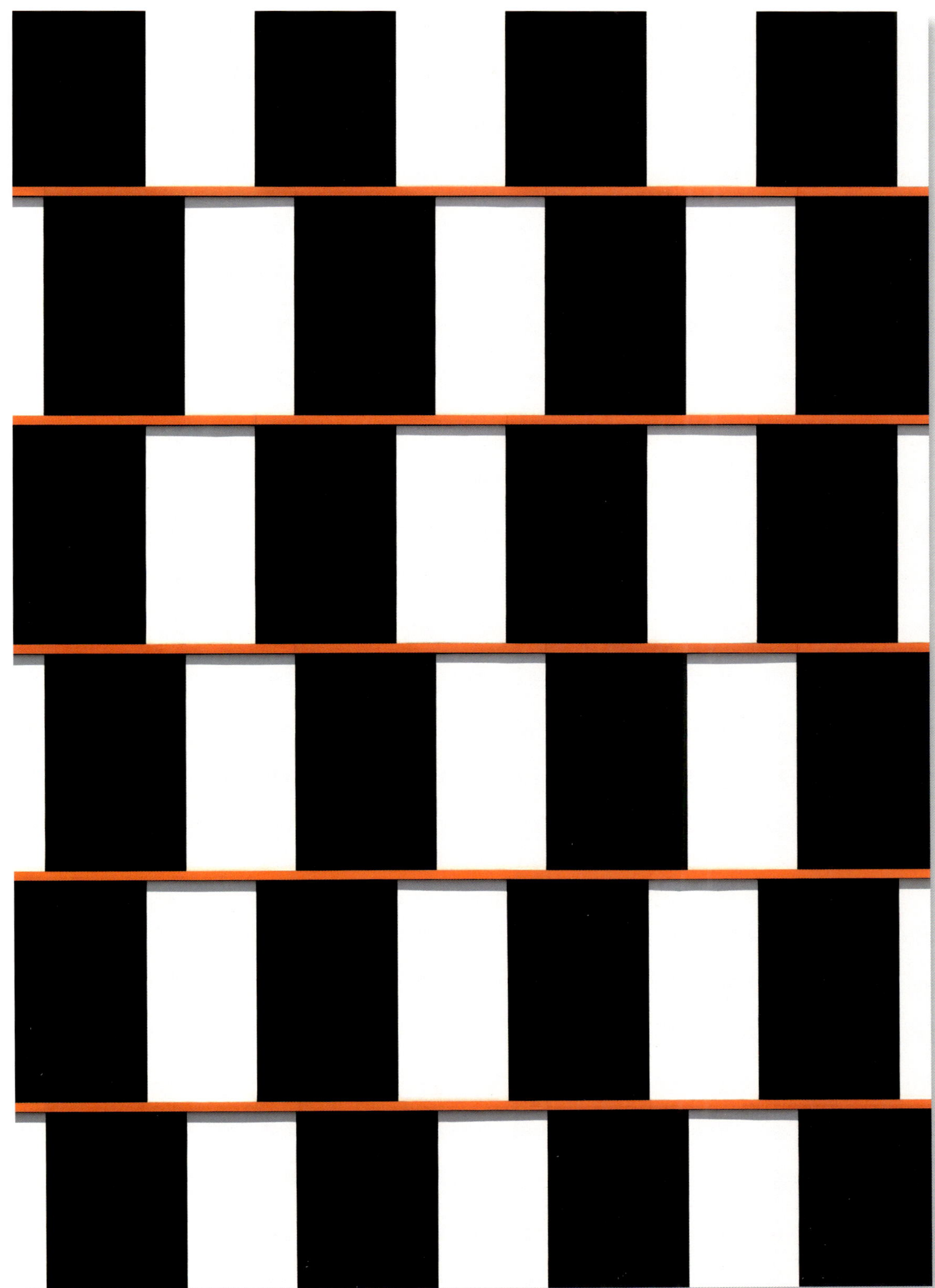

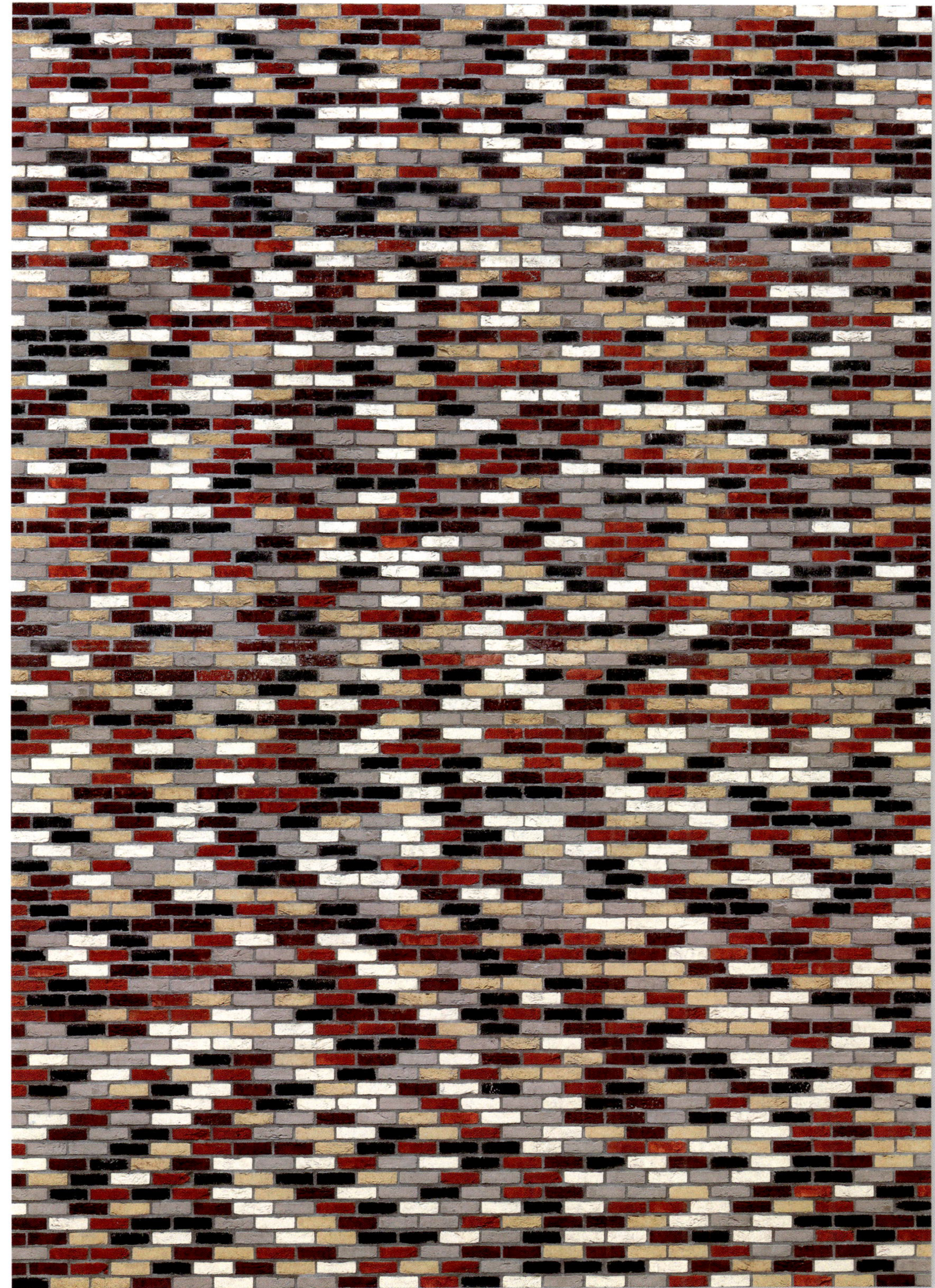

LUCAS AVE
LOS ANGELES
2002

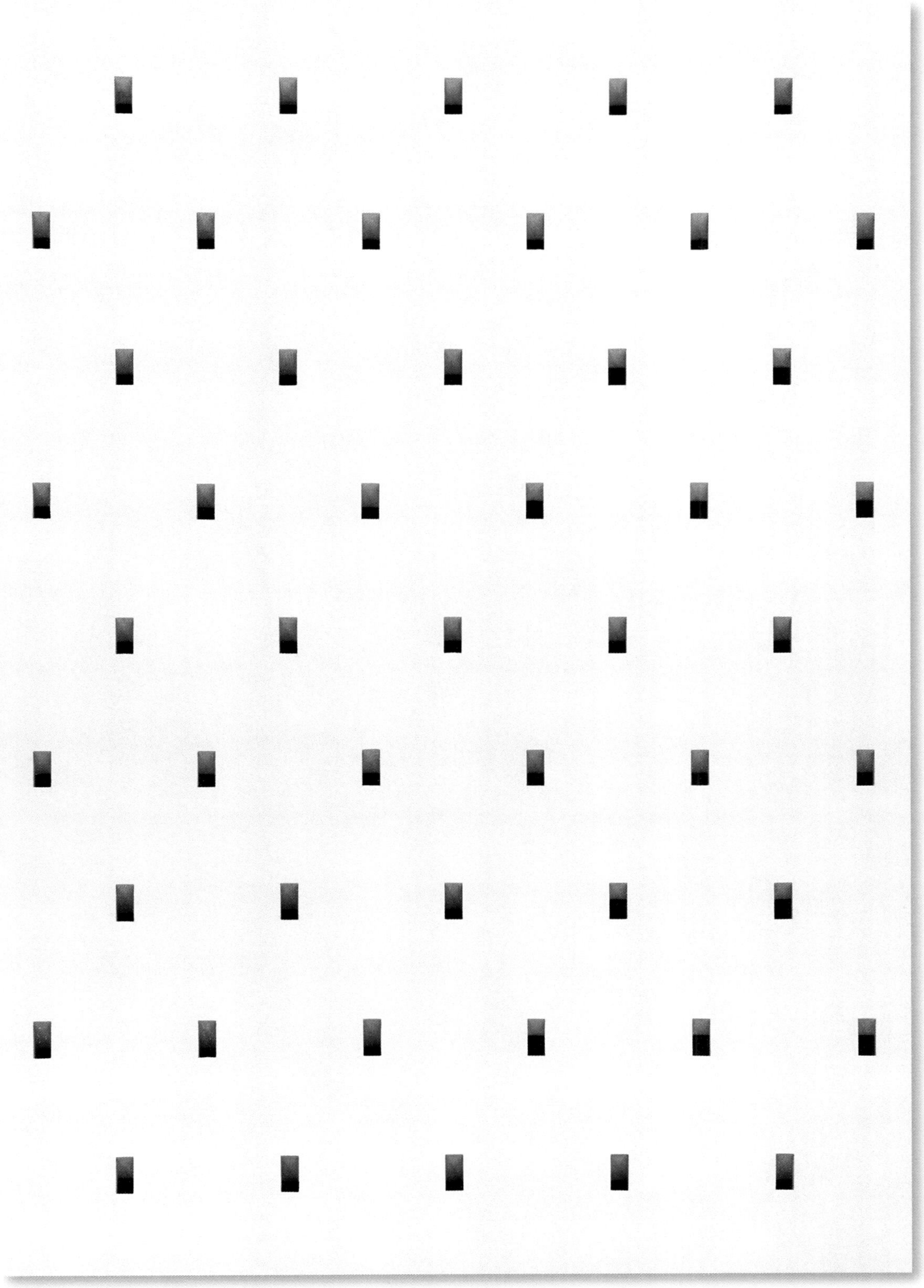

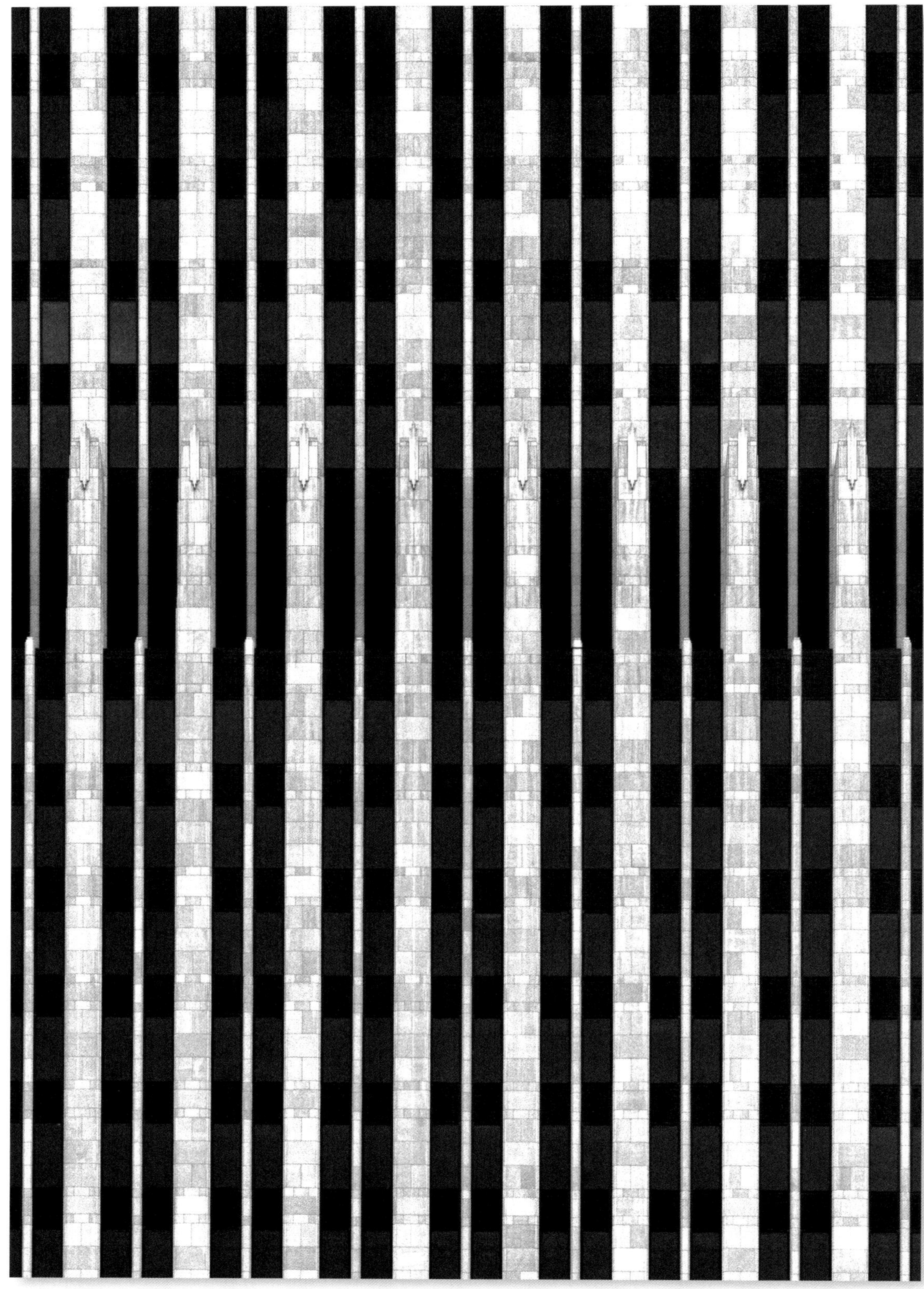

CHICAGO
2001

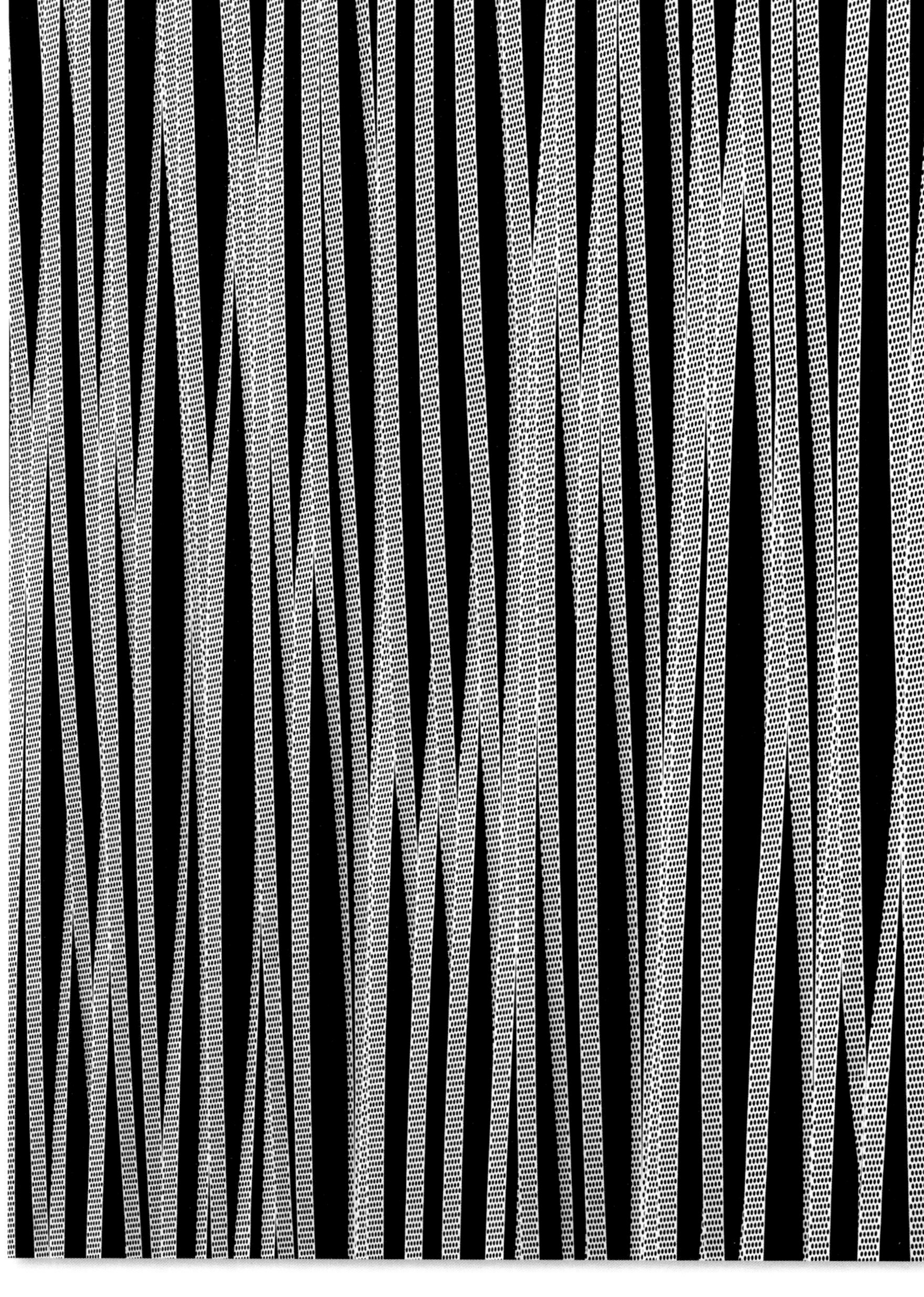

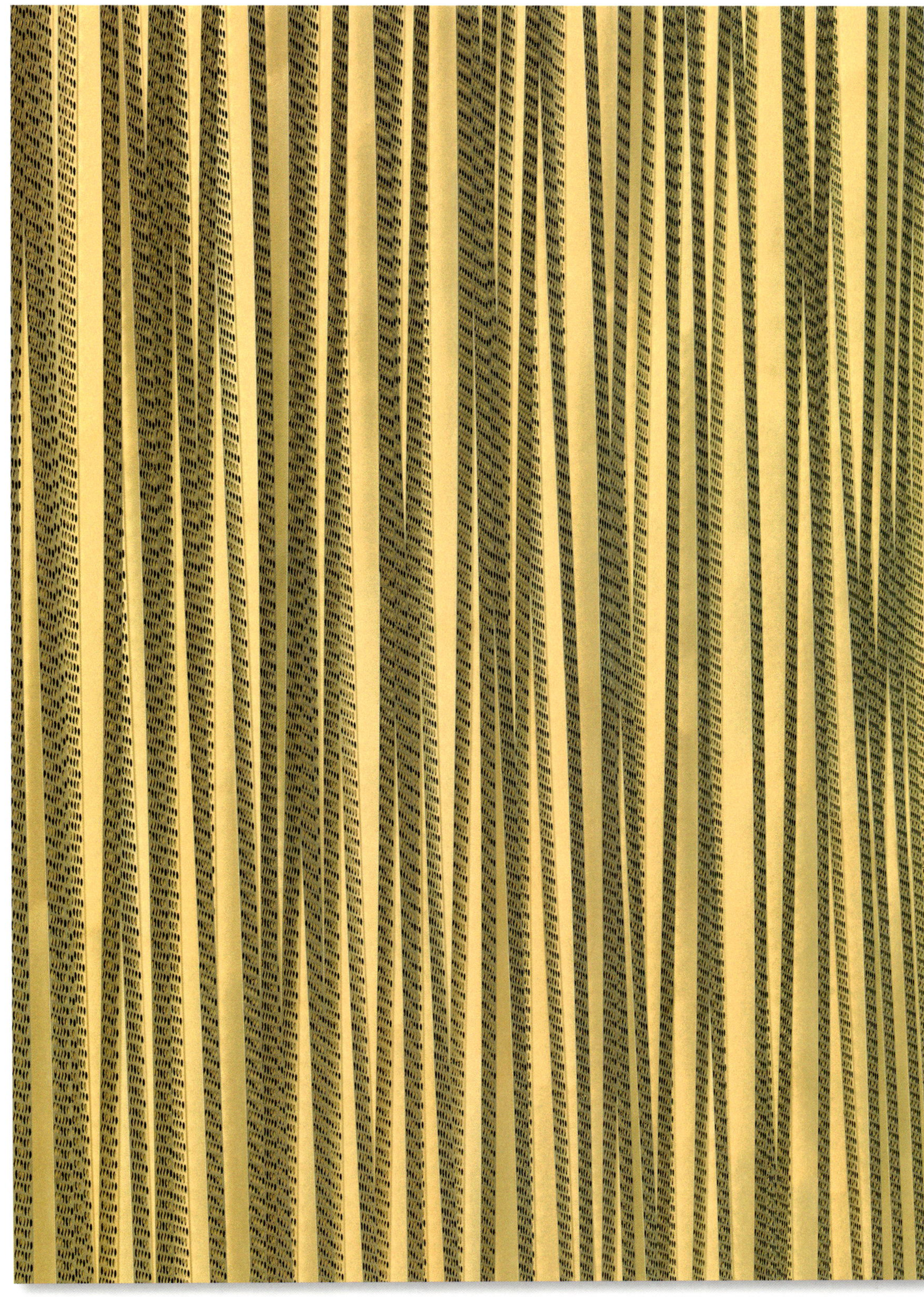

< WUKESONG
BEIJING
2010

< WUKESONG #2
BEIJING
2013

IGLESIAS
MEXICO CITY
2011

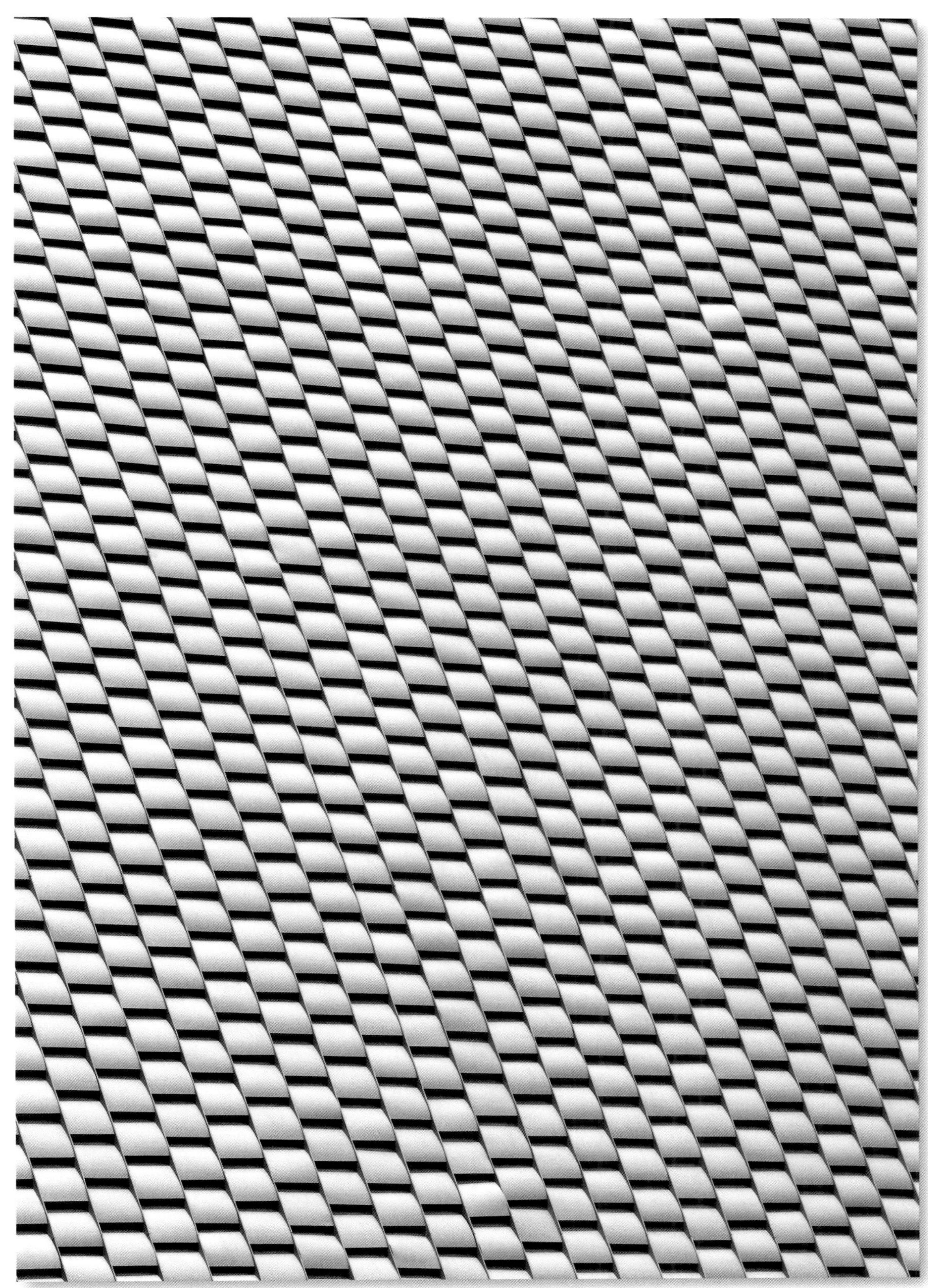

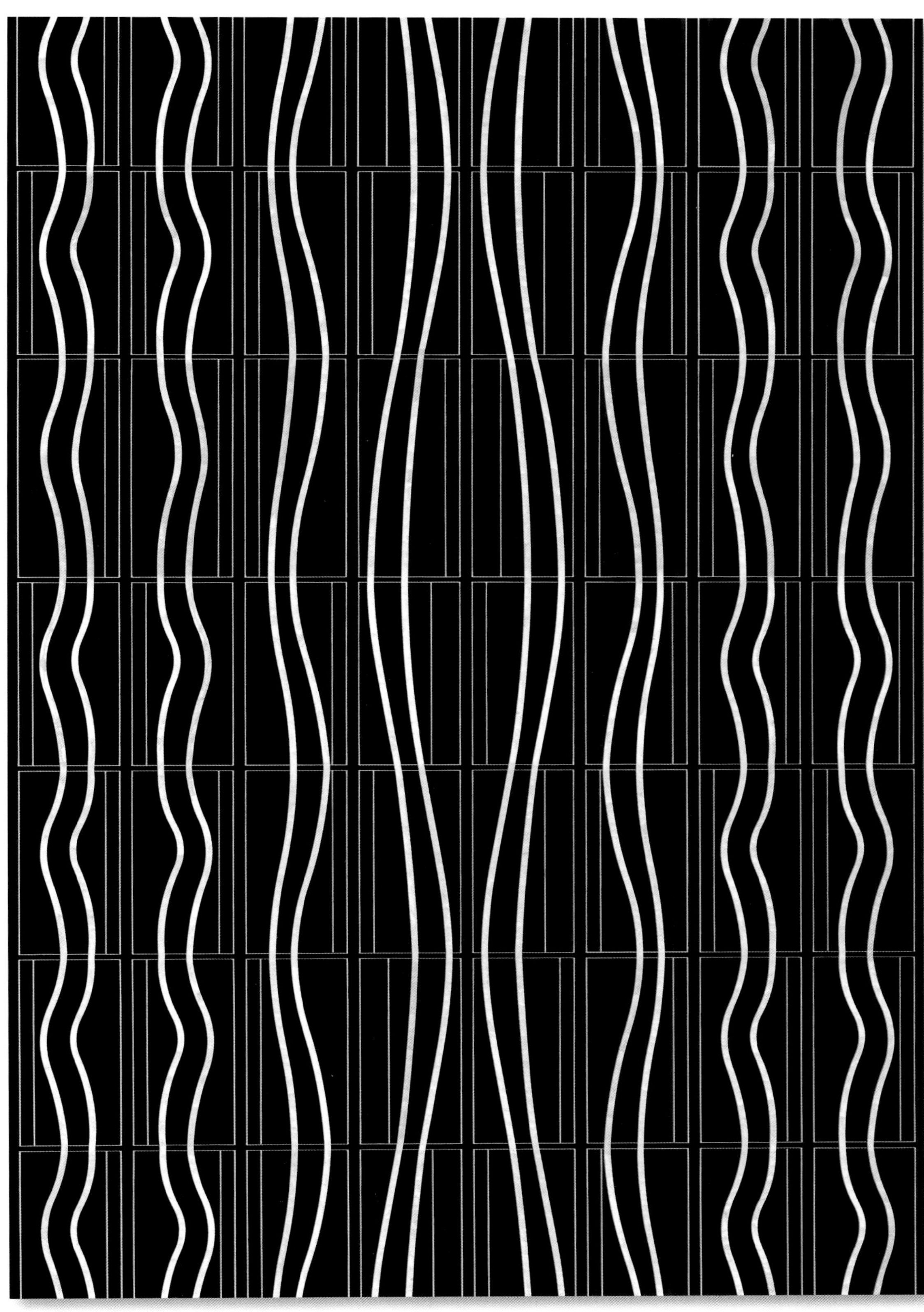

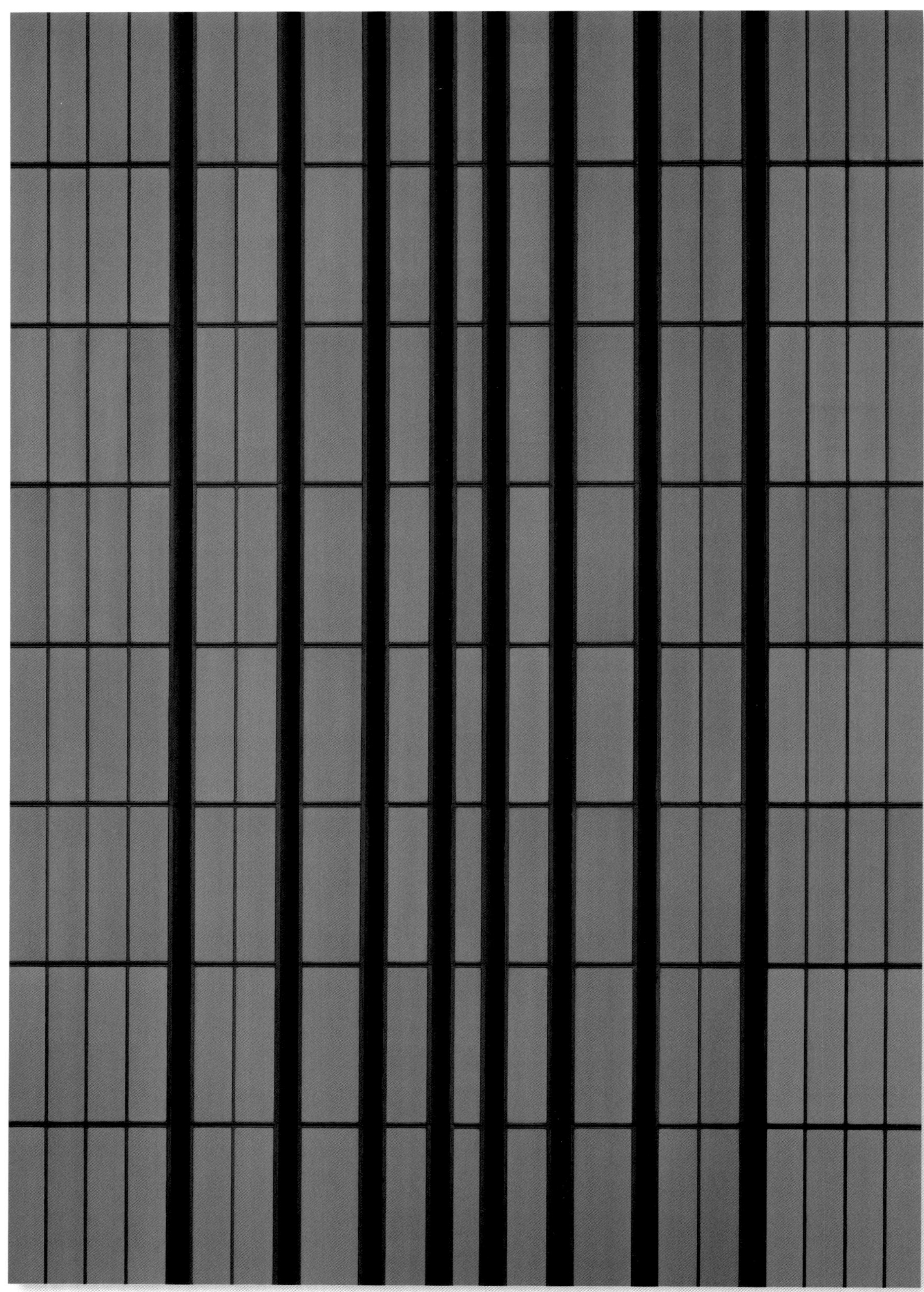

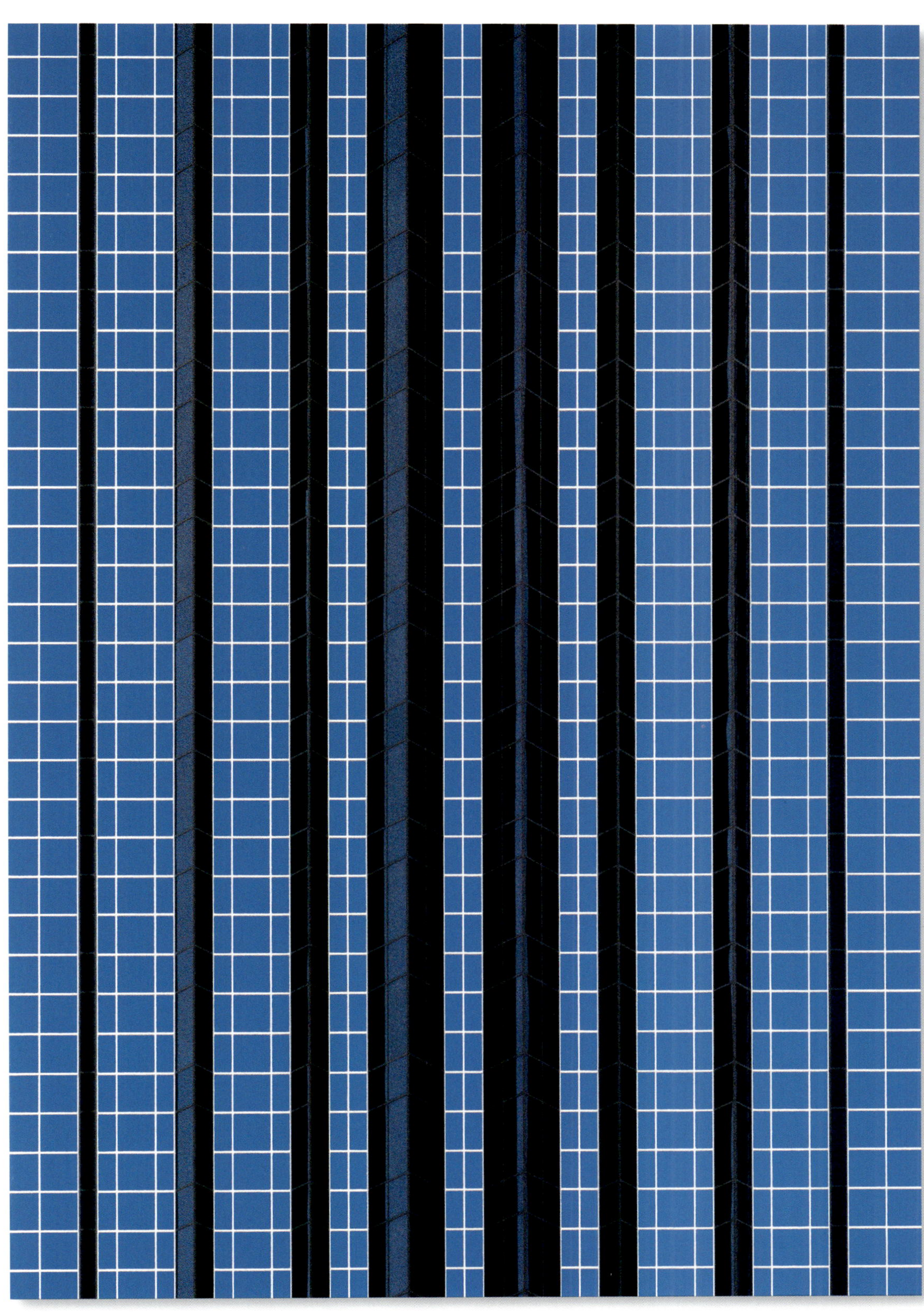

< SAT
MEXICO CITY
2010

< WILLIAMS TOWER
HOUSTON
2004

PPG
PITTSBURGH
2004

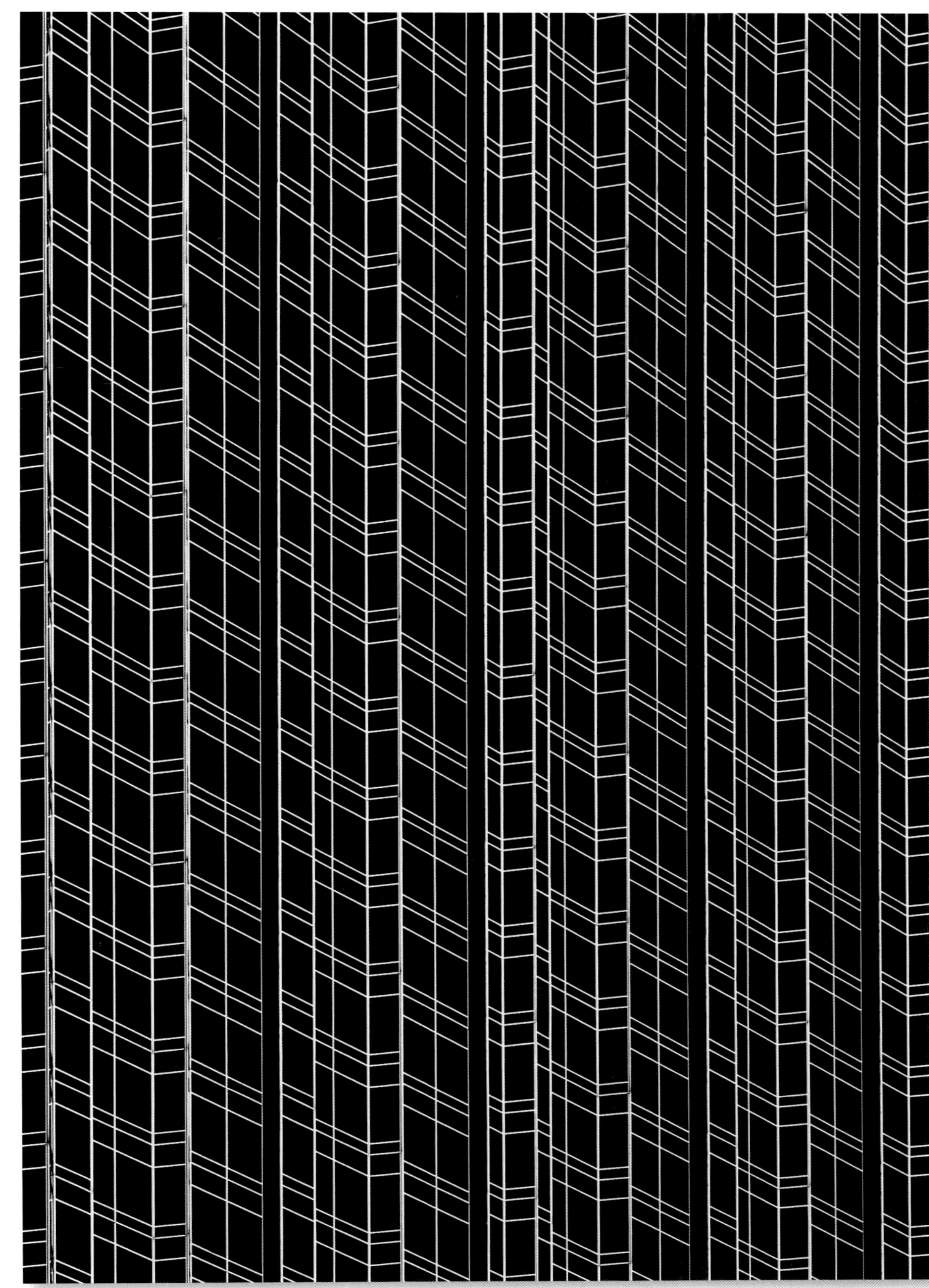

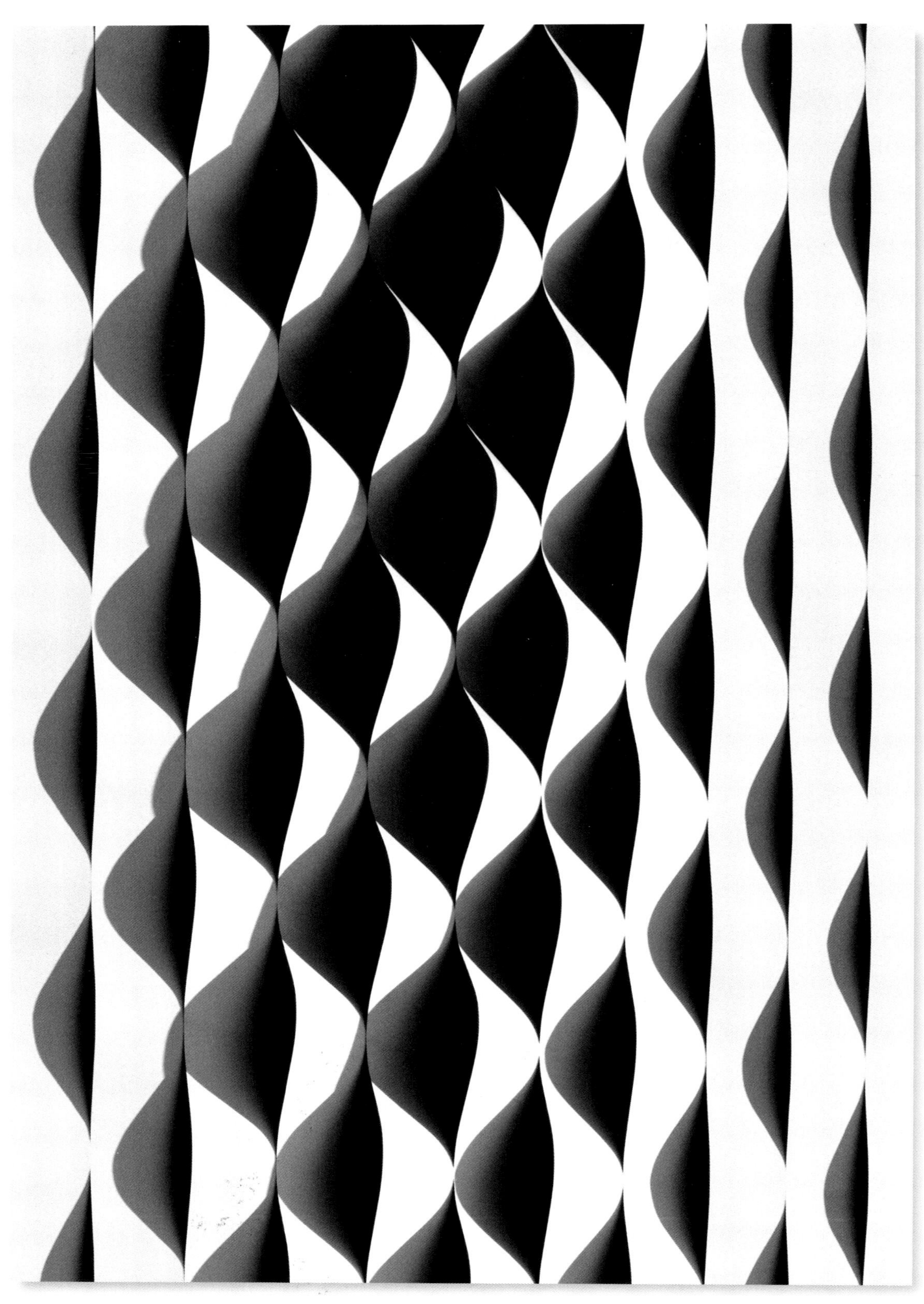

BANK OF AMERICA
ATLANTA
2005

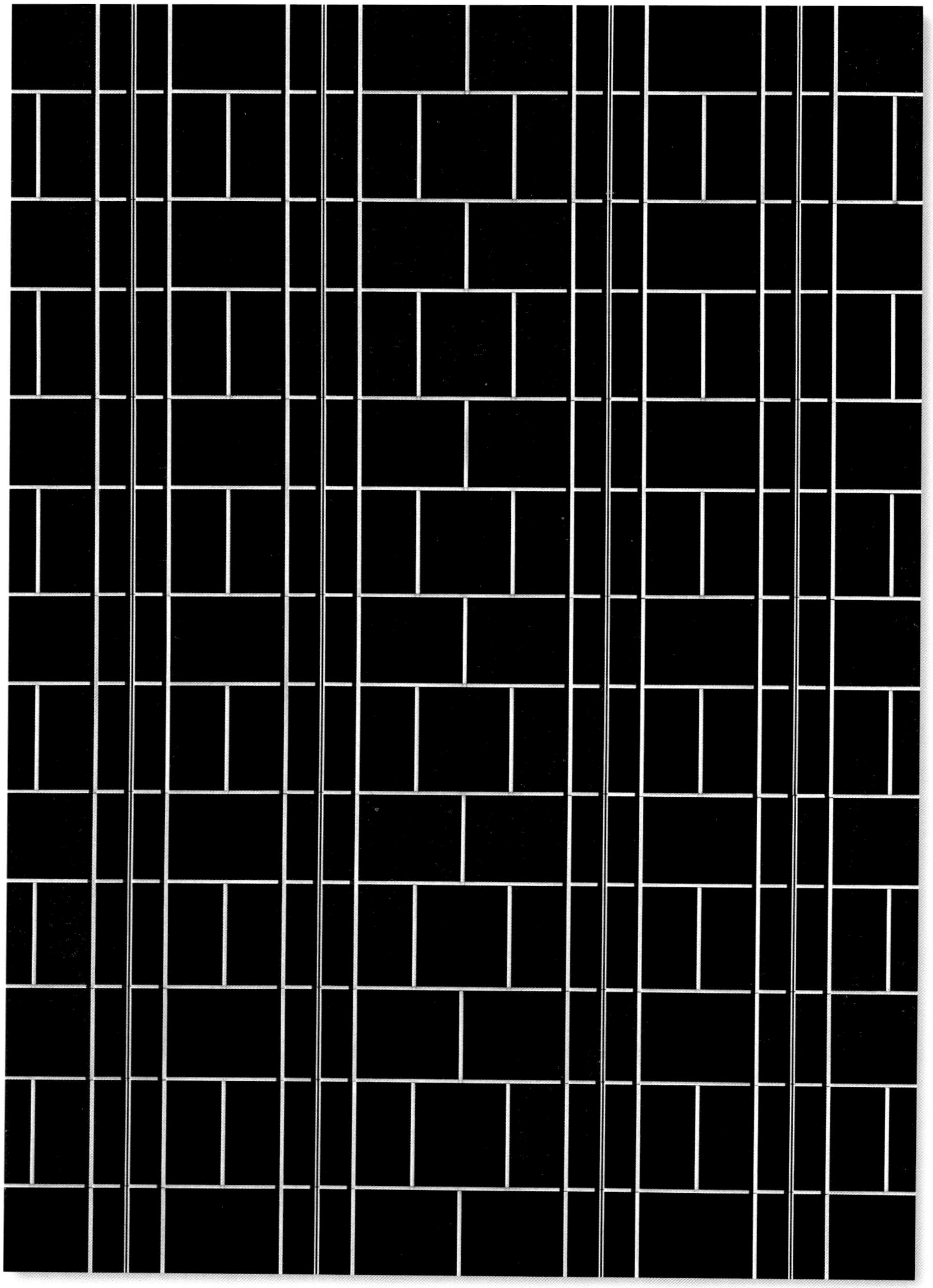

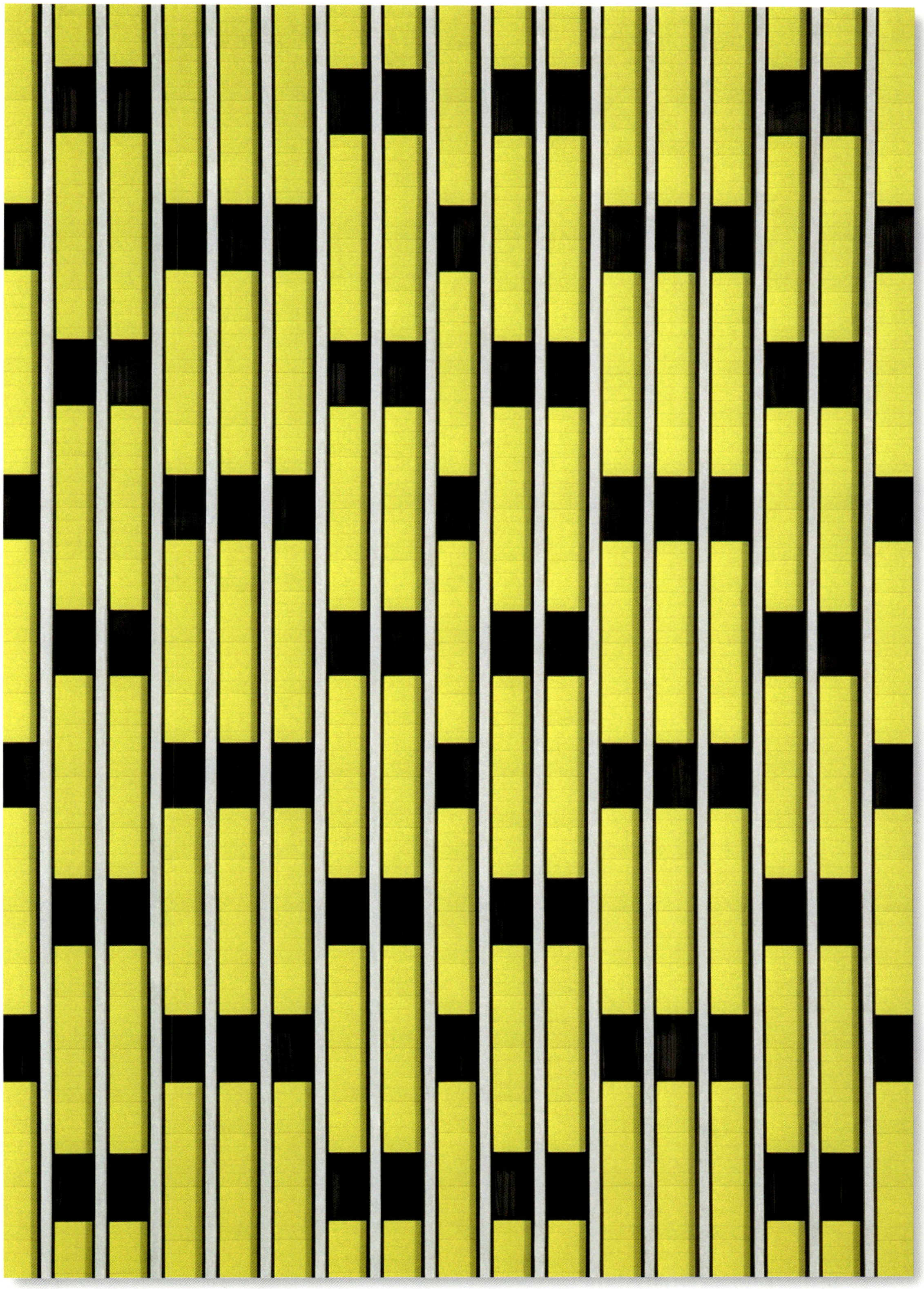

< SNC
MONTREAL
2014

< HOLIDAY INN
SÃO PAOLO
2010

LA DEFENSE #2
PARIS
2002

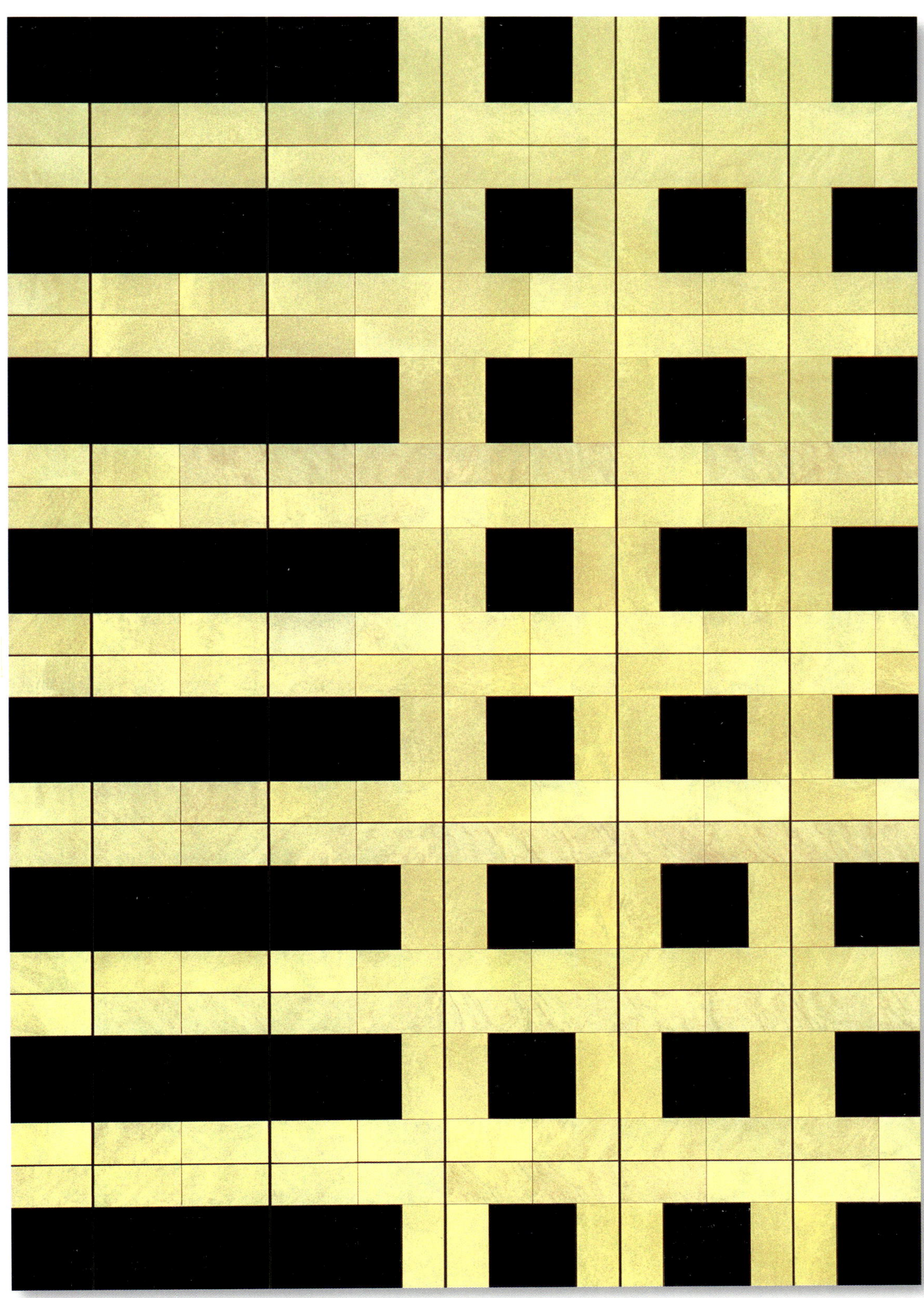

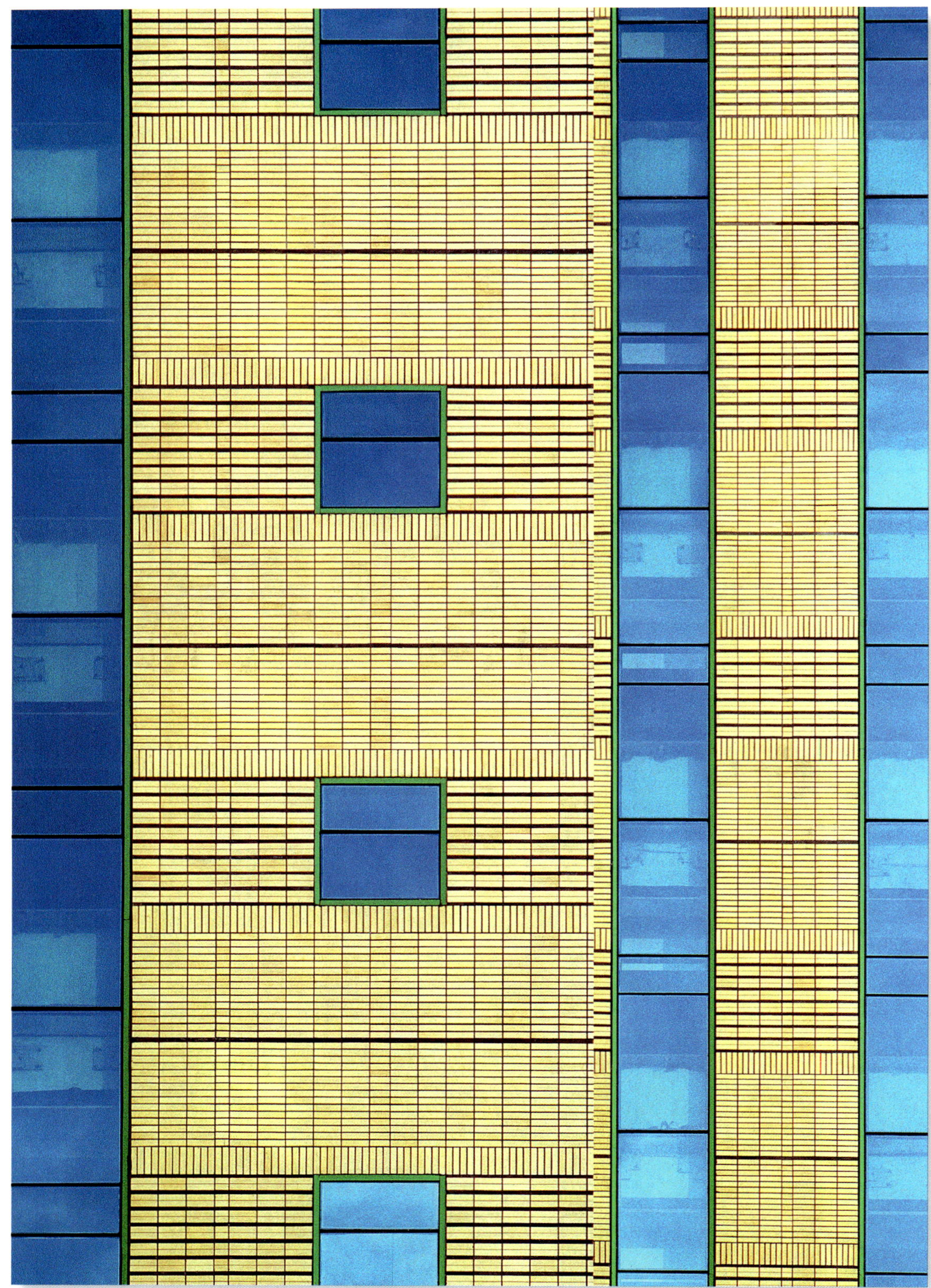

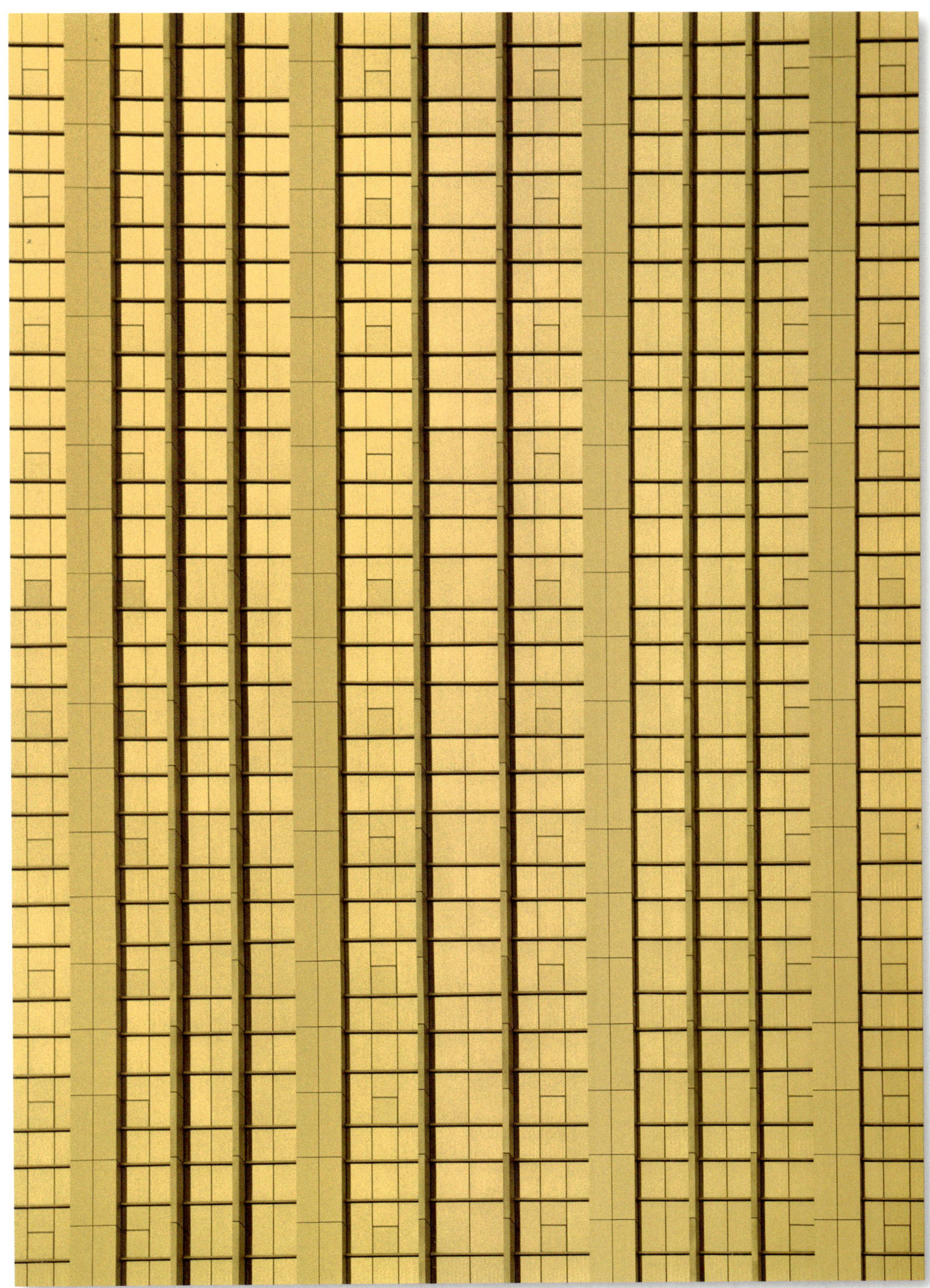

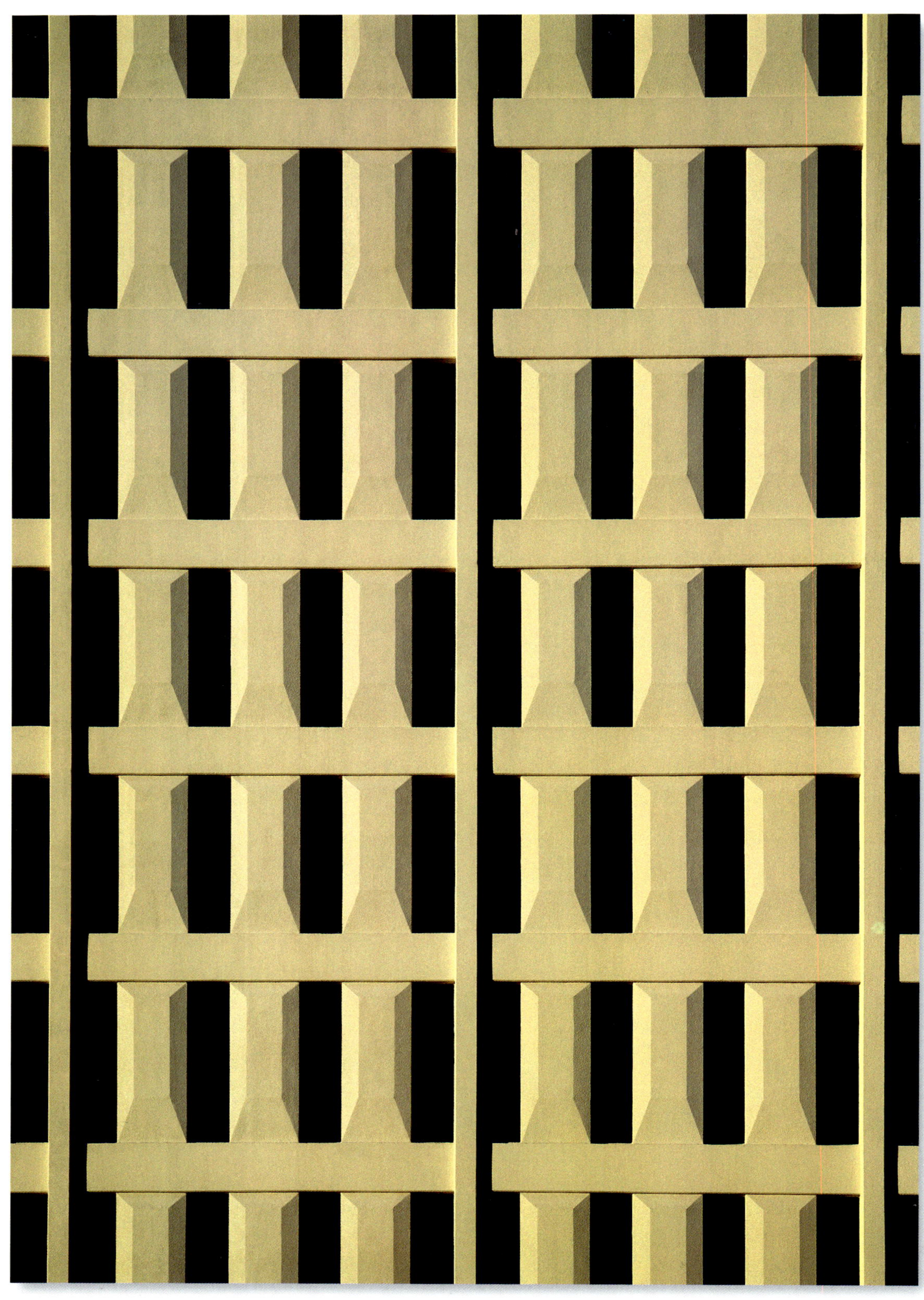

WELLS FARGO
DALLAS
2013

< XI ERHUAN
BEIJING
1998

< BINHE LU
SHENZHEN
2010

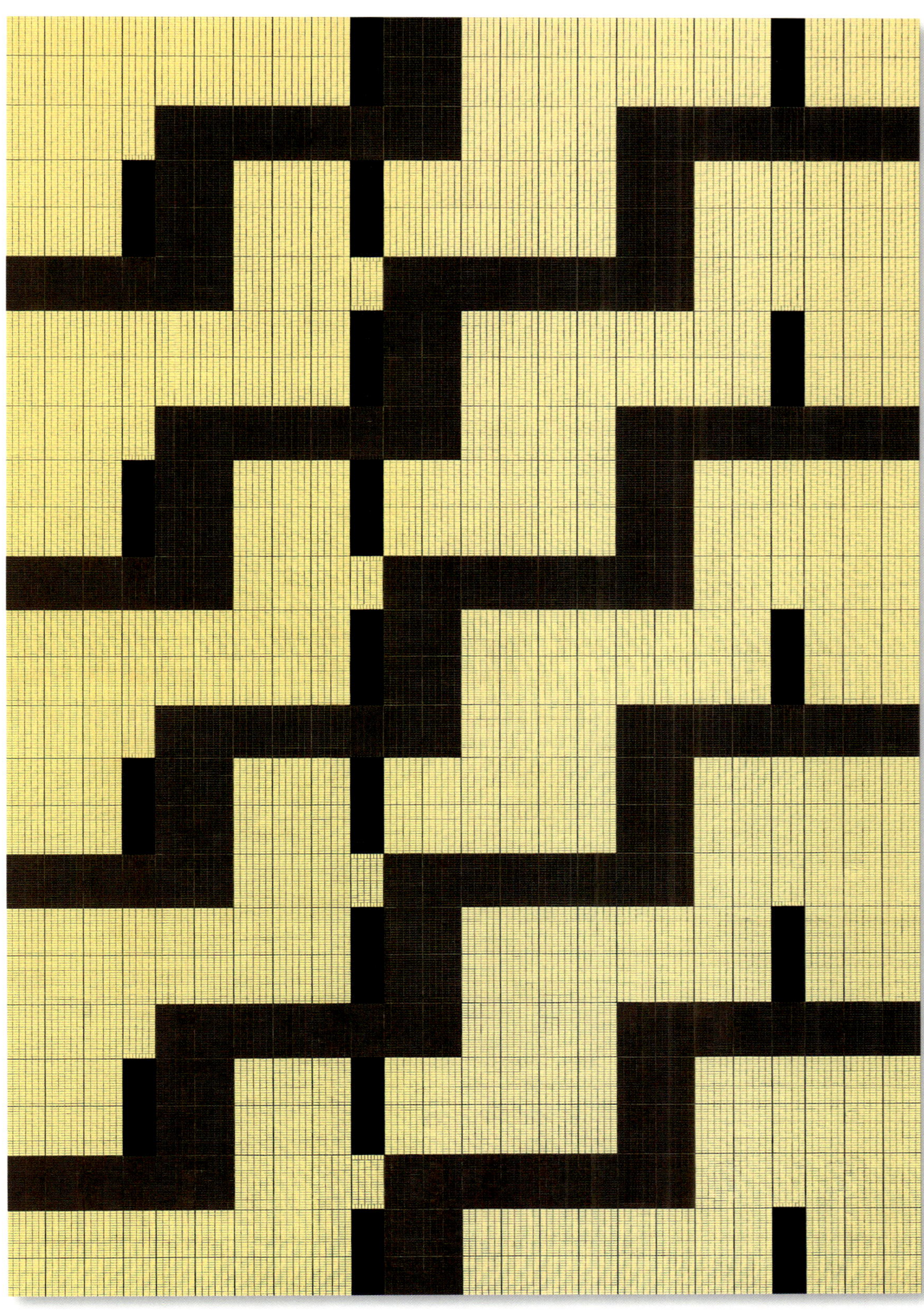

3WTC
NEW YORK
1999

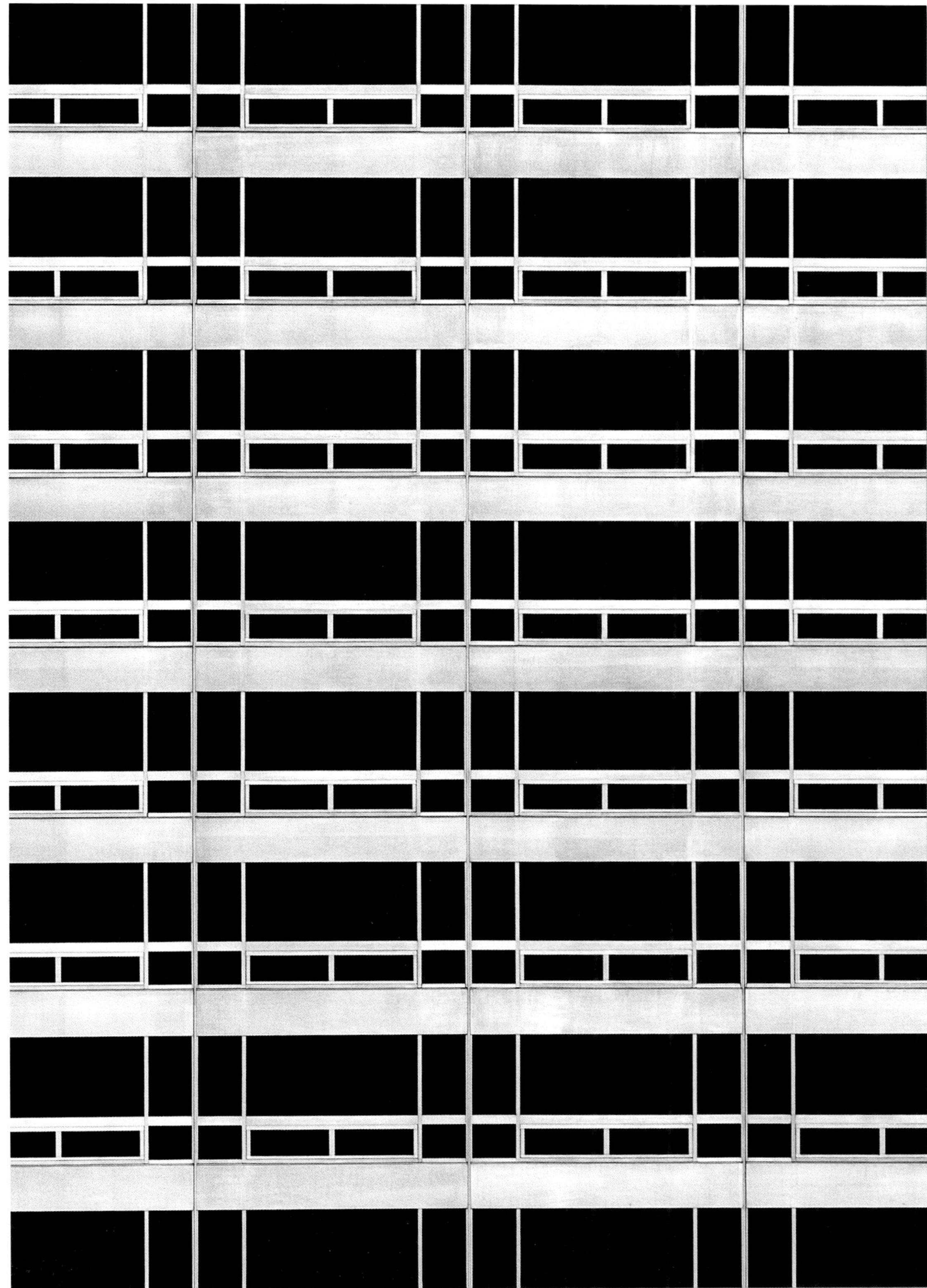

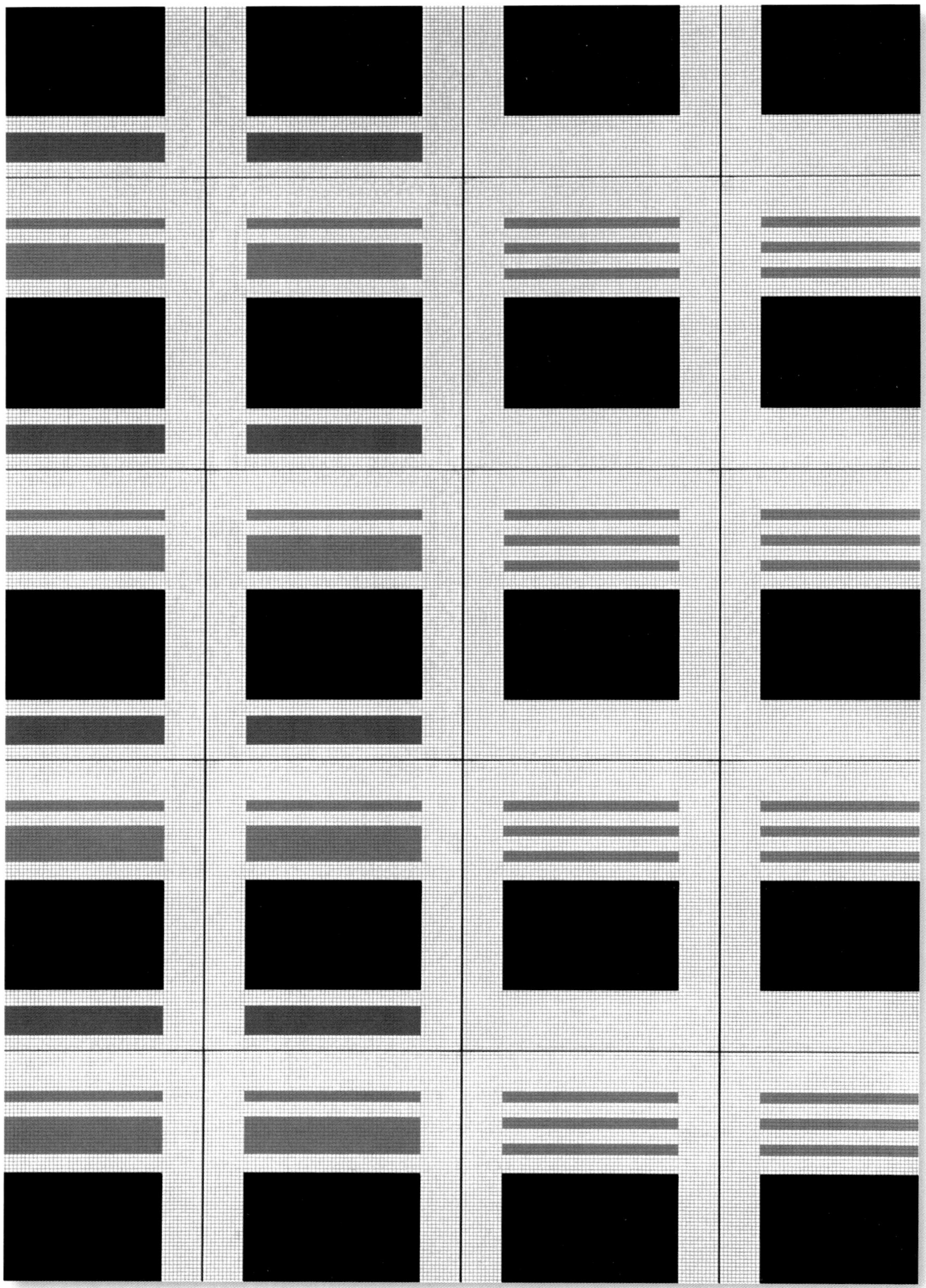

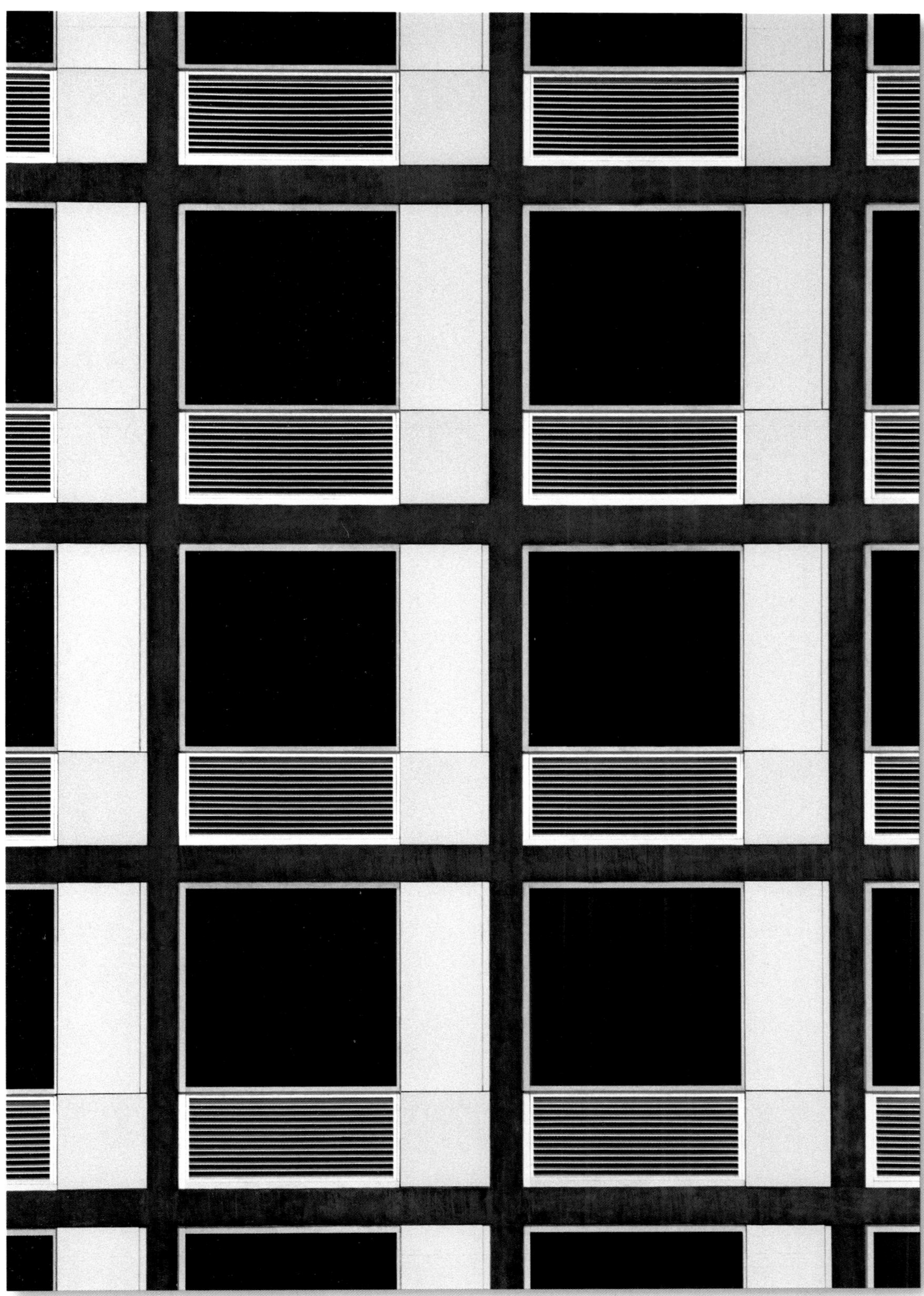

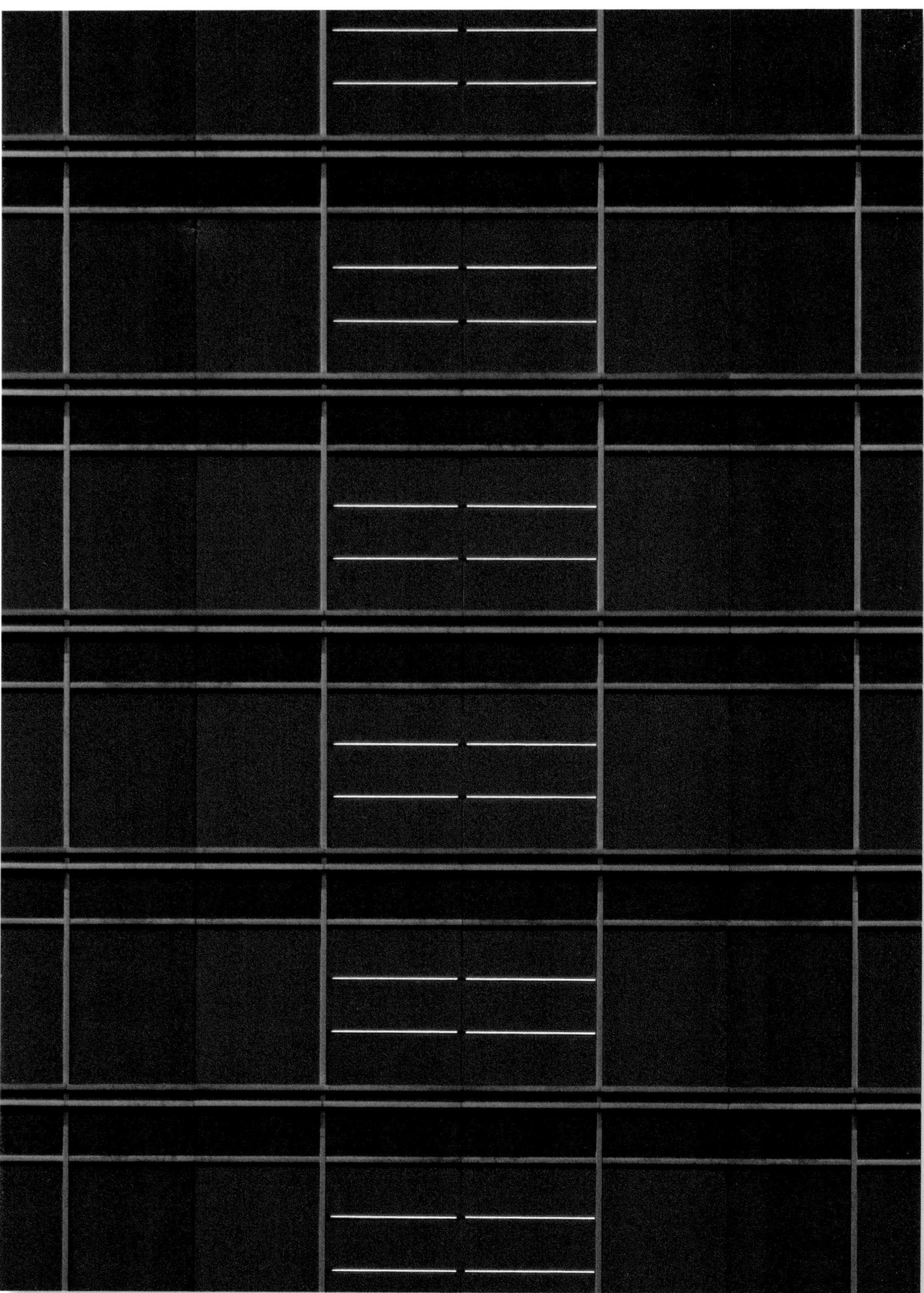

SHEUNG WAN
HONG KONG
1998

< DOCOMO
TOKYO
2004

< MCM
BEIJING
2005

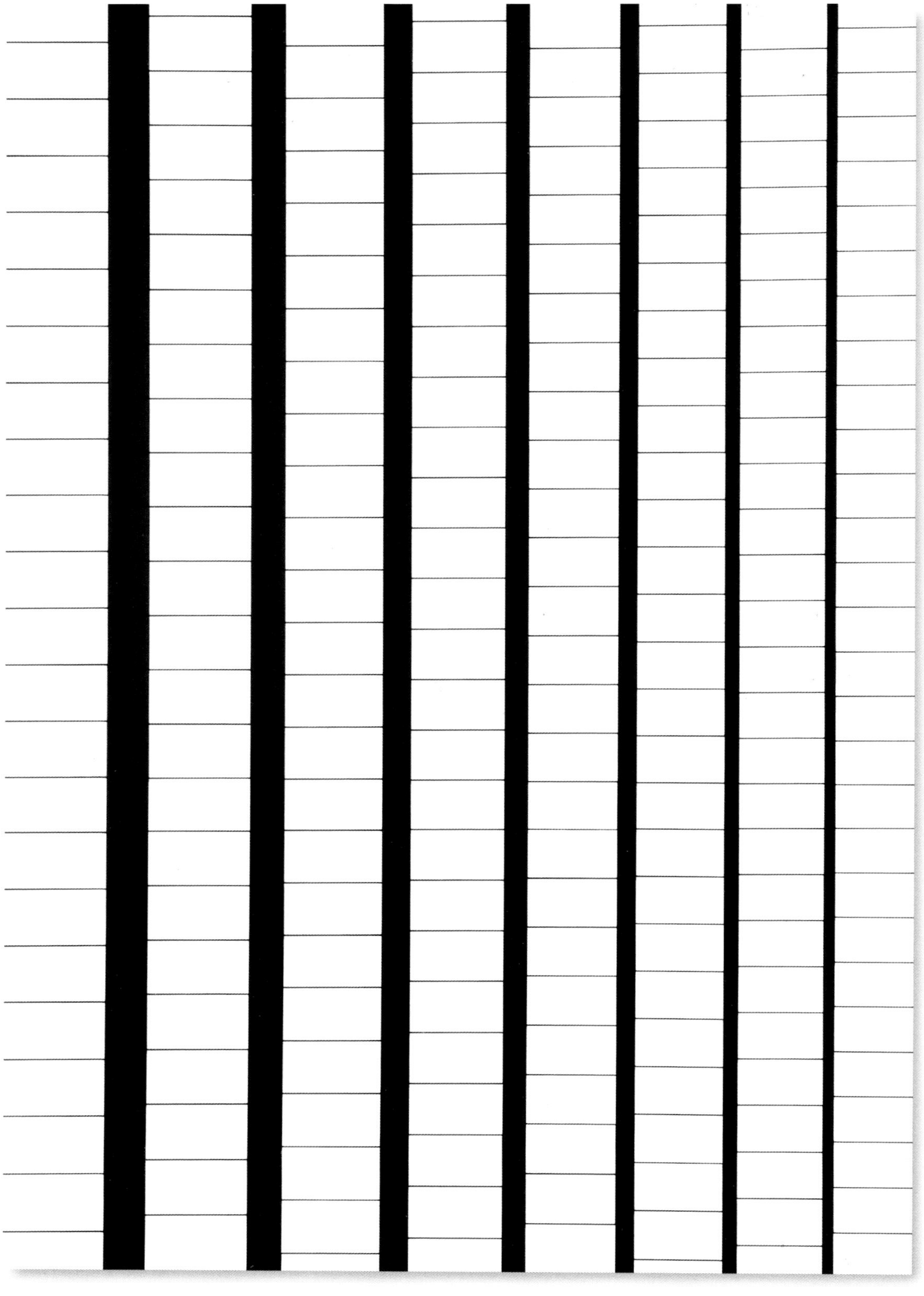

BANK OF BANGKOK
SINGAPORE
2002

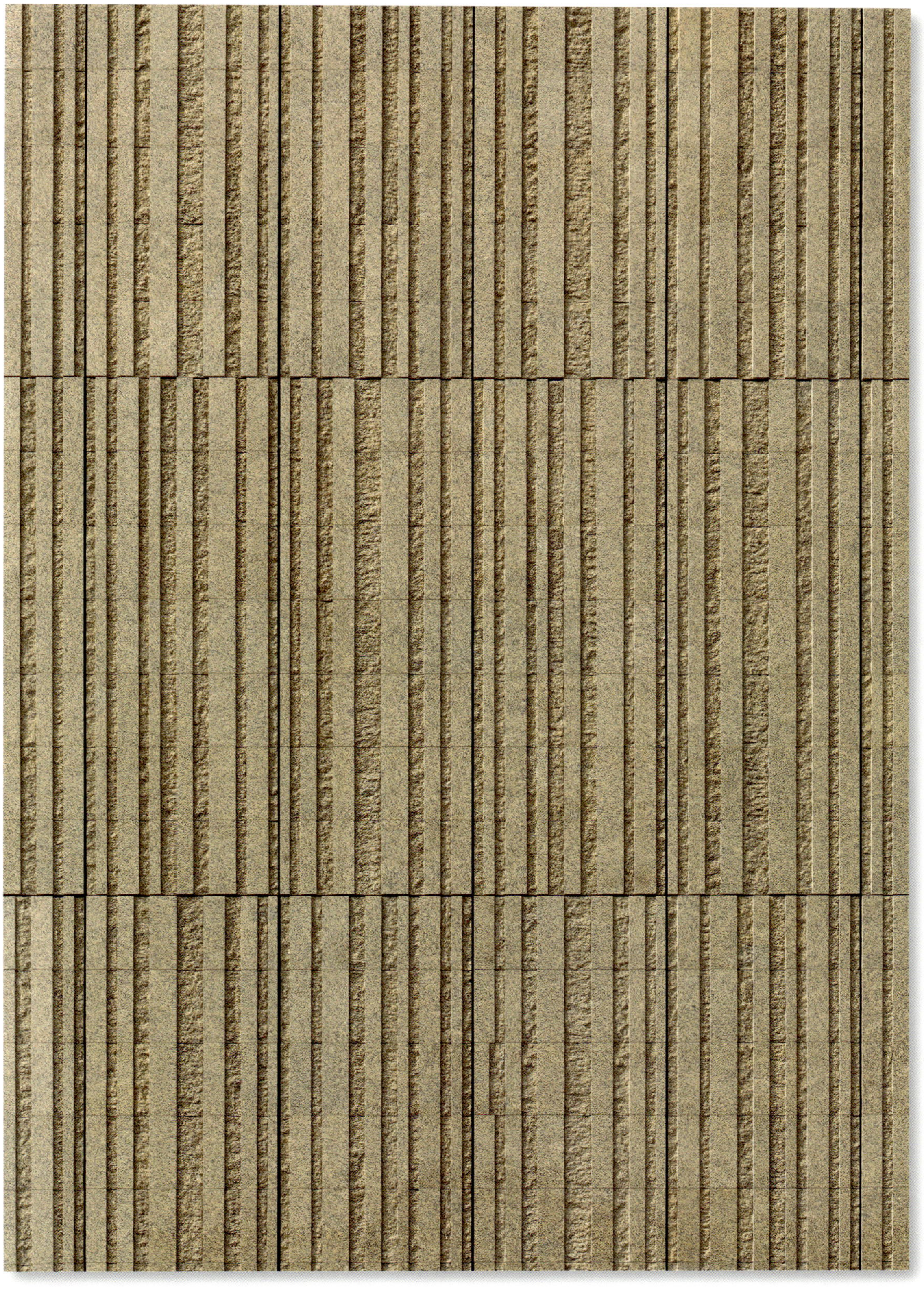

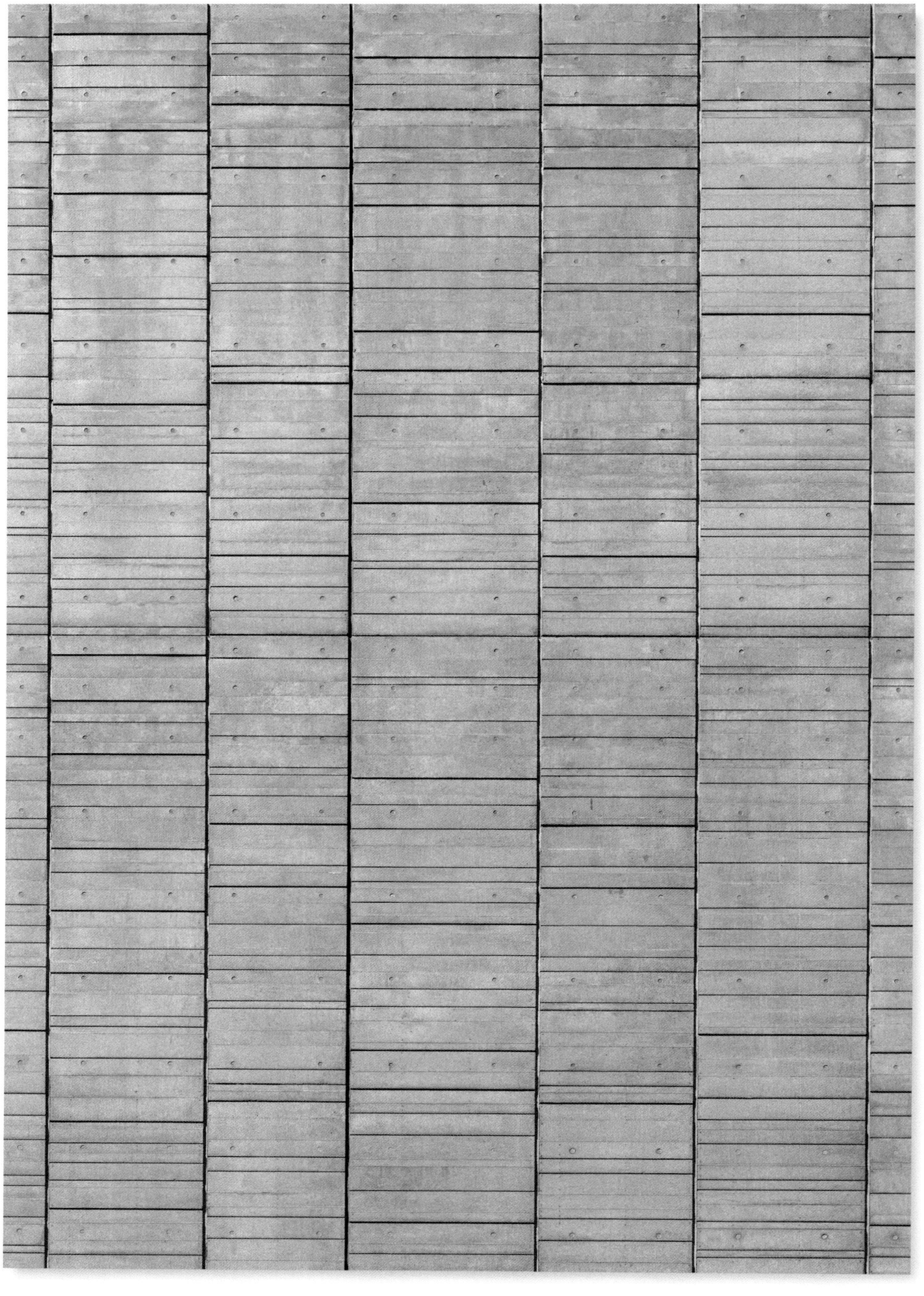

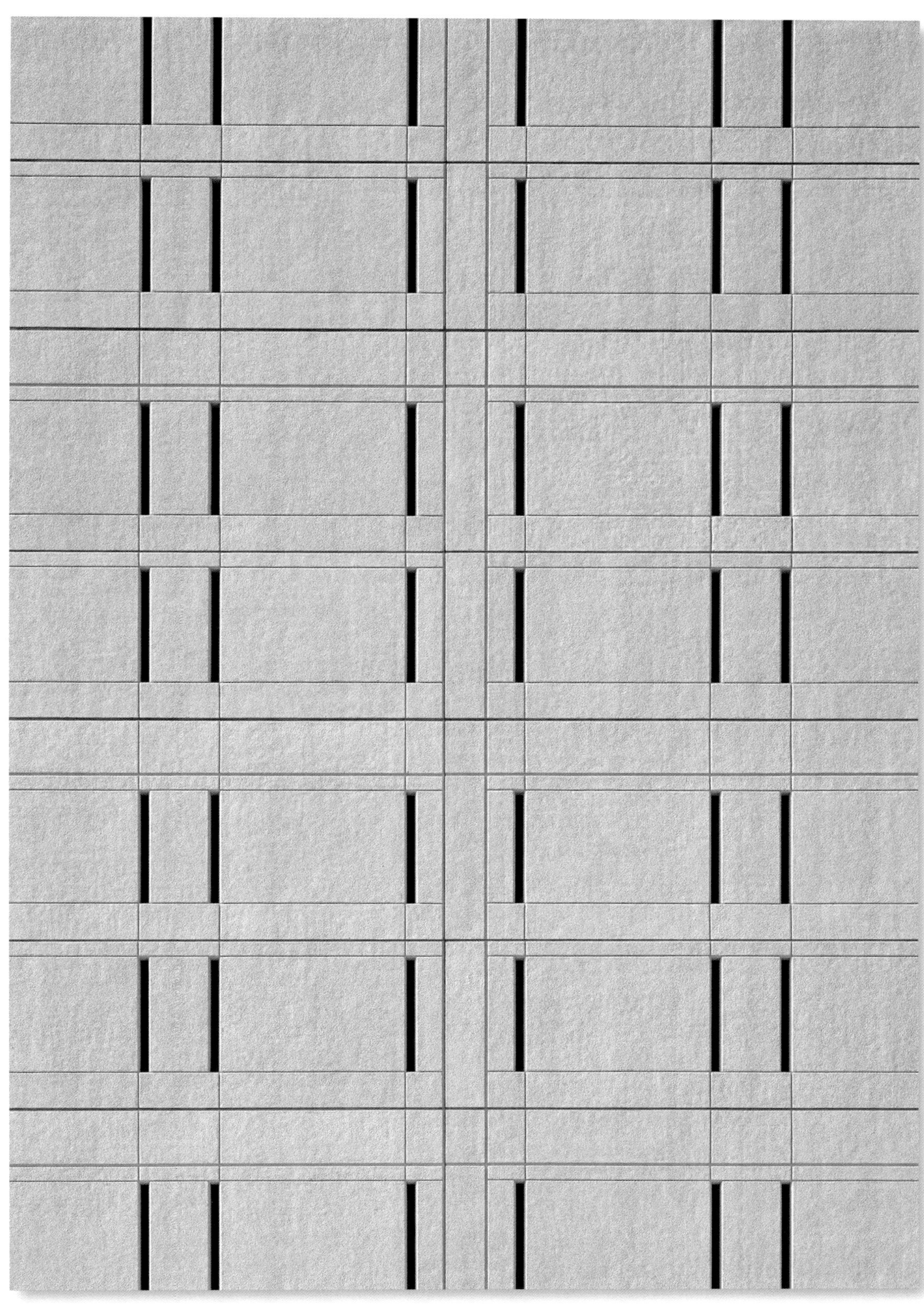

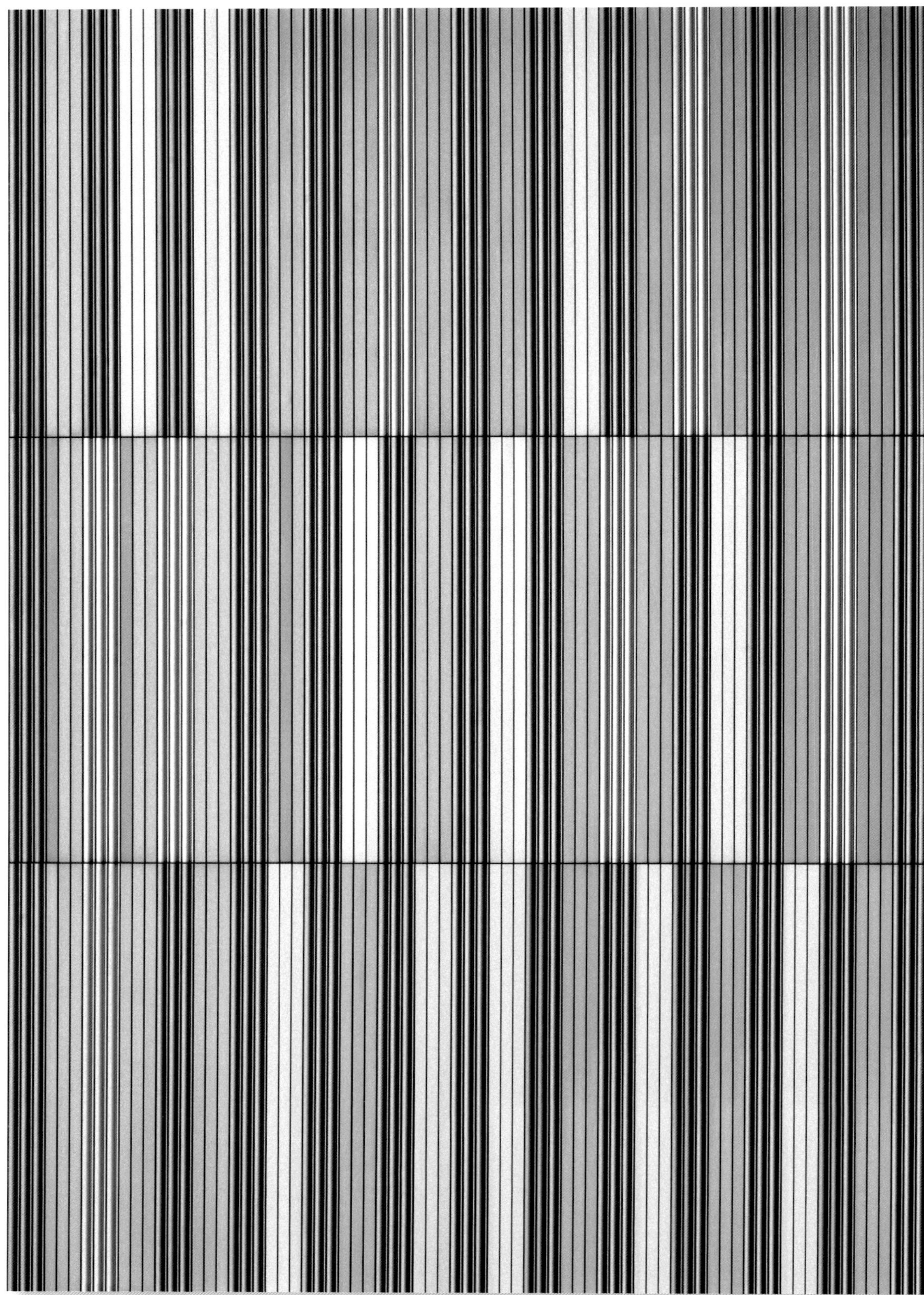

ICC
THE HAGUE
2013

< ARUKAS
OSAKA
2014

< FDC
HOUSTON
2014

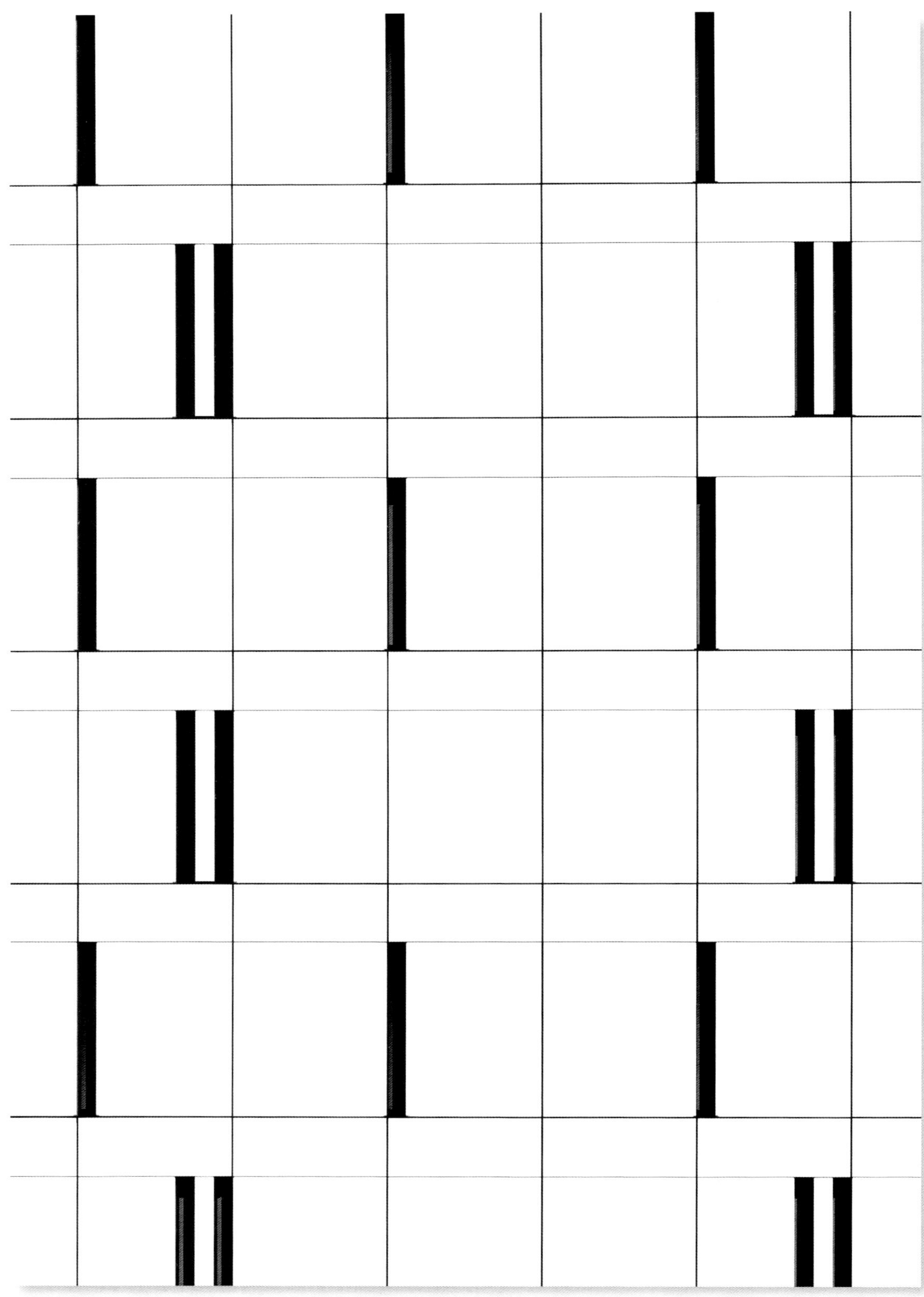

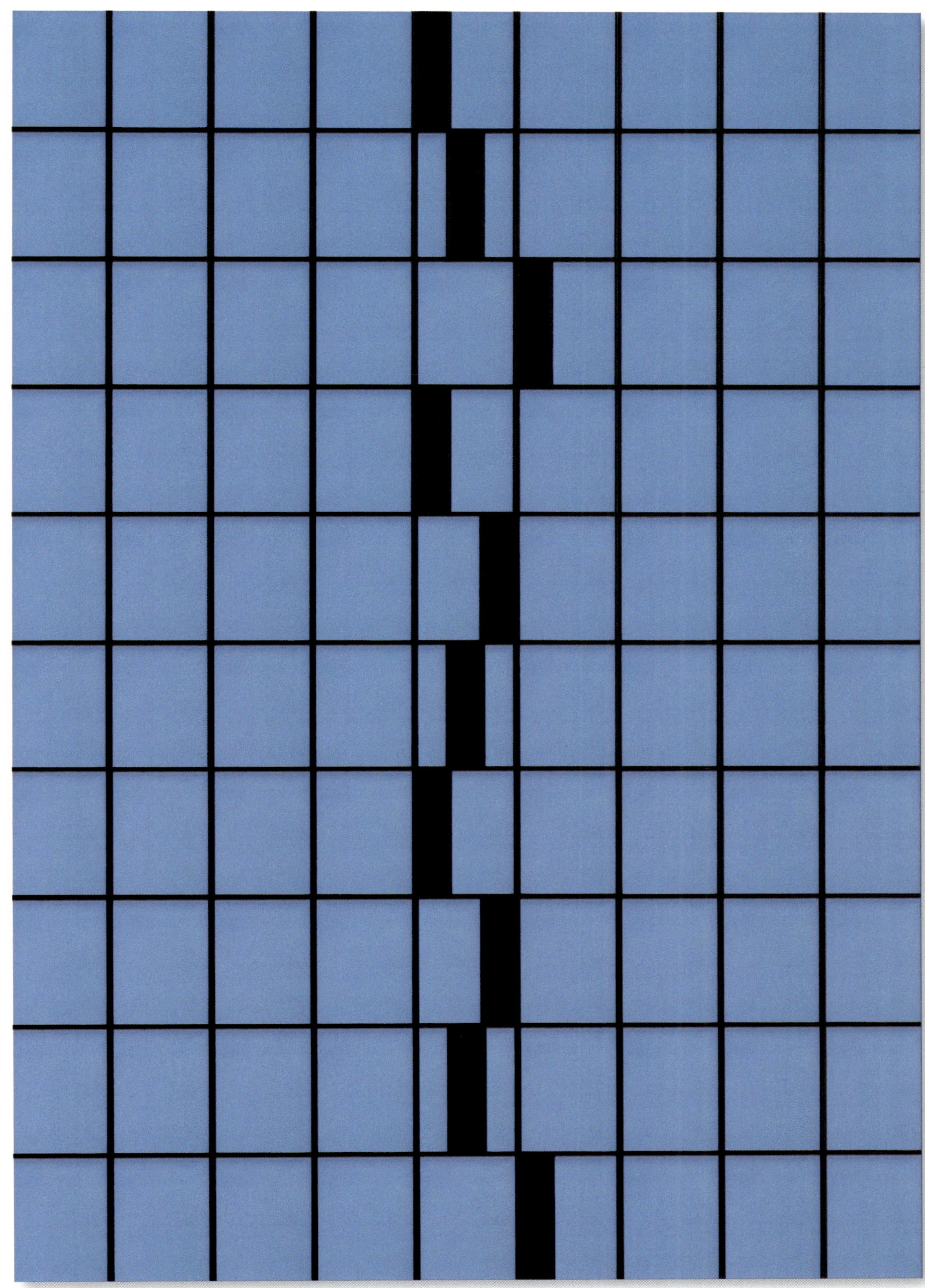

< SAKURA DORI
NAGOYA
2014

< MIYAKOJIMA DORI
OSAKA
2014

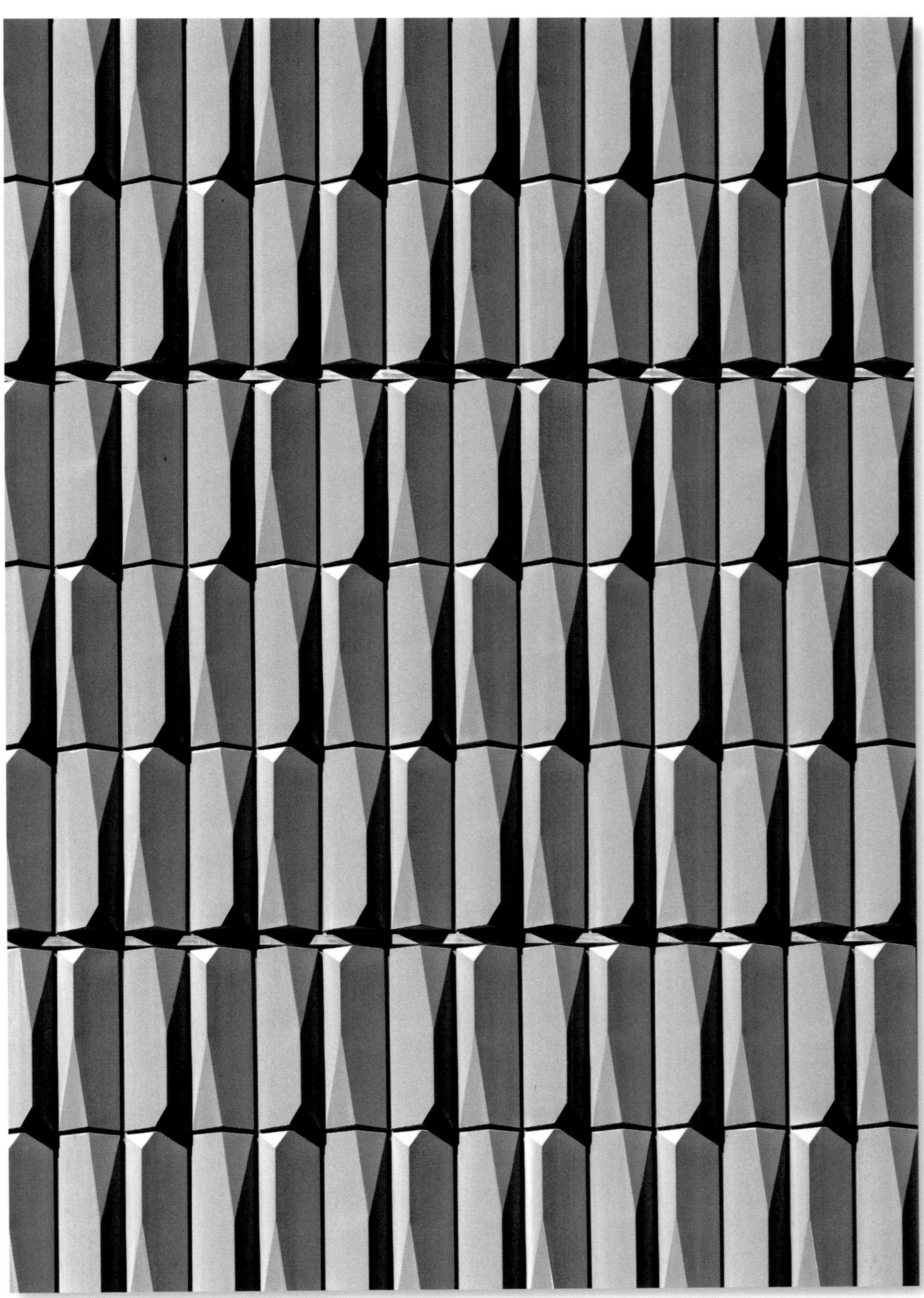

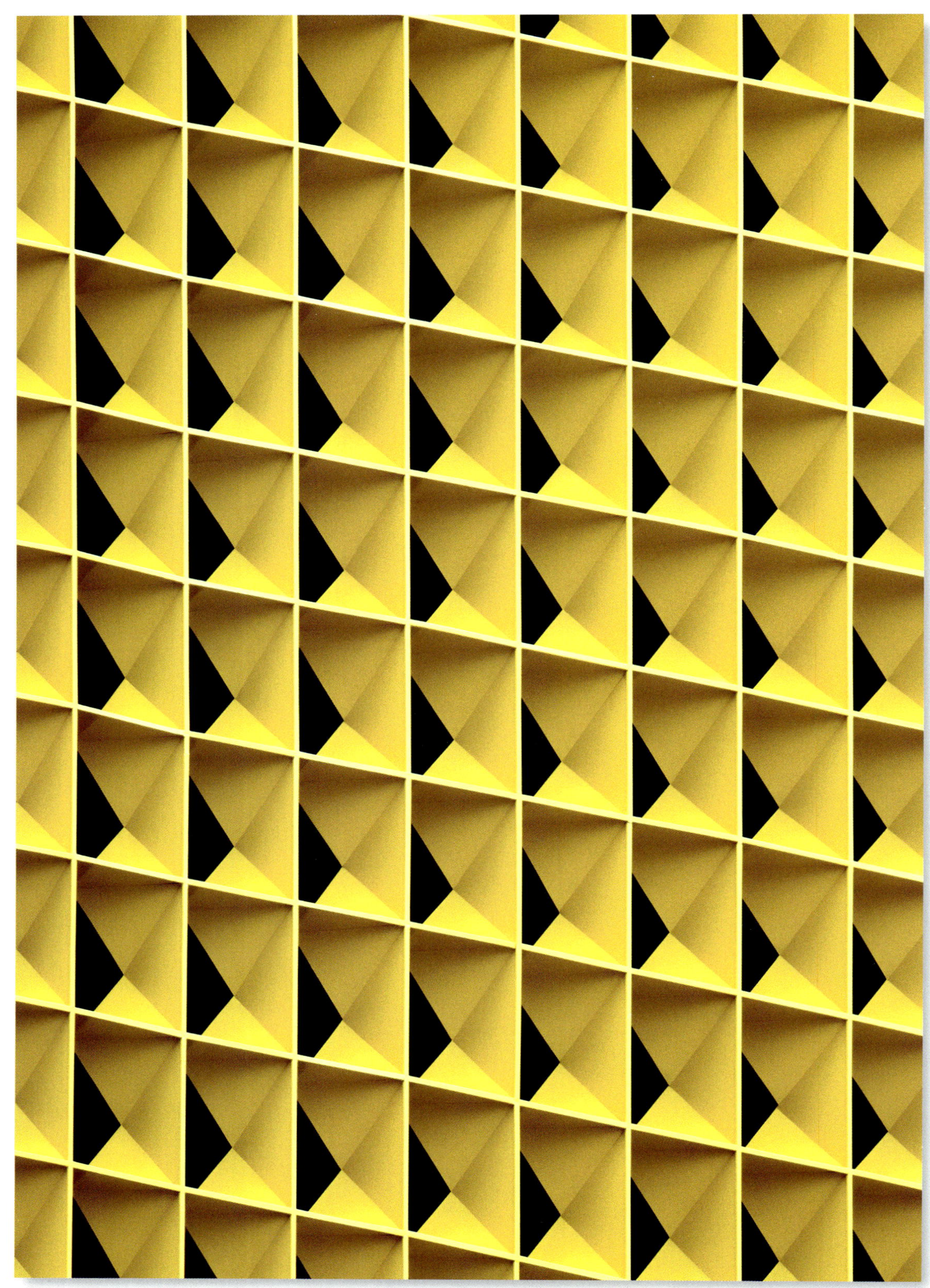

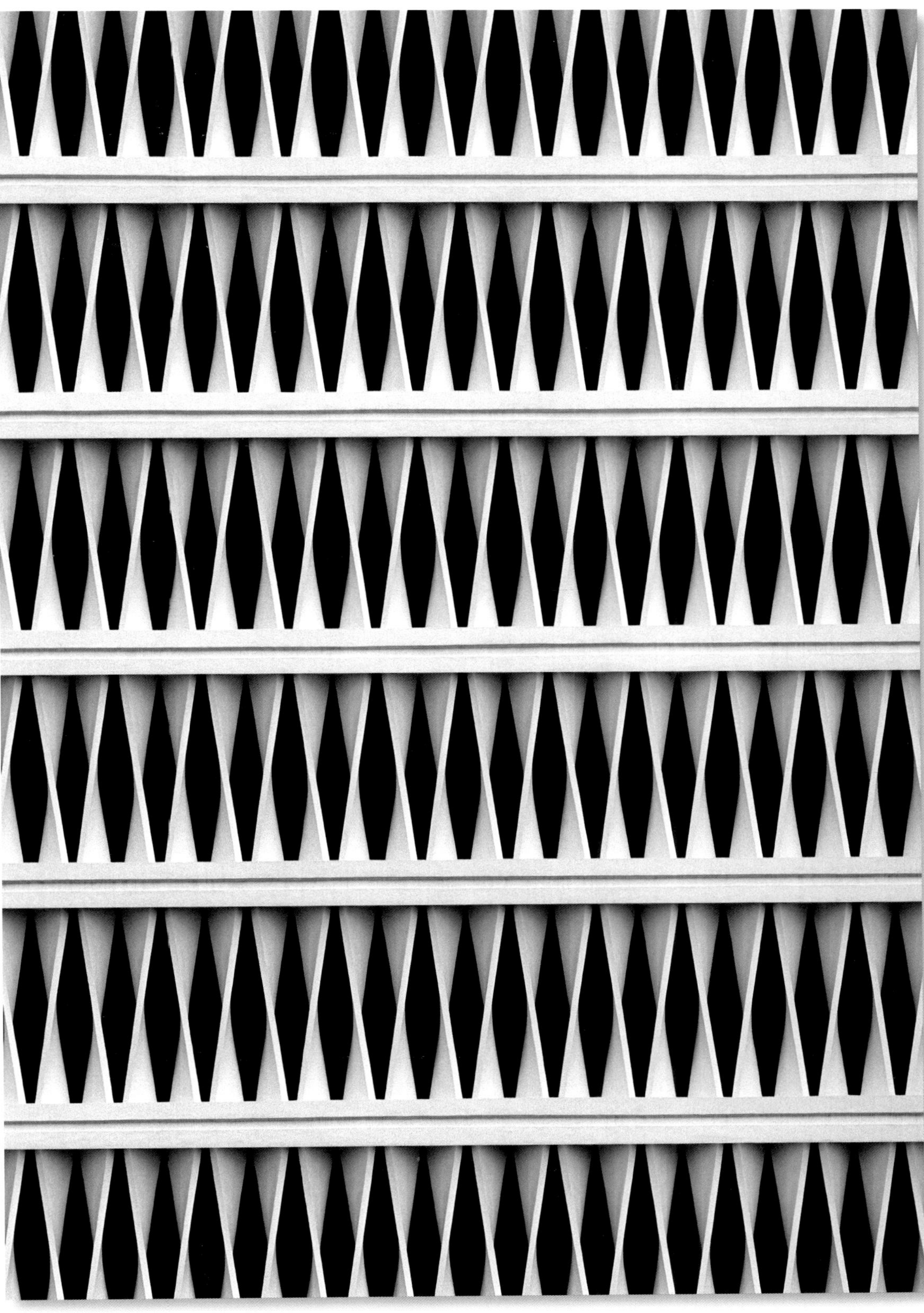

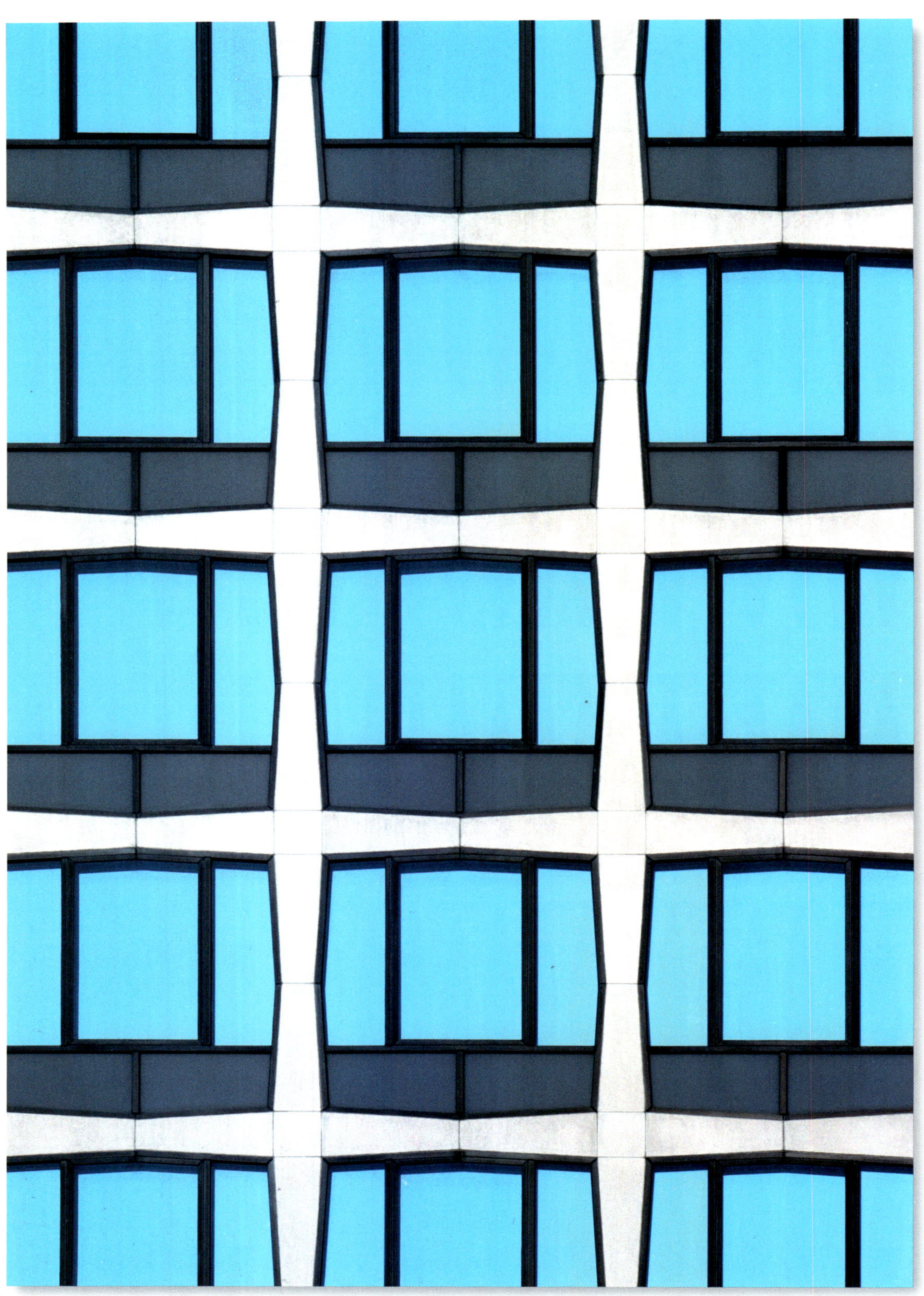

PENN AVE
WASHINGTON
2005

< ELDORADO
BRASILIA
2006

< CICIL STREET
SINGAPORE
2002

PRISON
CHICAGO
2002

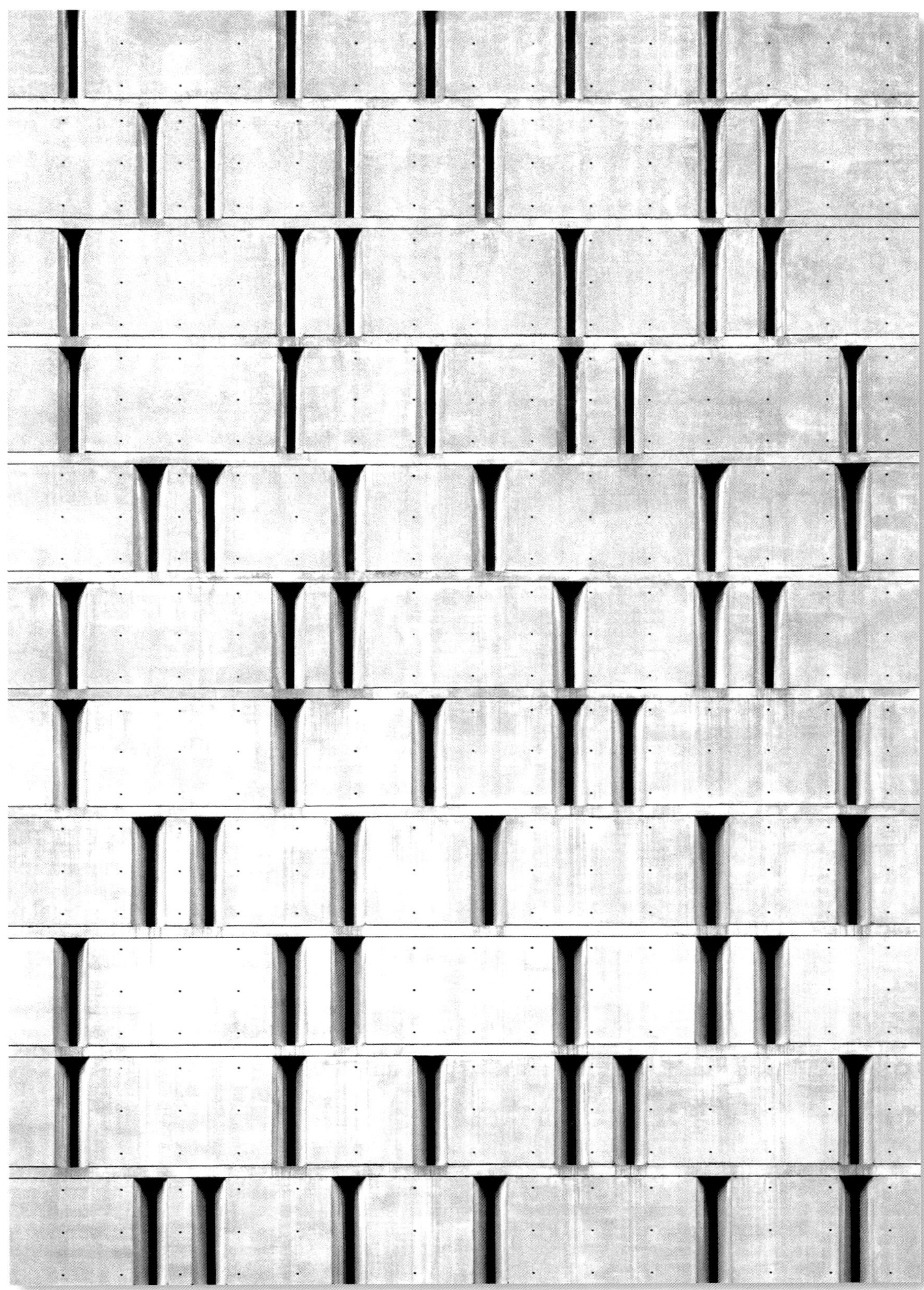

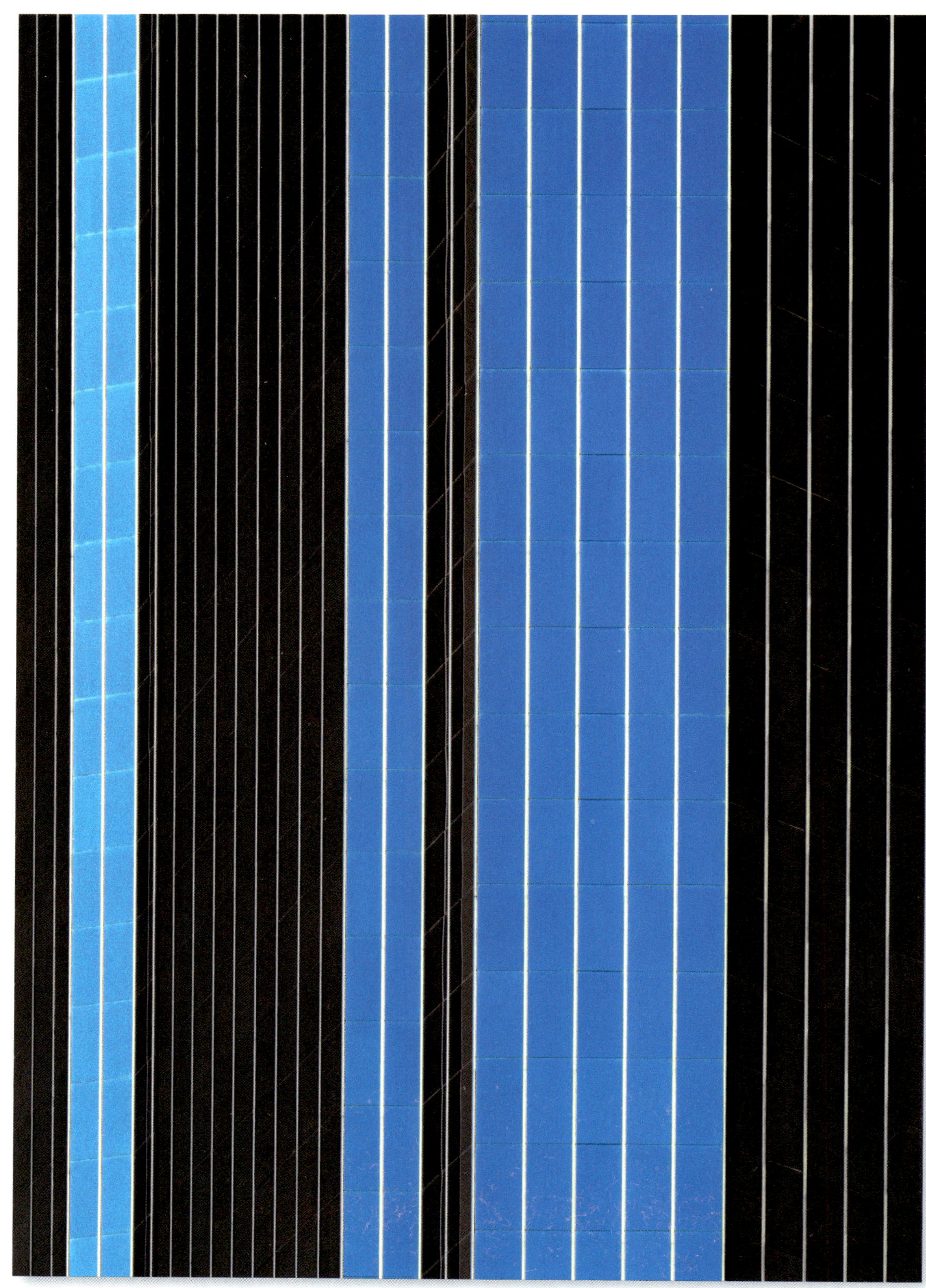

TSIM SHA TSUI EAST
HONG KONG
1998

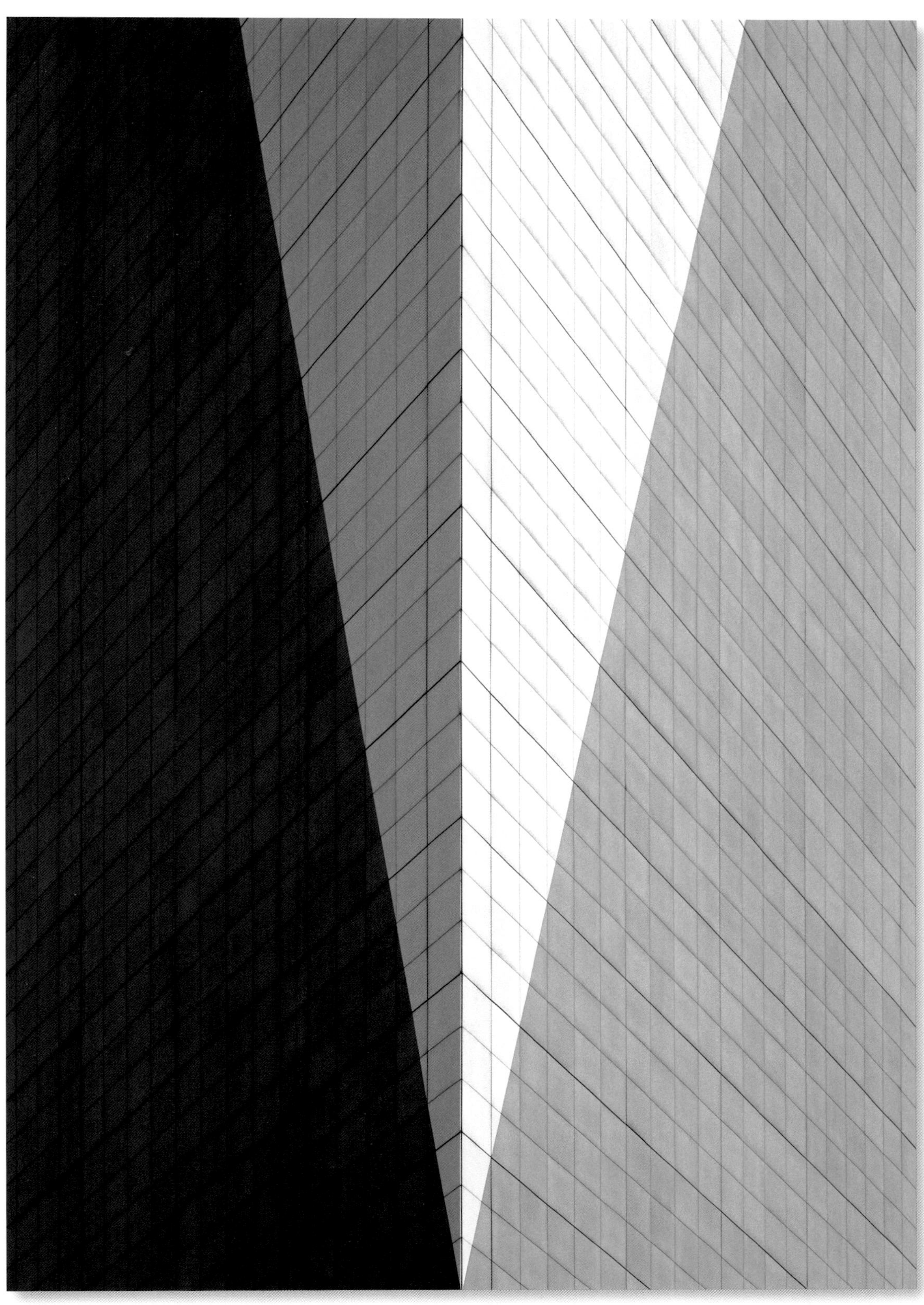

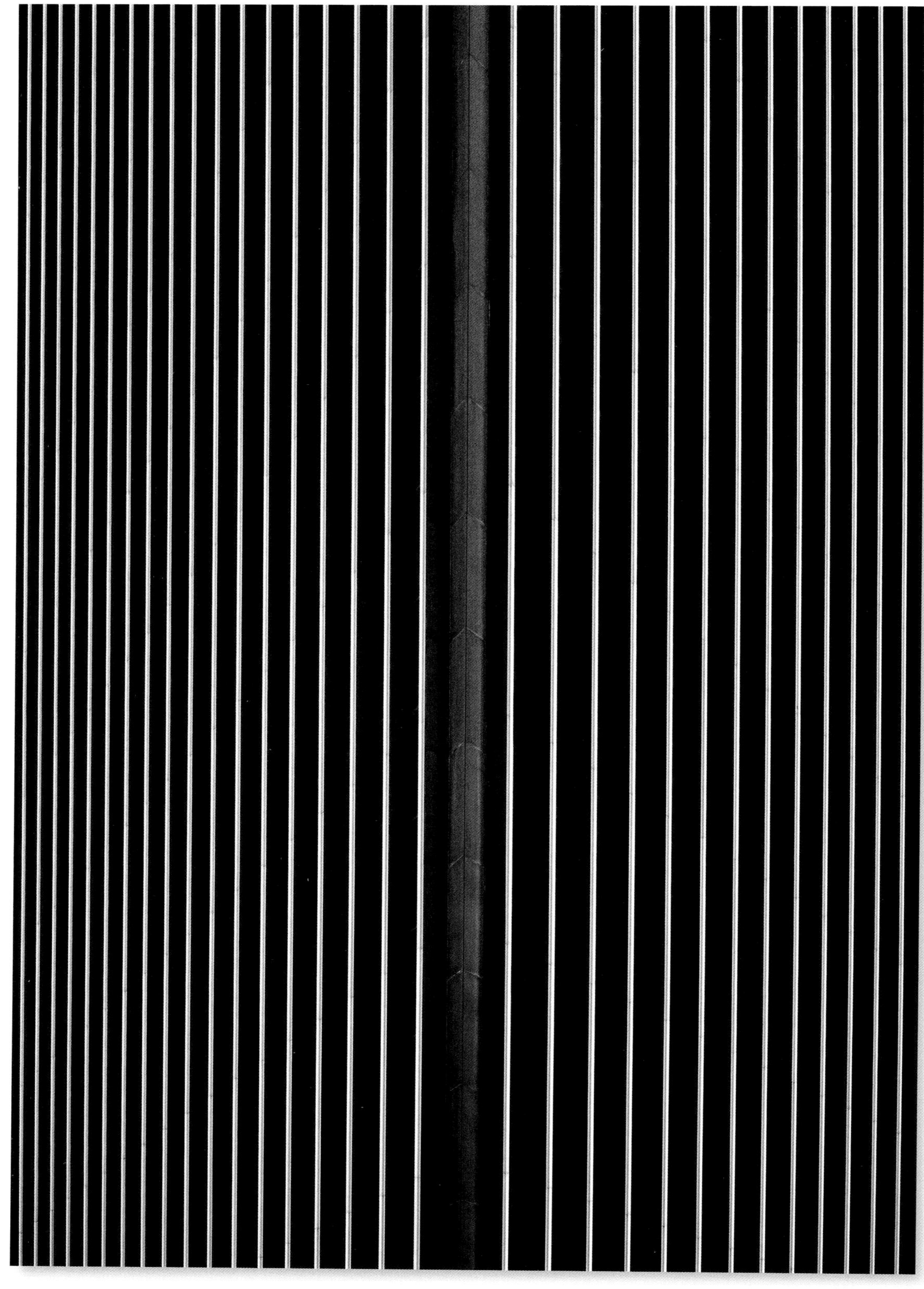

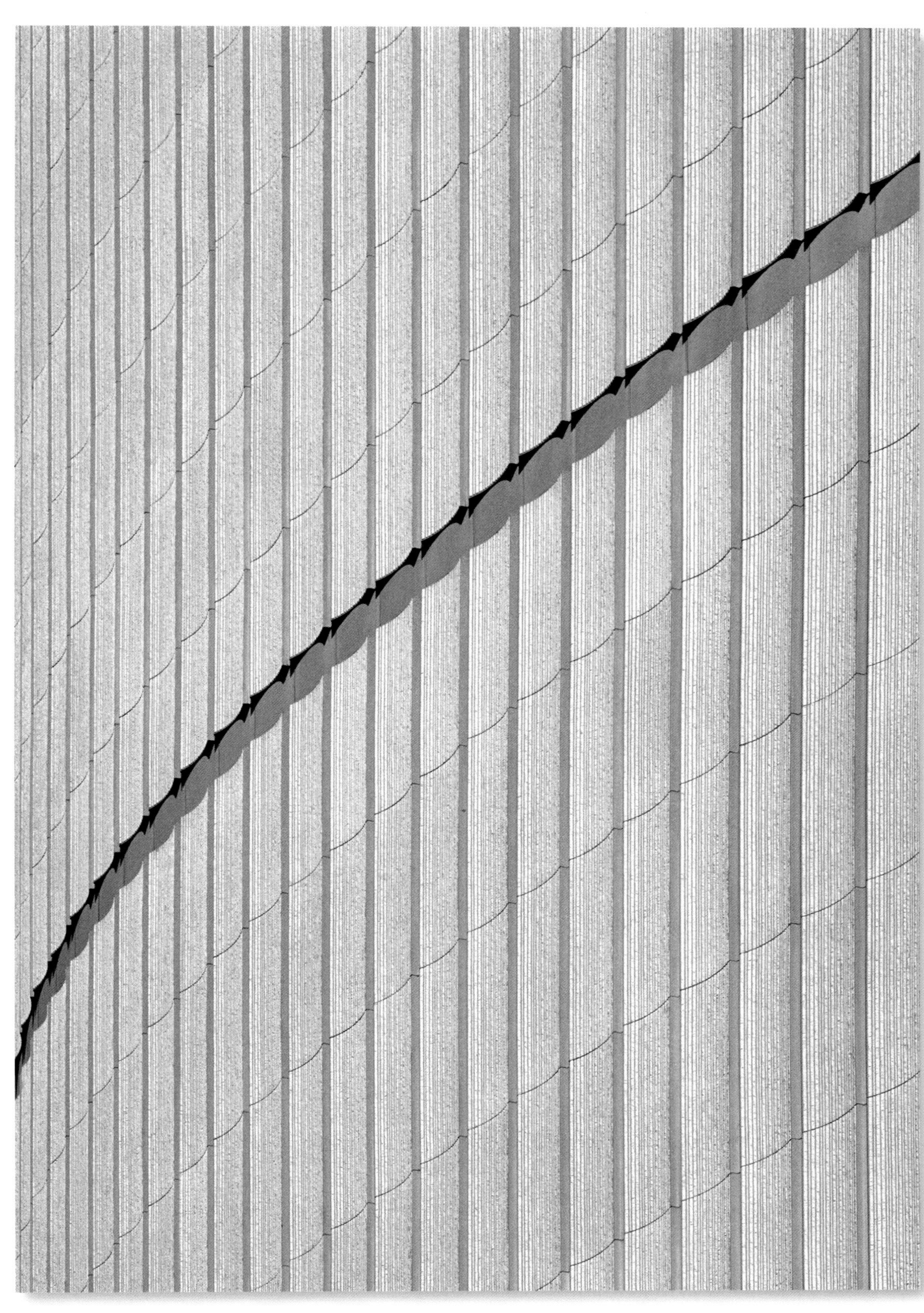

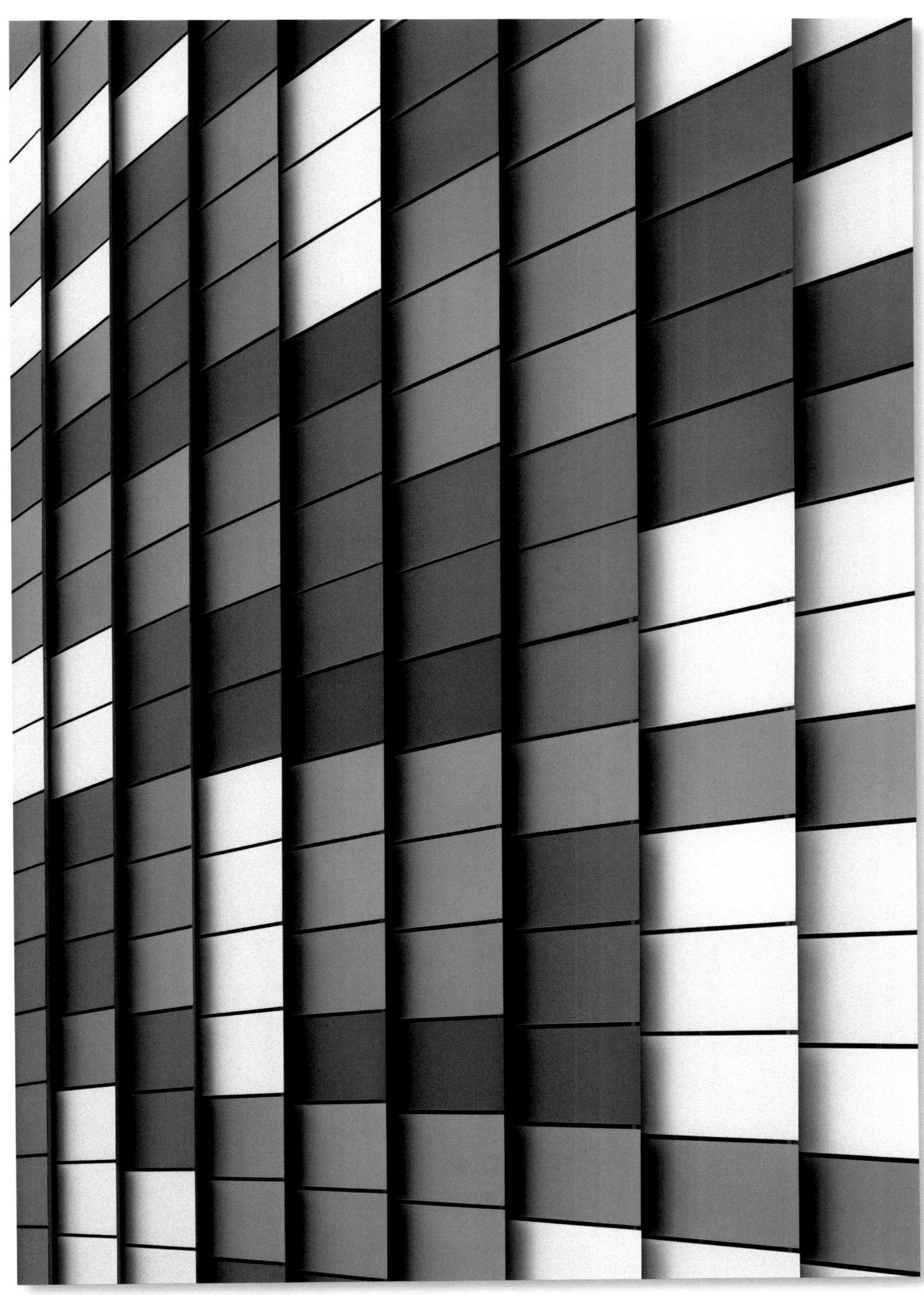

PUDONG
SHANGHAI
1998

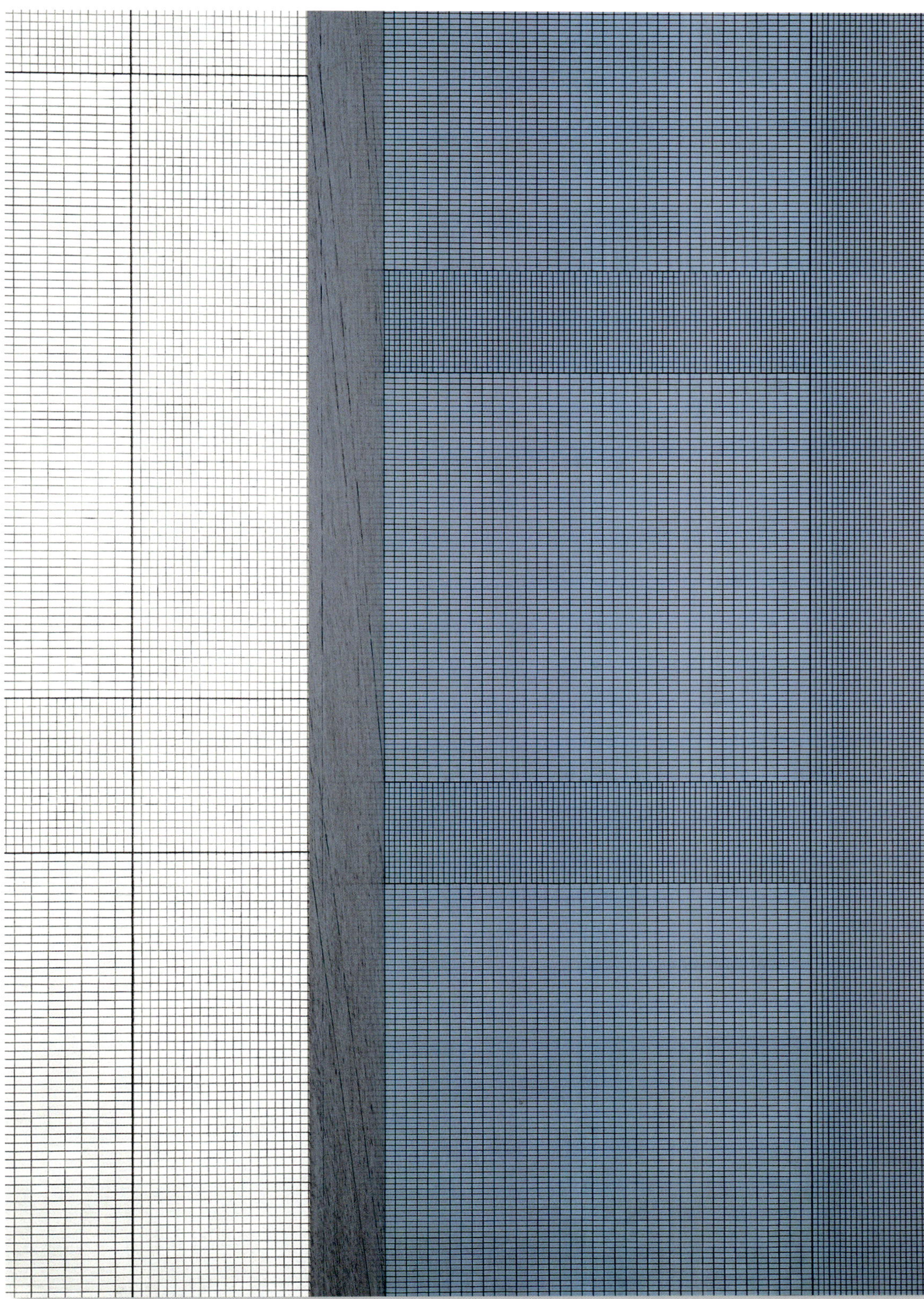

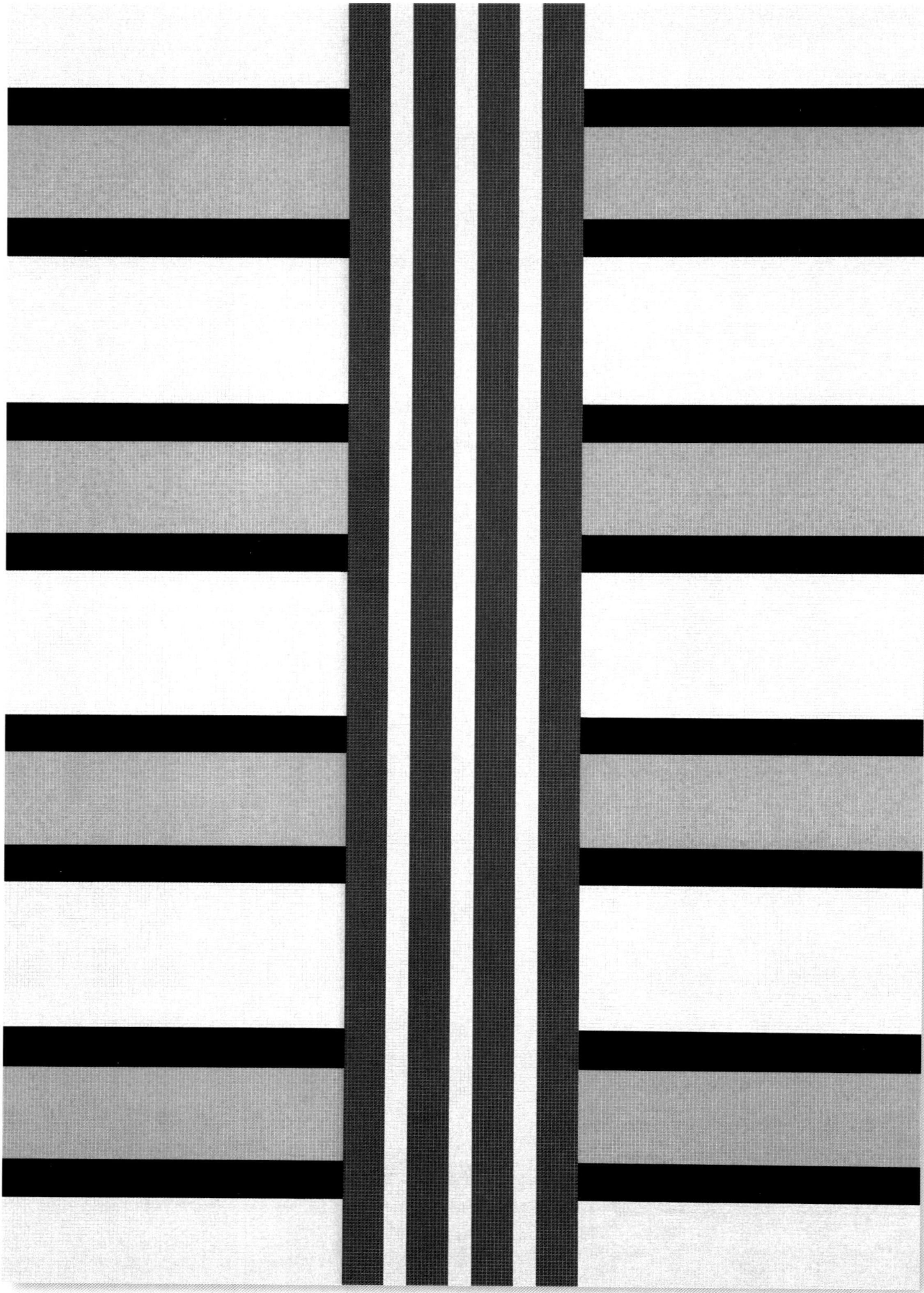

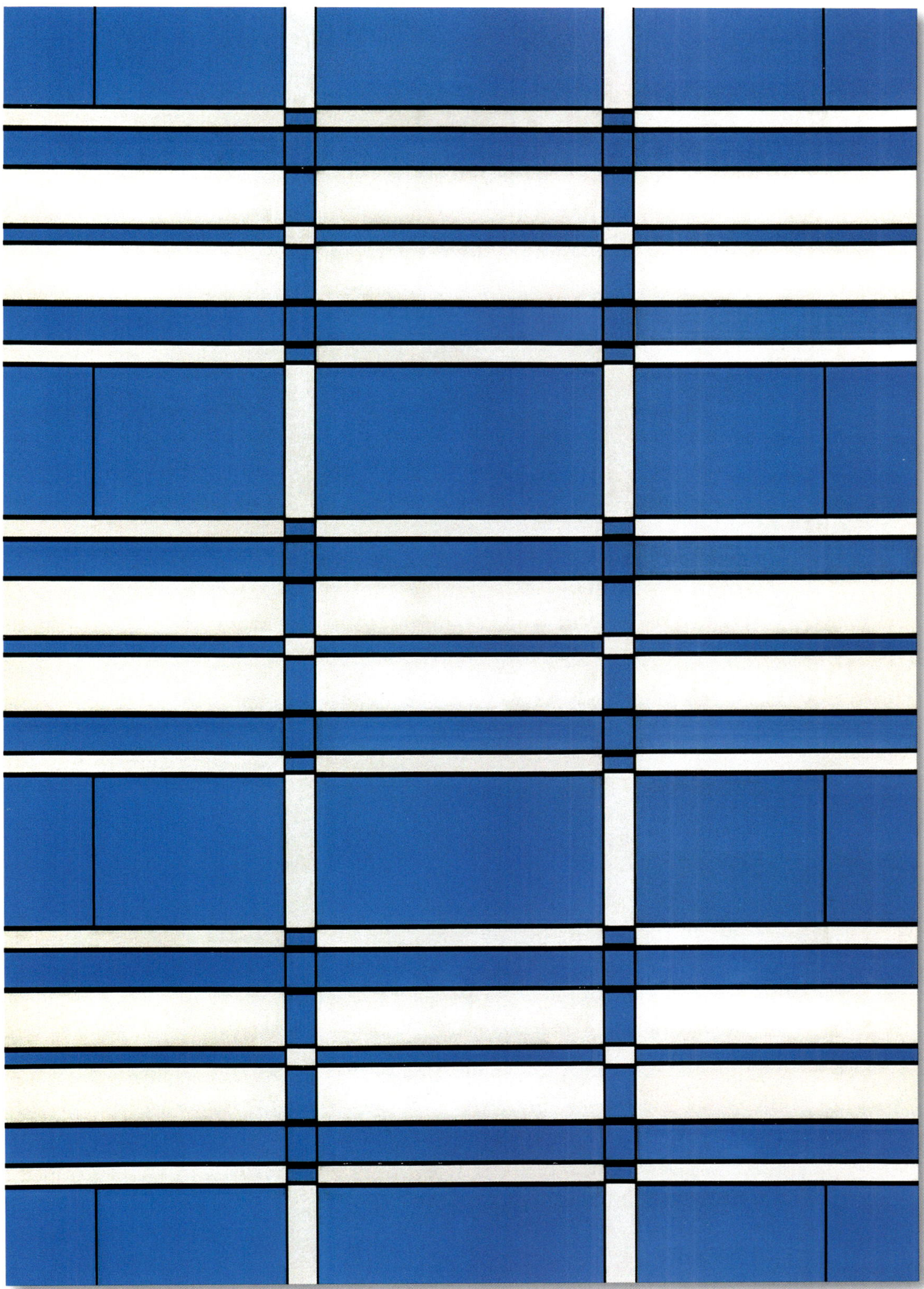

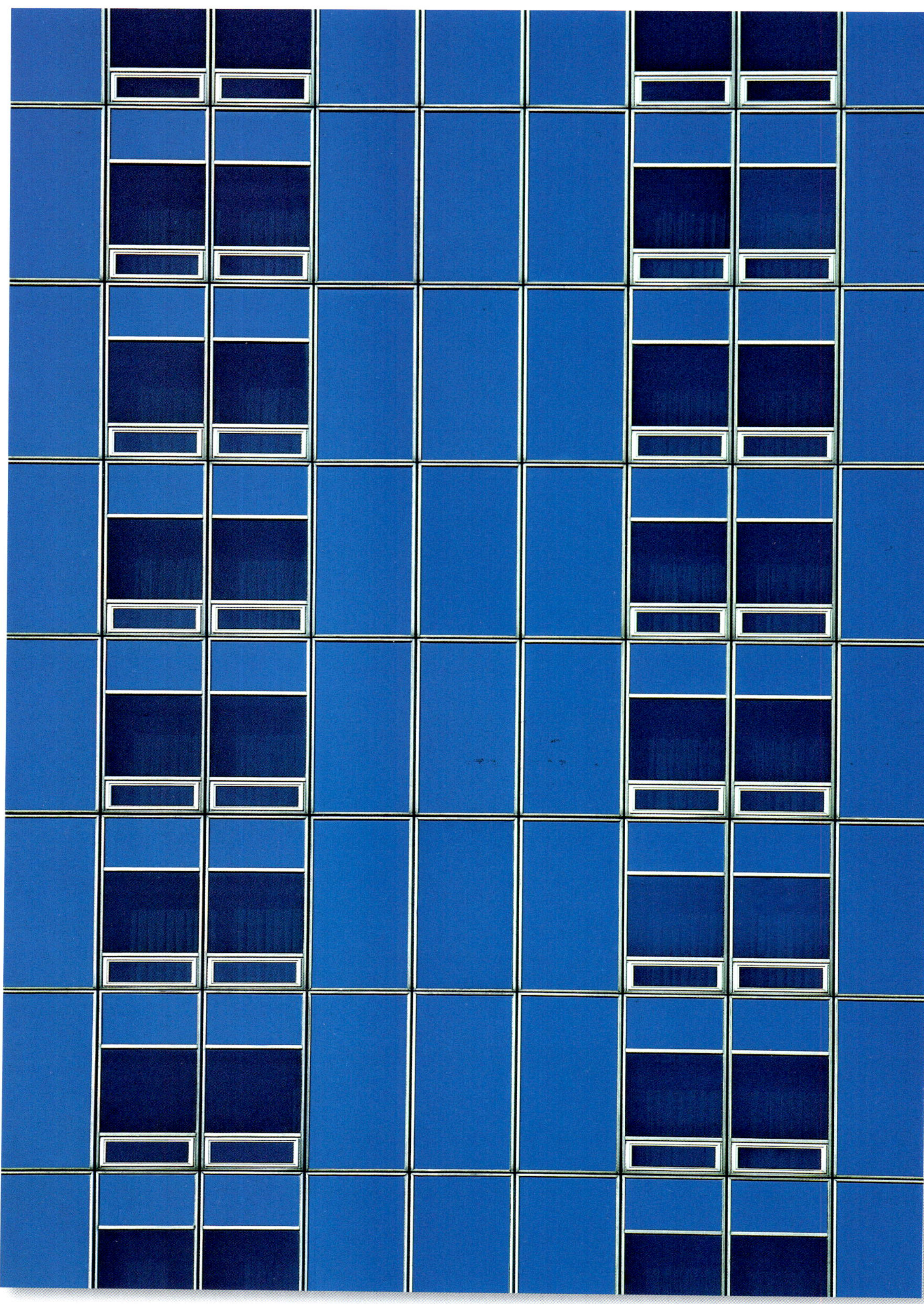

DONG SAN HUAN
BEIJING
1998

< N-2
BRASILIA
2006

< XING YA
TOKYO
2012

SEDUS
“BLACK FOREST”
DOGERN
2007

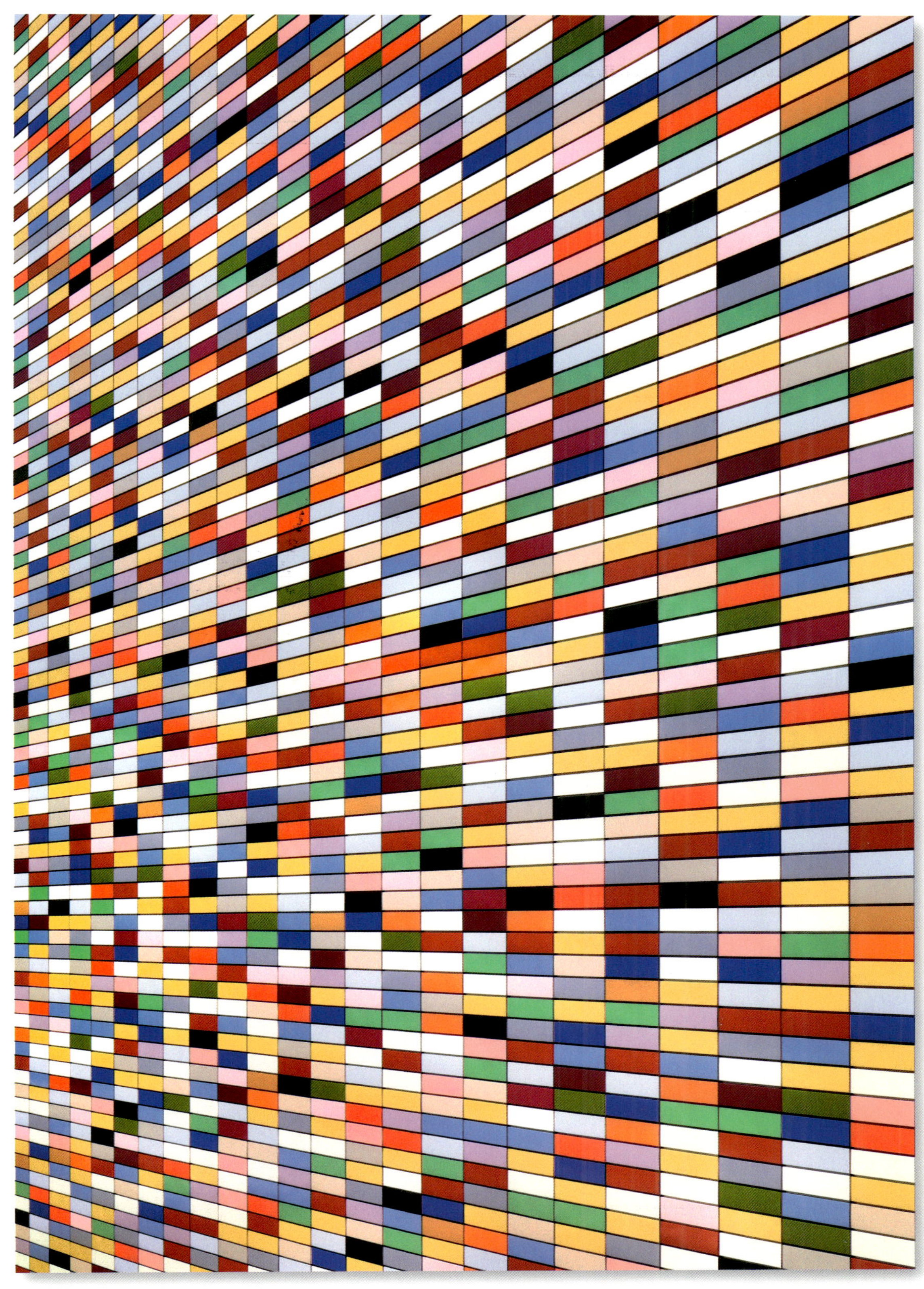

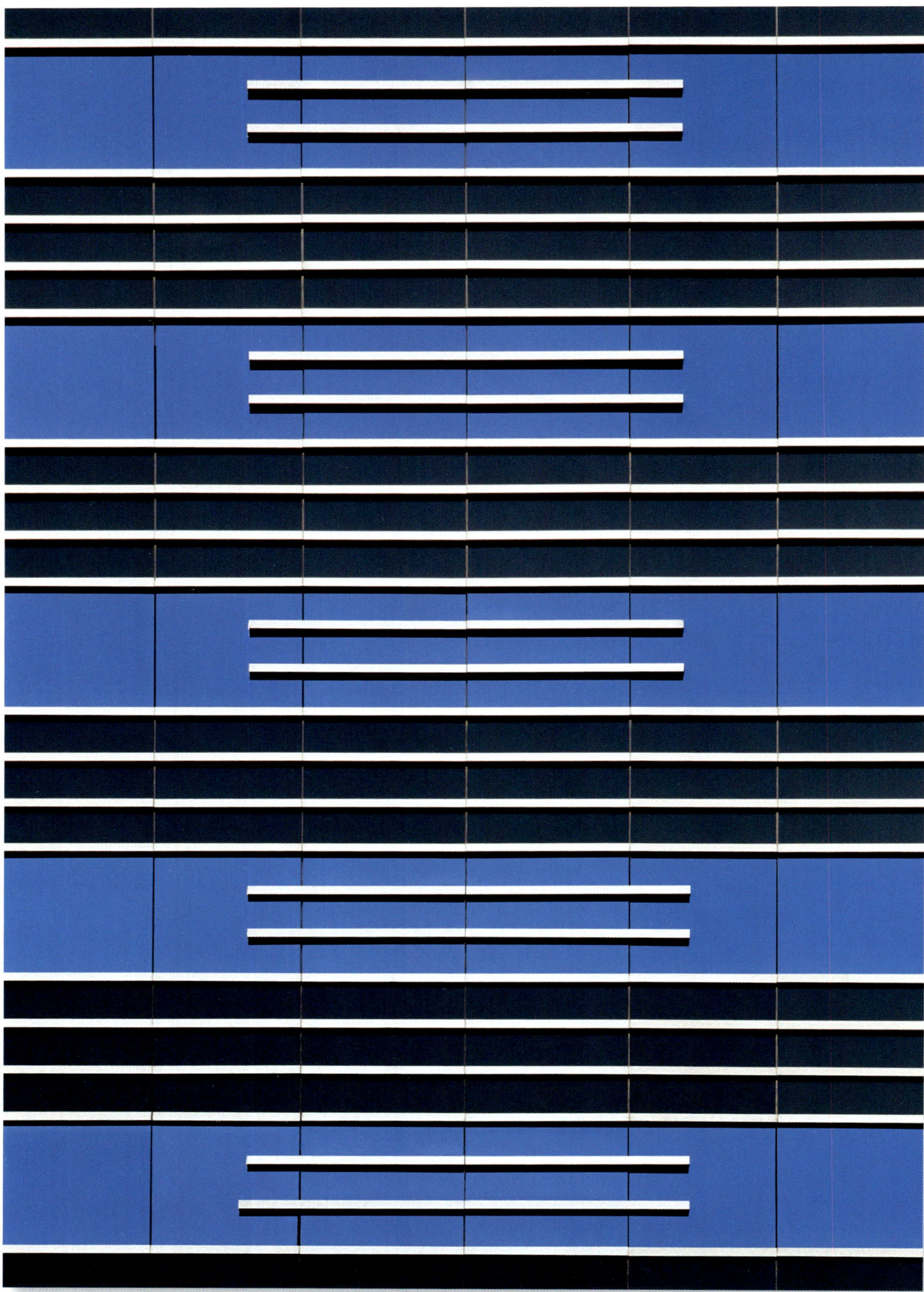

BEIJING ZHAN
BEIJING
1998

SPRING STREET
SEATTLE
2005

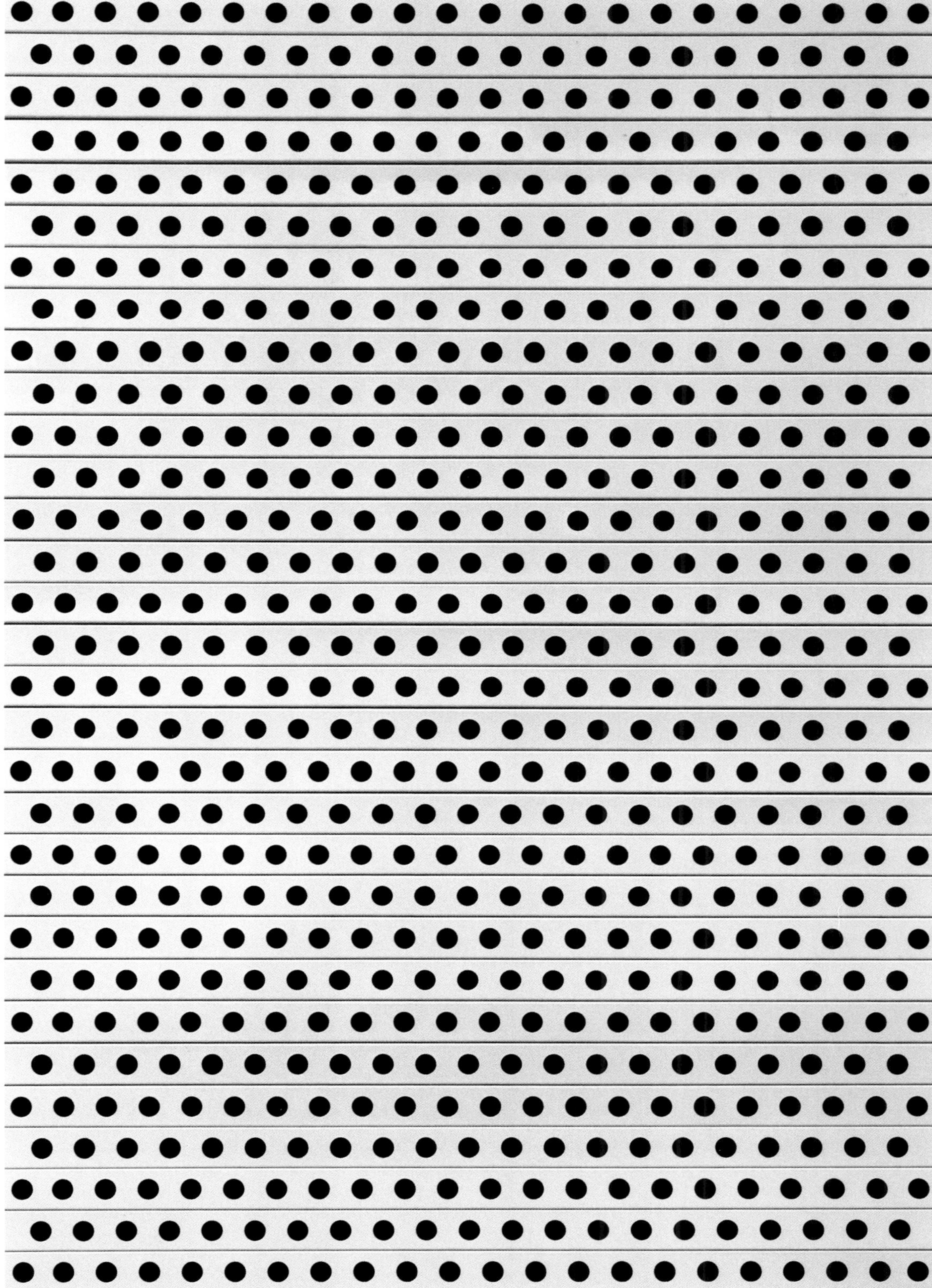

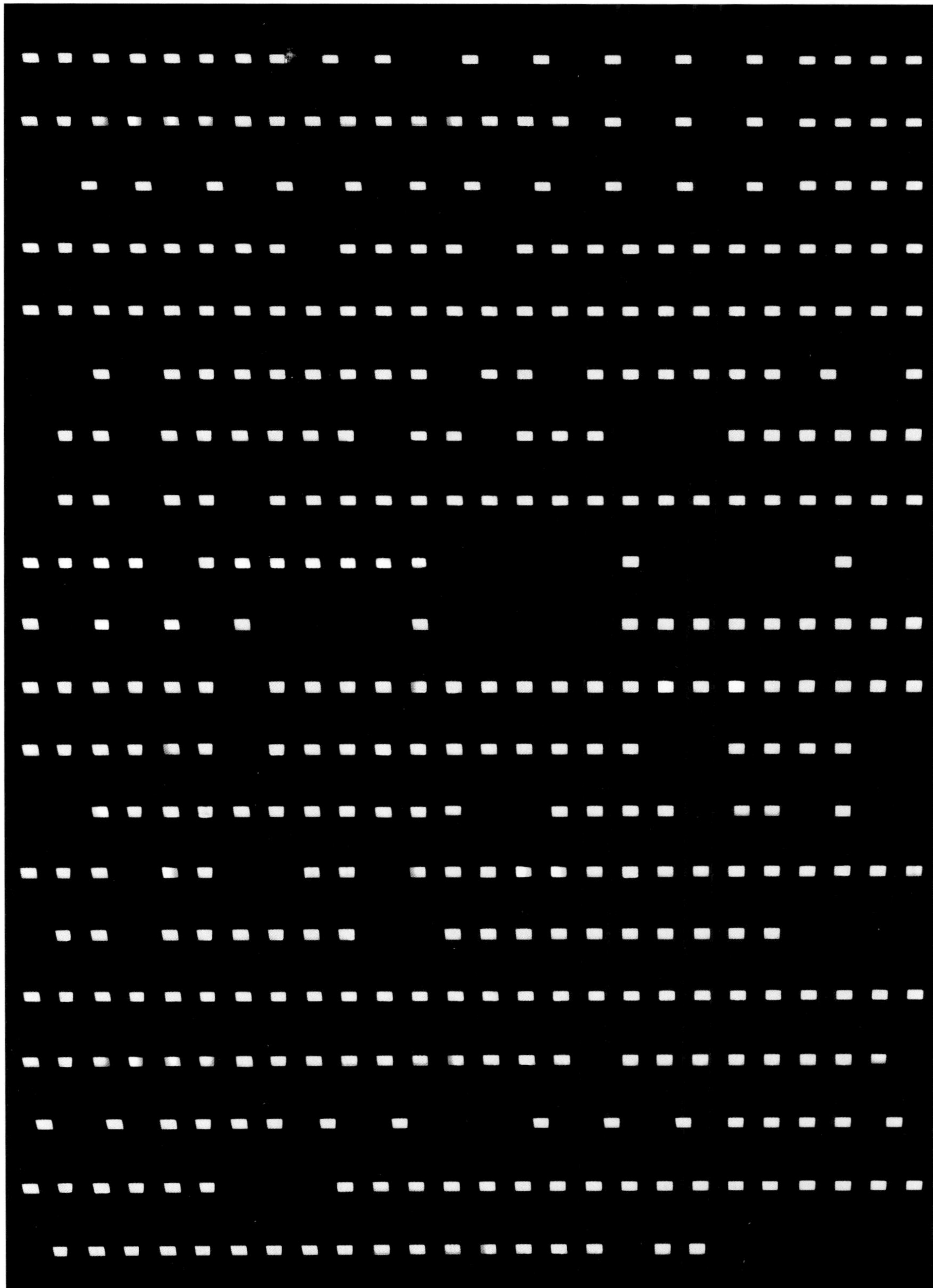

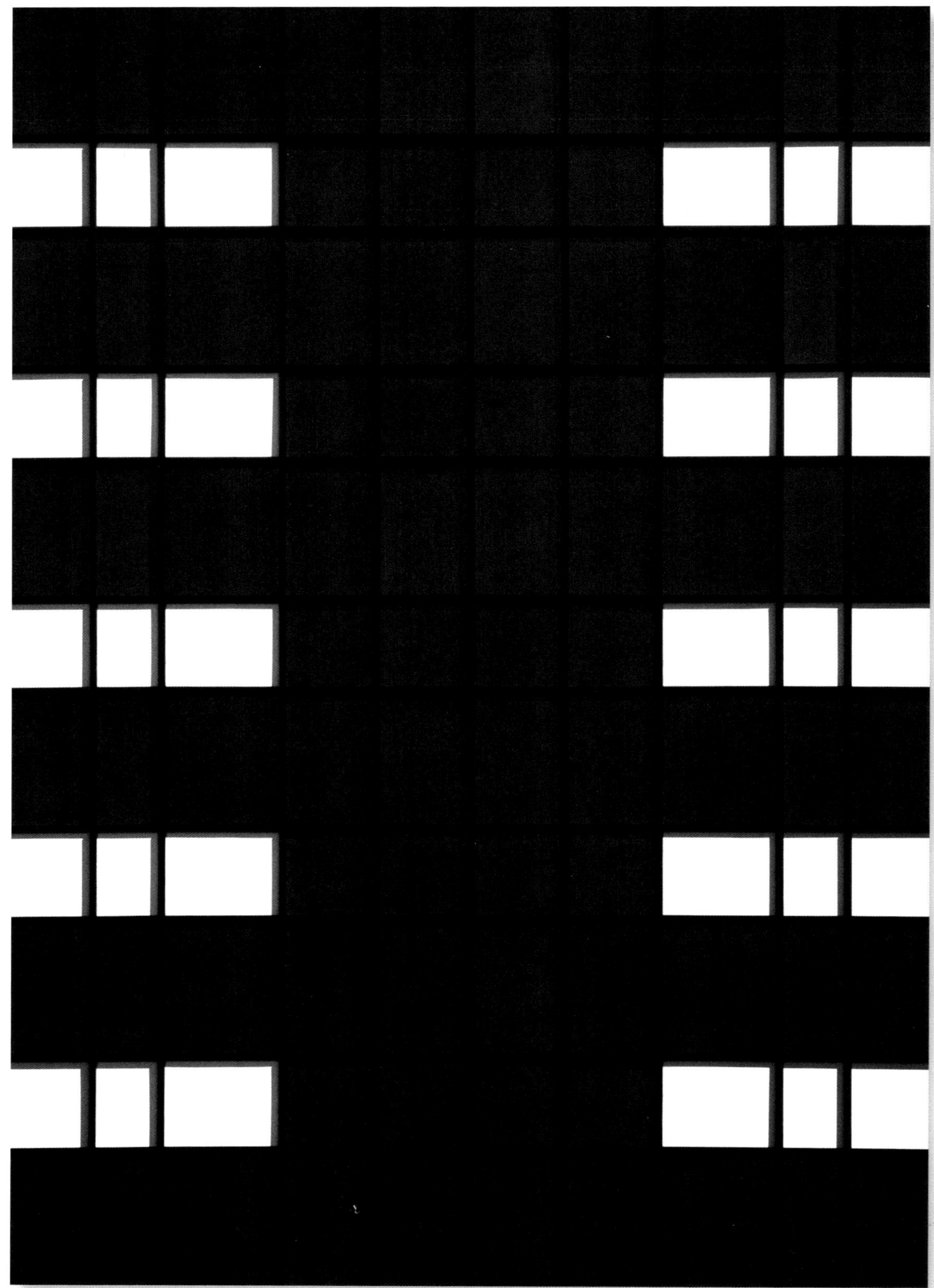

WAN CHAI
HONG KONG
1999

< S1
BRASILIA
2014

< BMO
TORONTO
2005

MINDRAY
SHENZHEN
2006

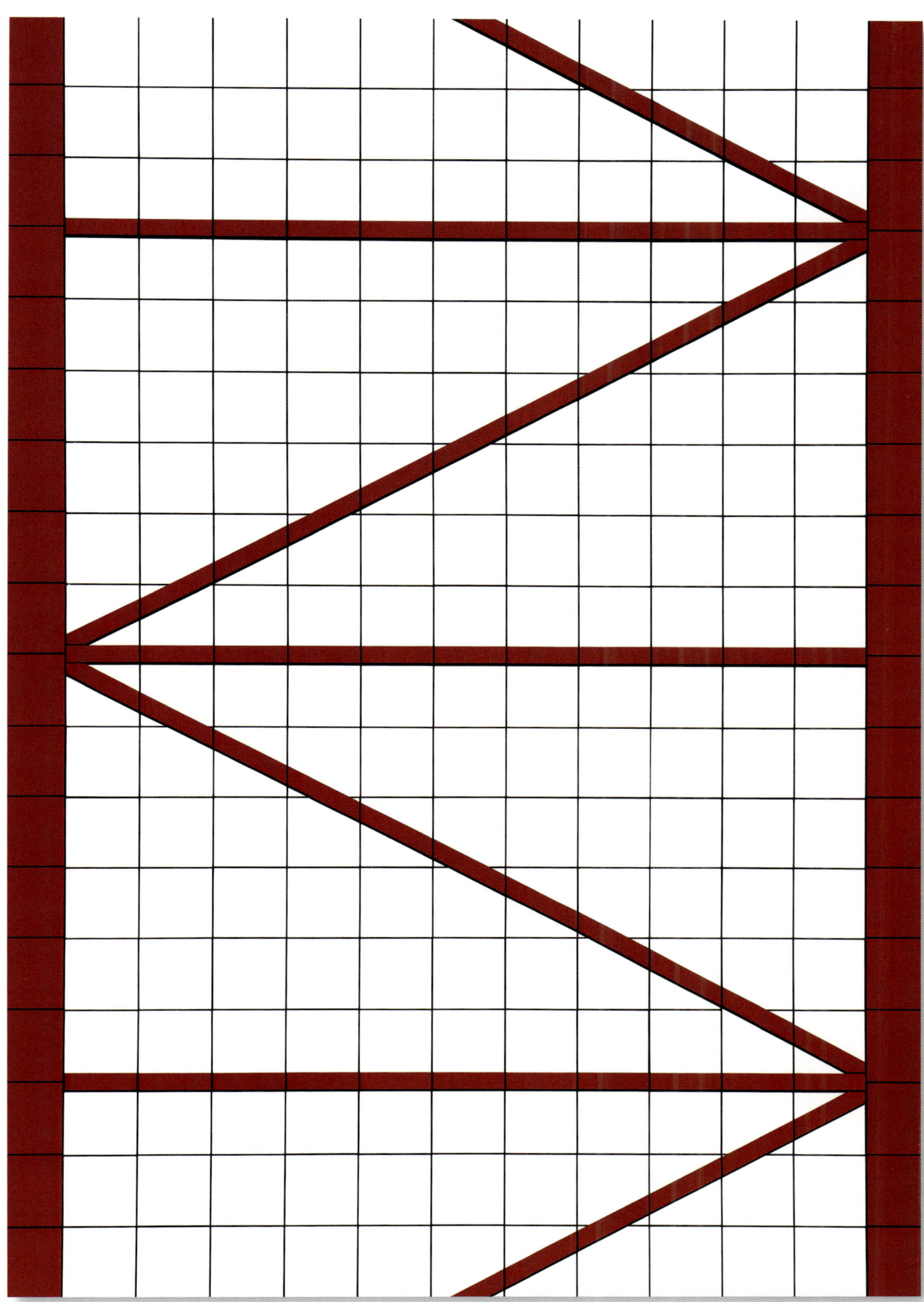

BANK OF CHINA
HONG KONG
1998

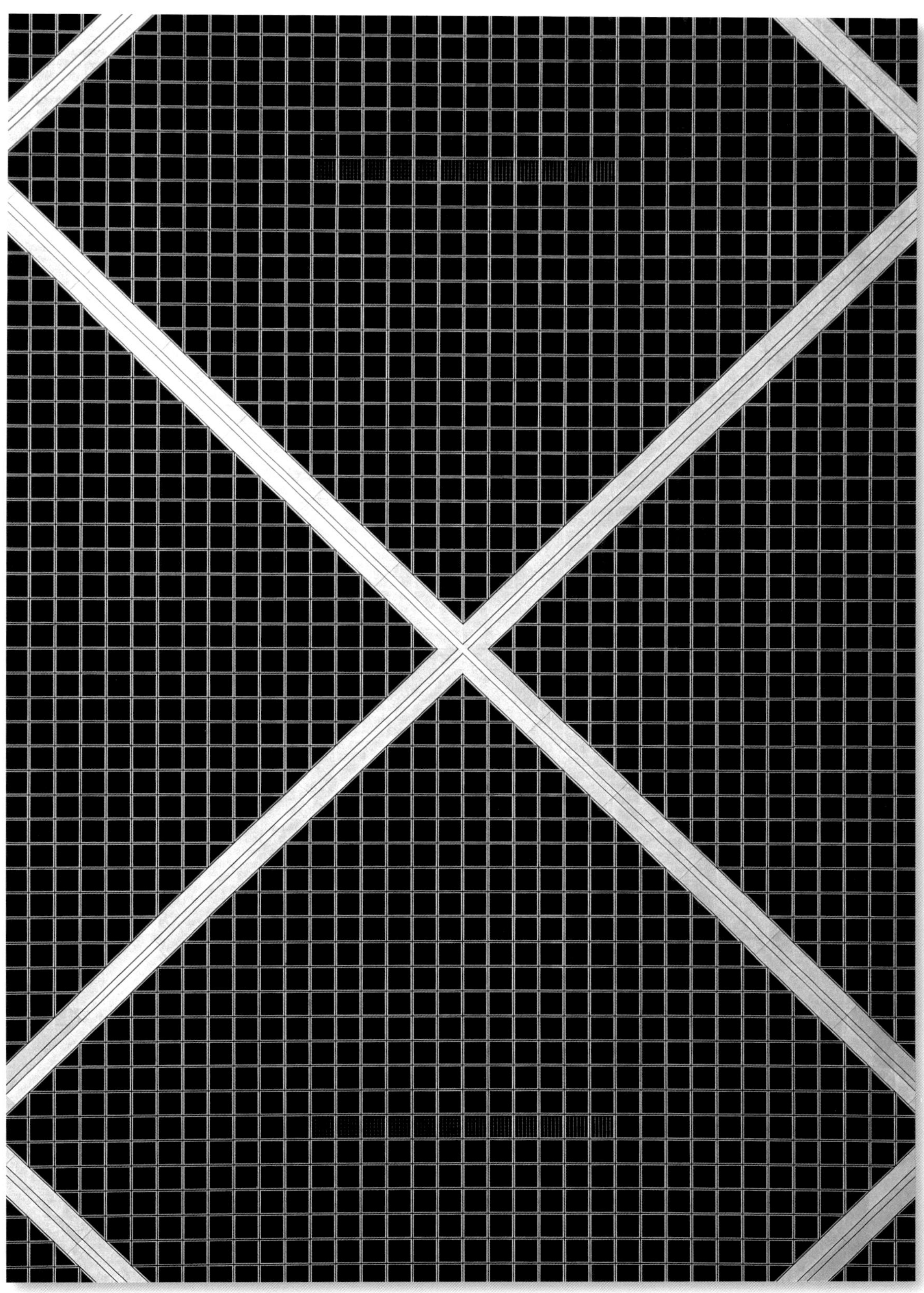

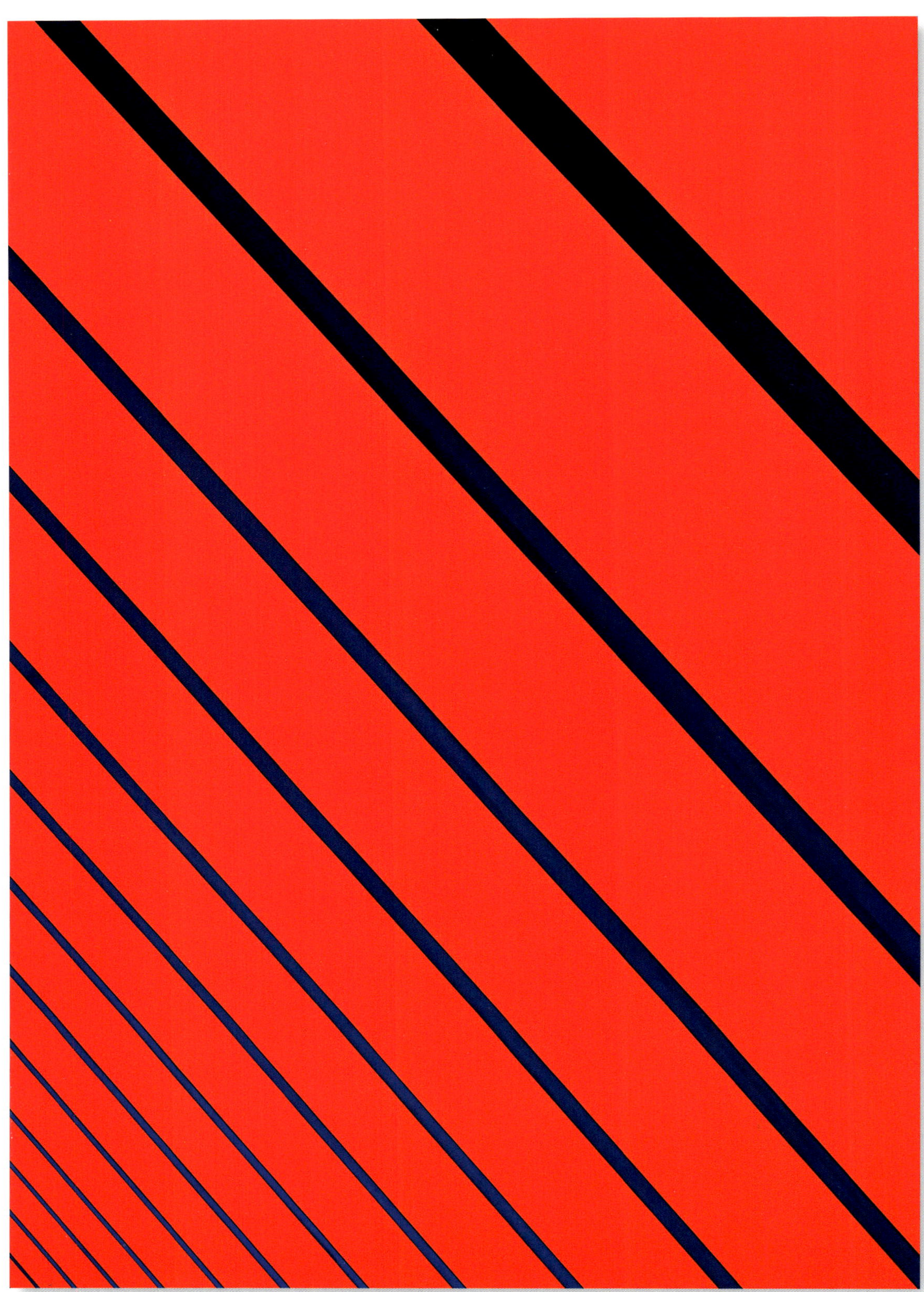

ROYAL PARK
MELBOURNE
2013

BERRINI
SÃO PAOLO
2006

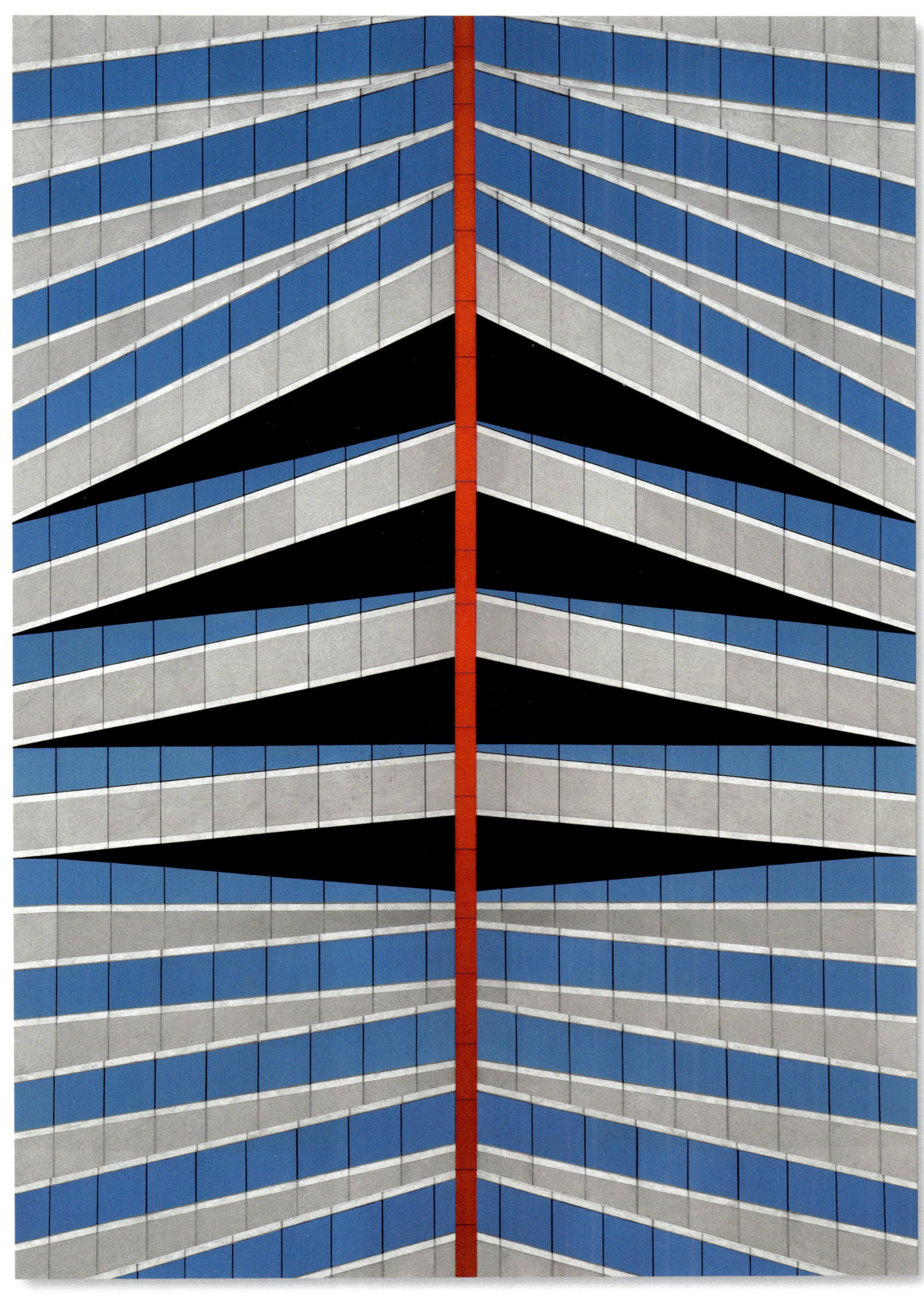

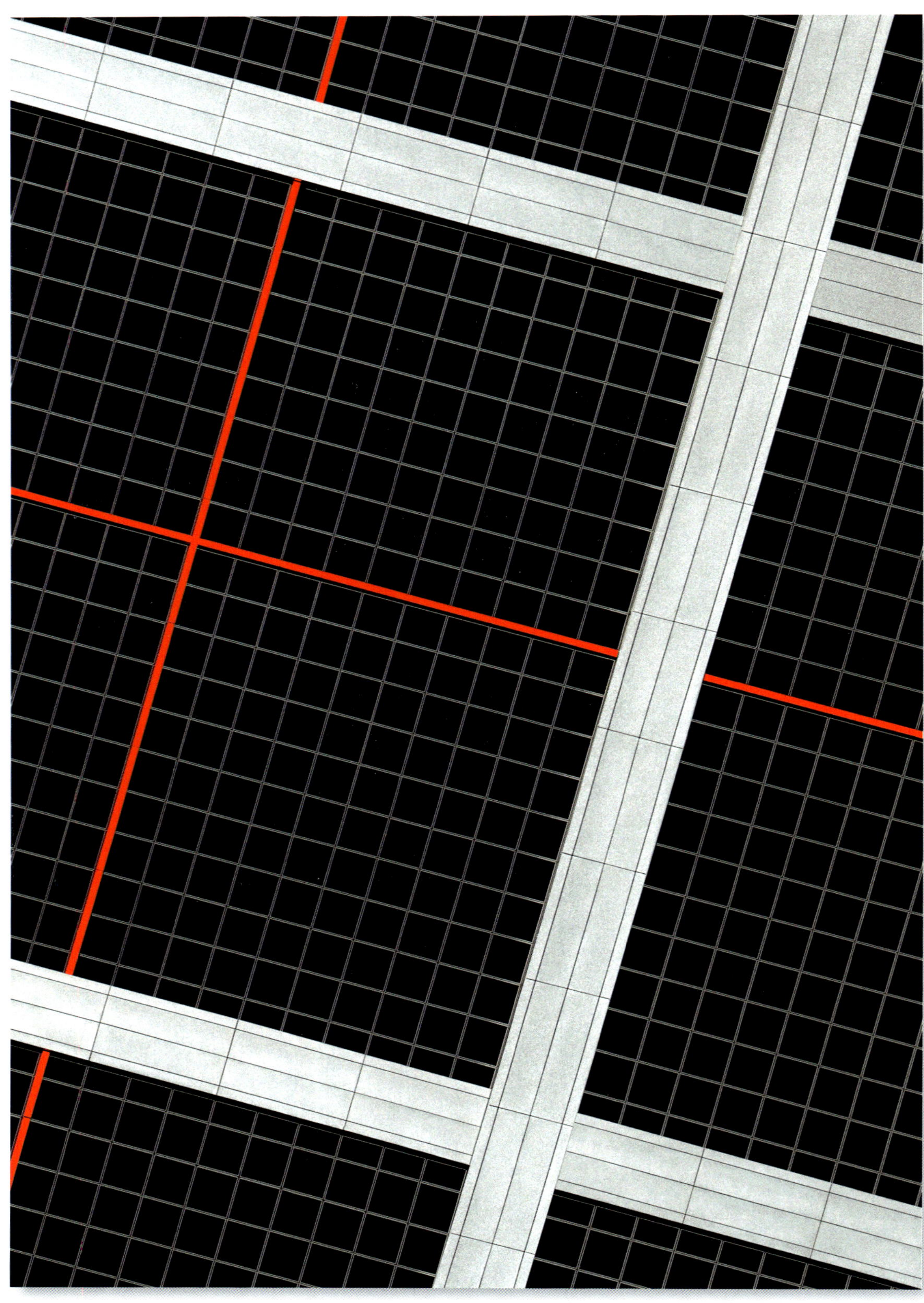

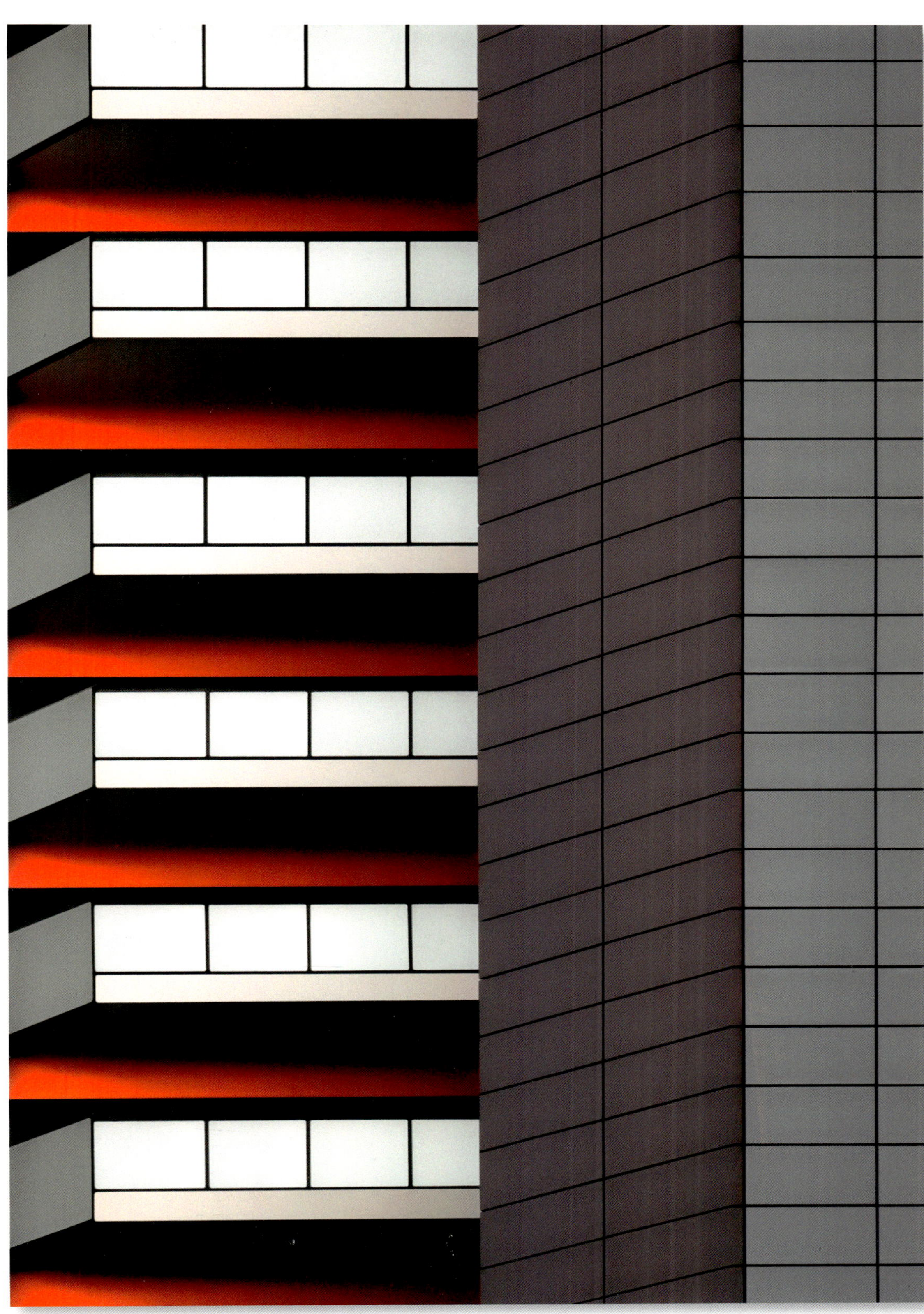

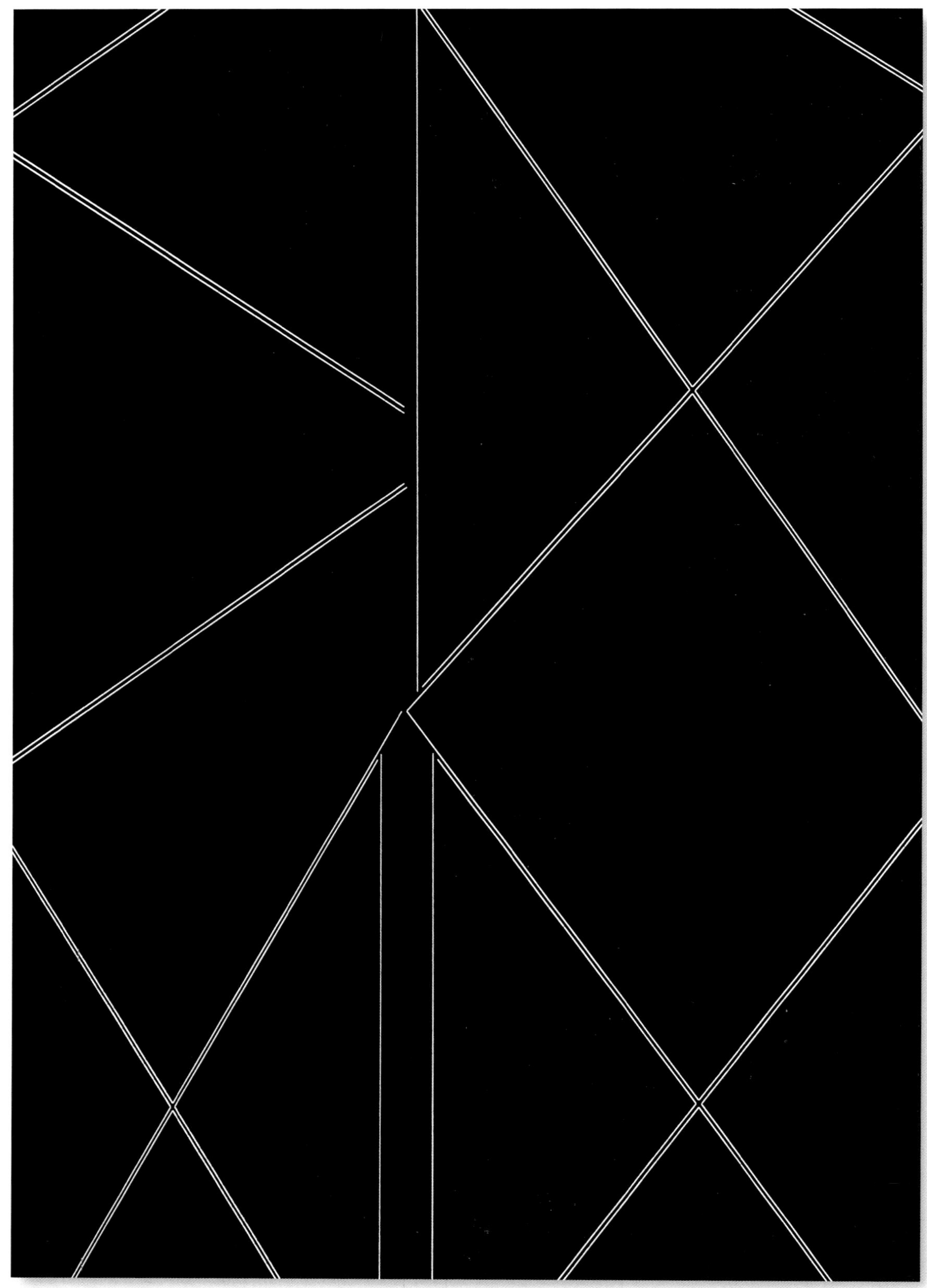

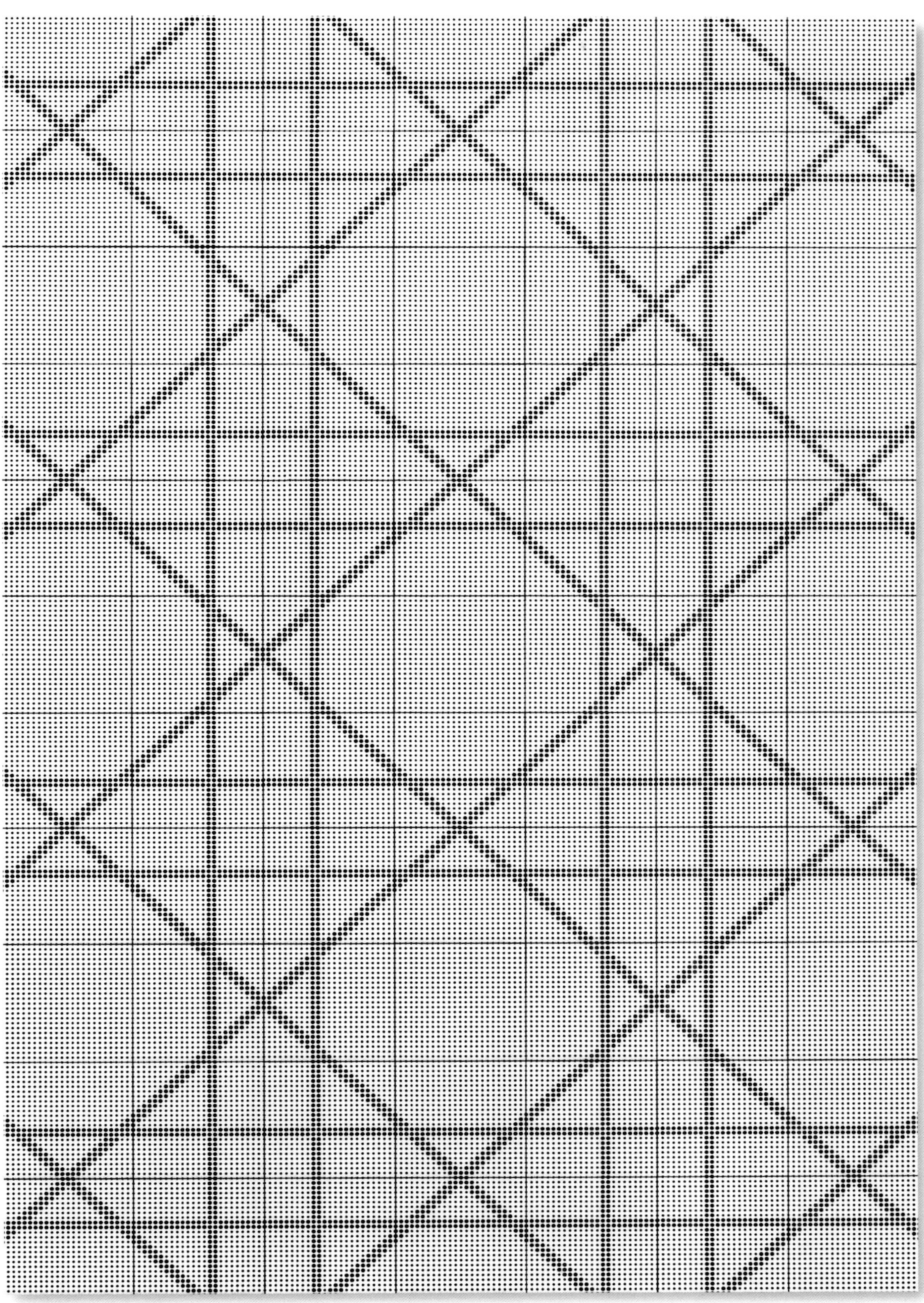

≪ PLAZA CASTILLA
MADRID
2004

≪ YOKOHAMA
TOKYO
2005

< BANK OF CHINA #2
HONG KONG
2008

< DIOR
TOKYO
2014

**UNIQLO
OSAKA
2013**

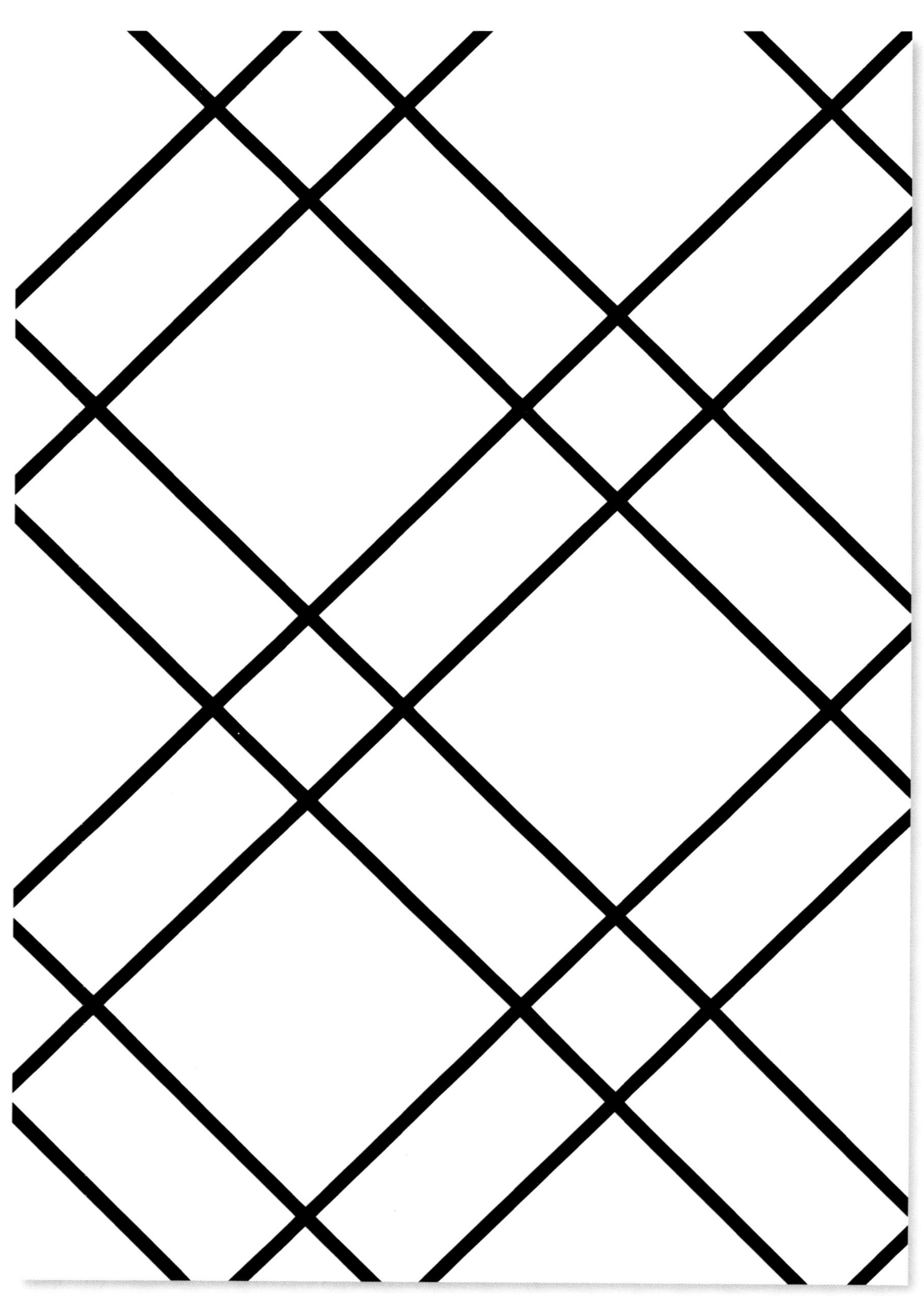

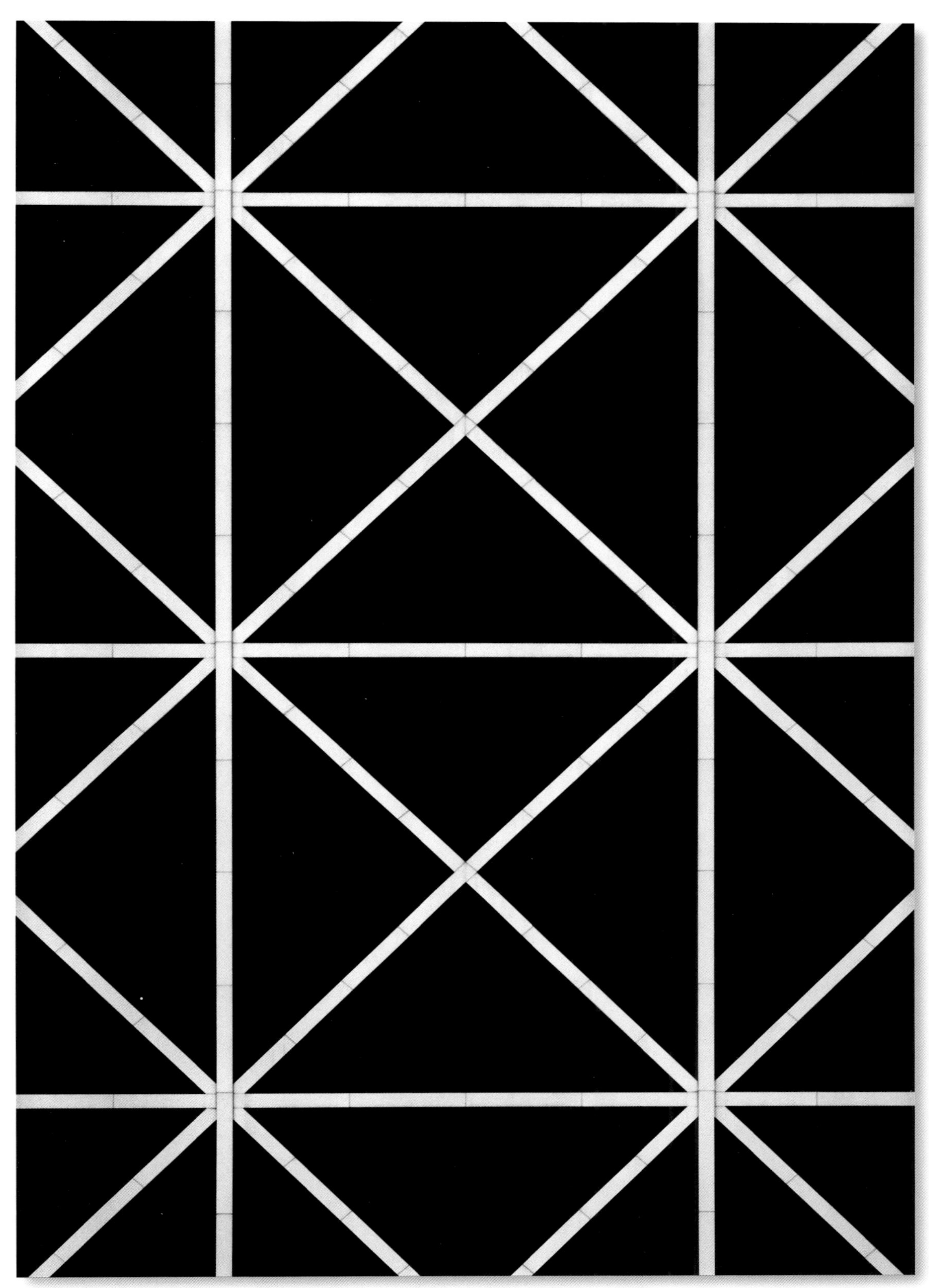

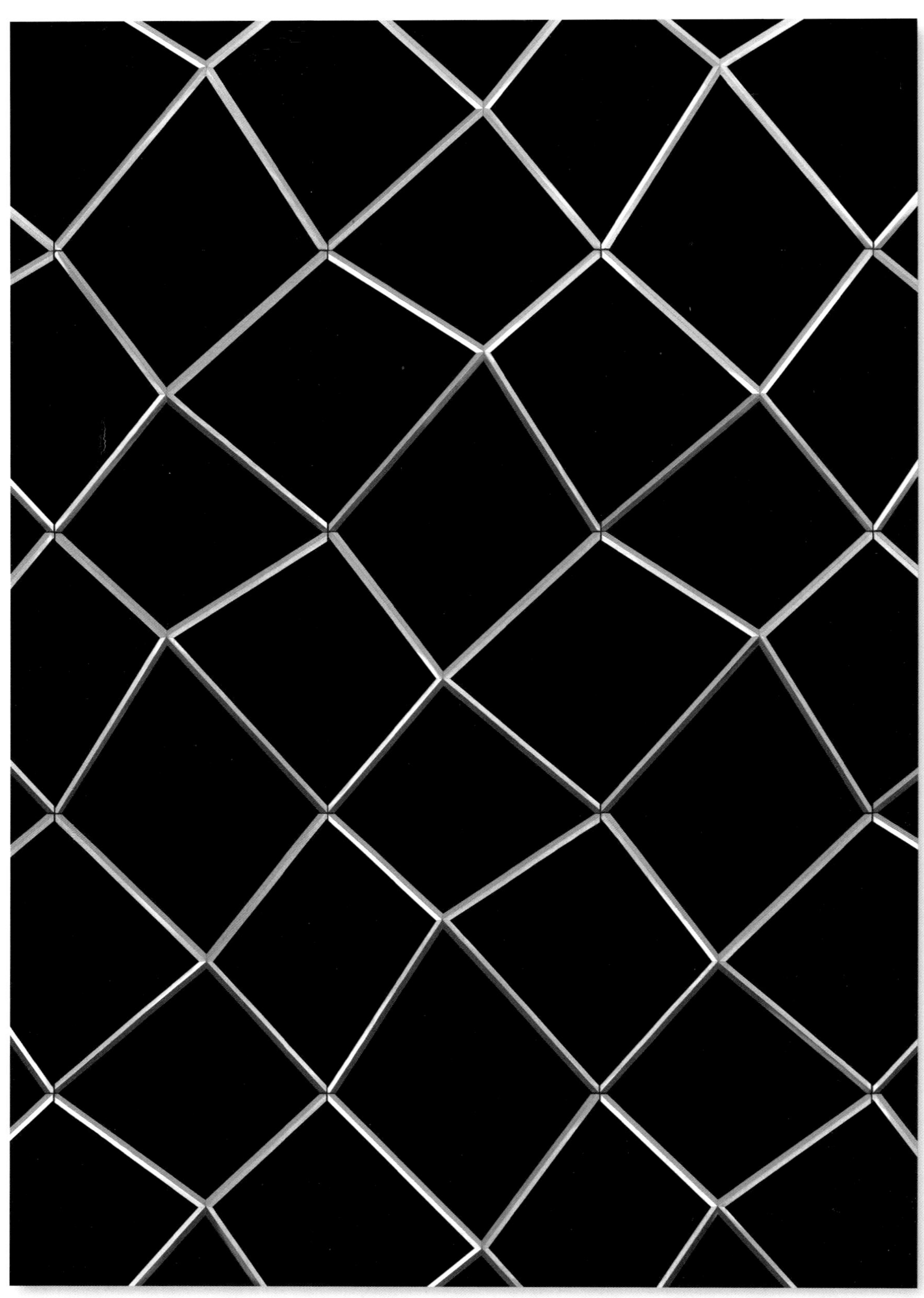

BBVA
MADRID
2014

< KAKUDACHO
OSAKA
2014

< TIANHE LU
GUANGZHOU
2006

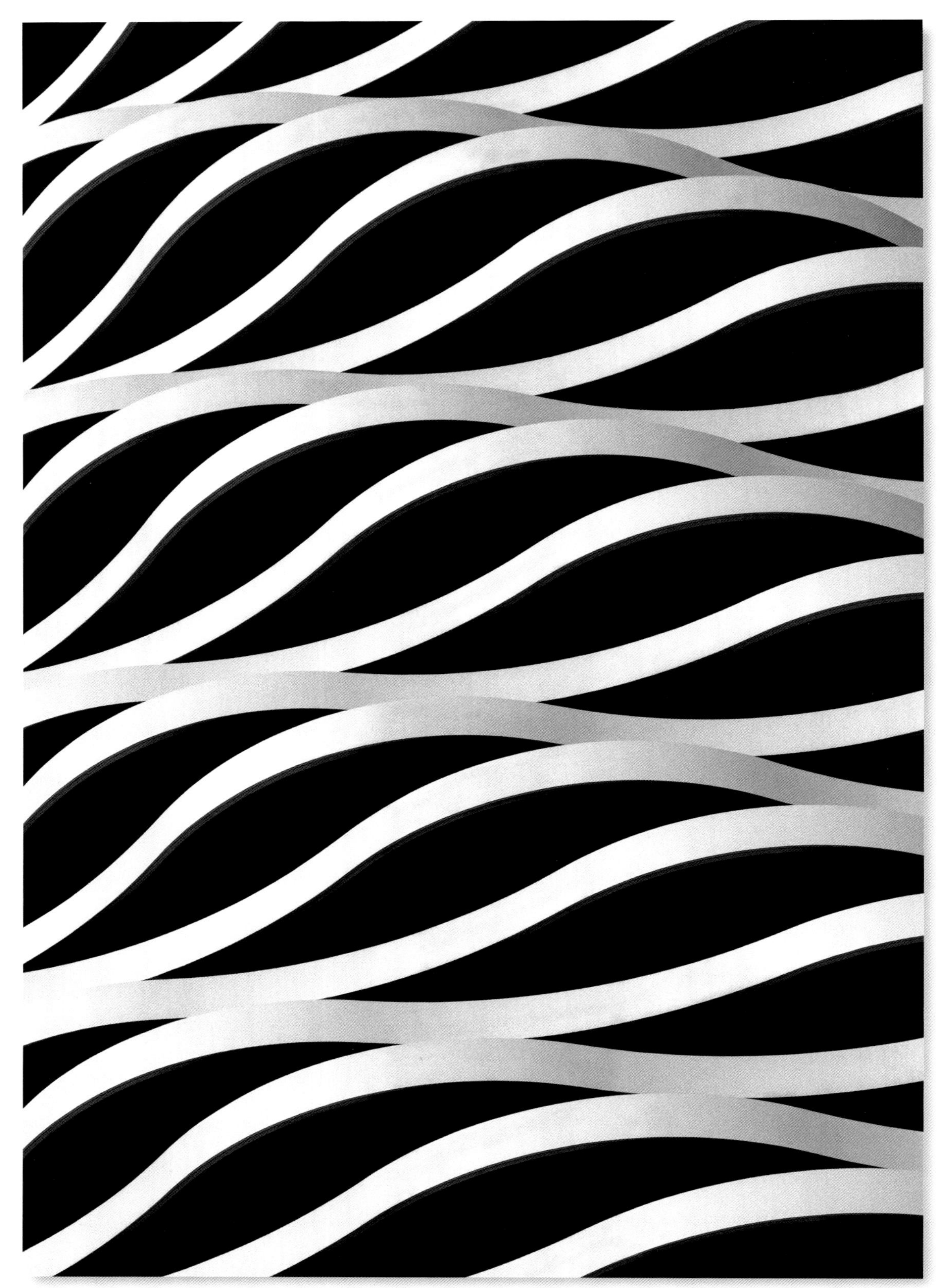

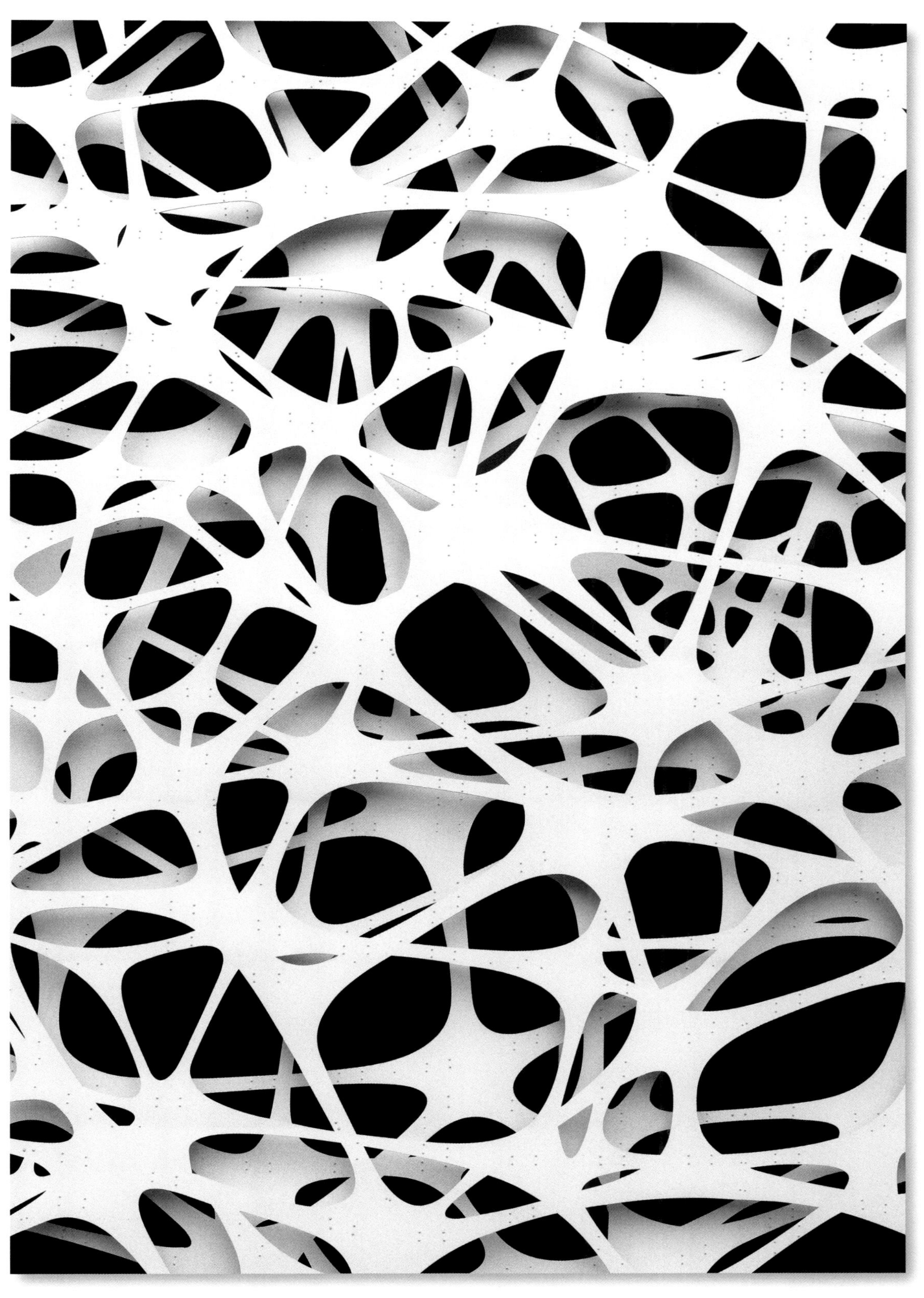

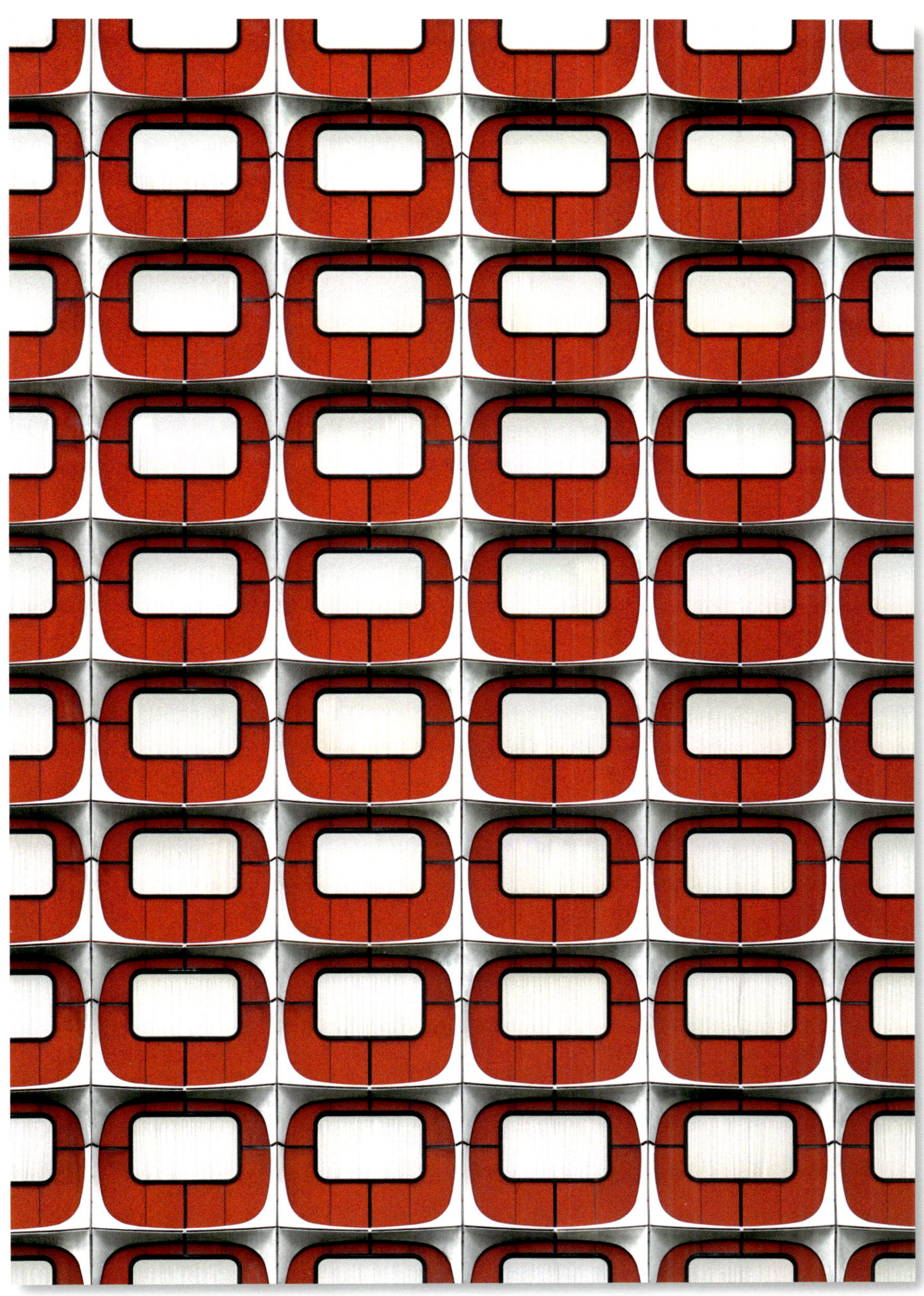

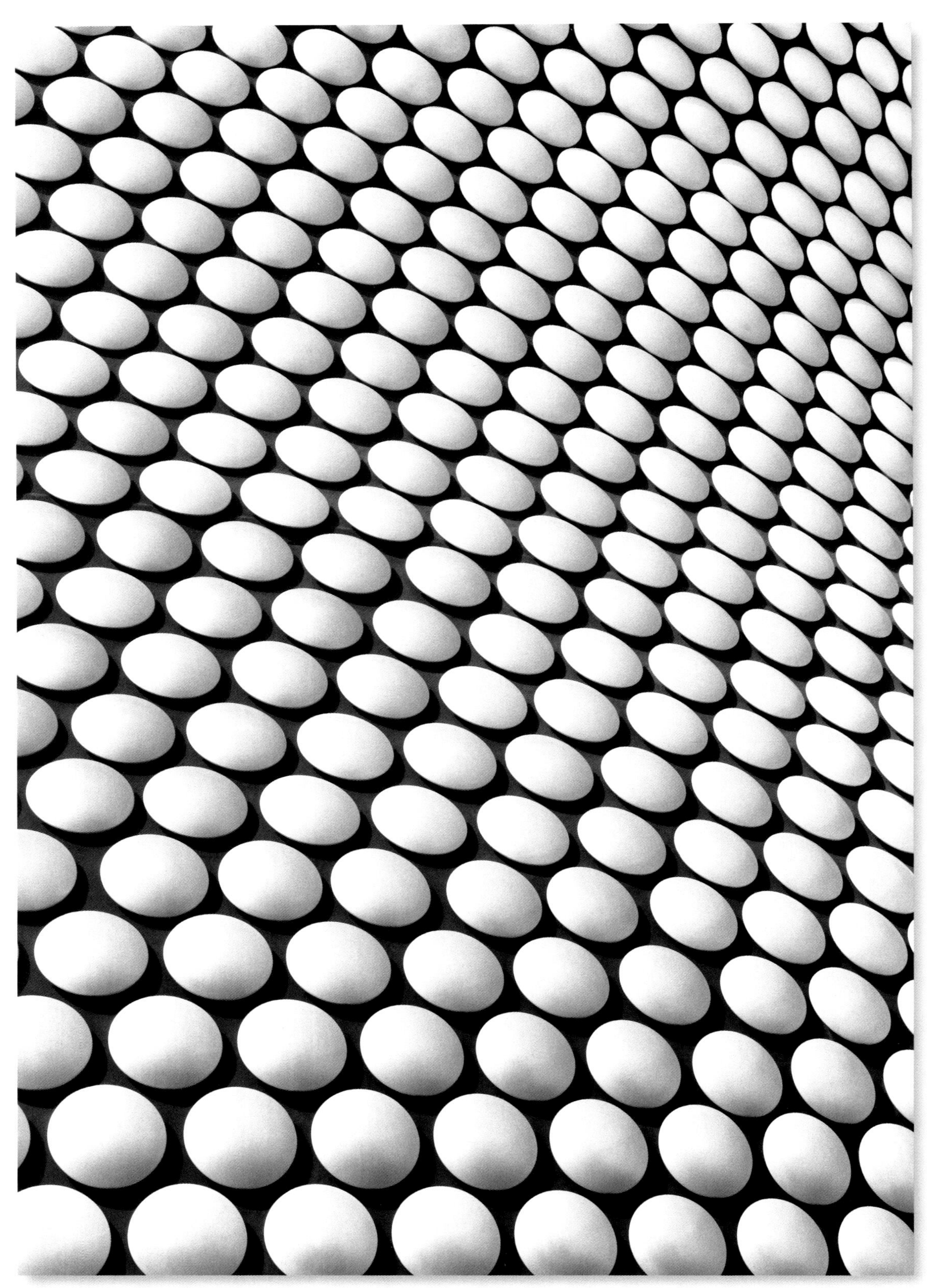

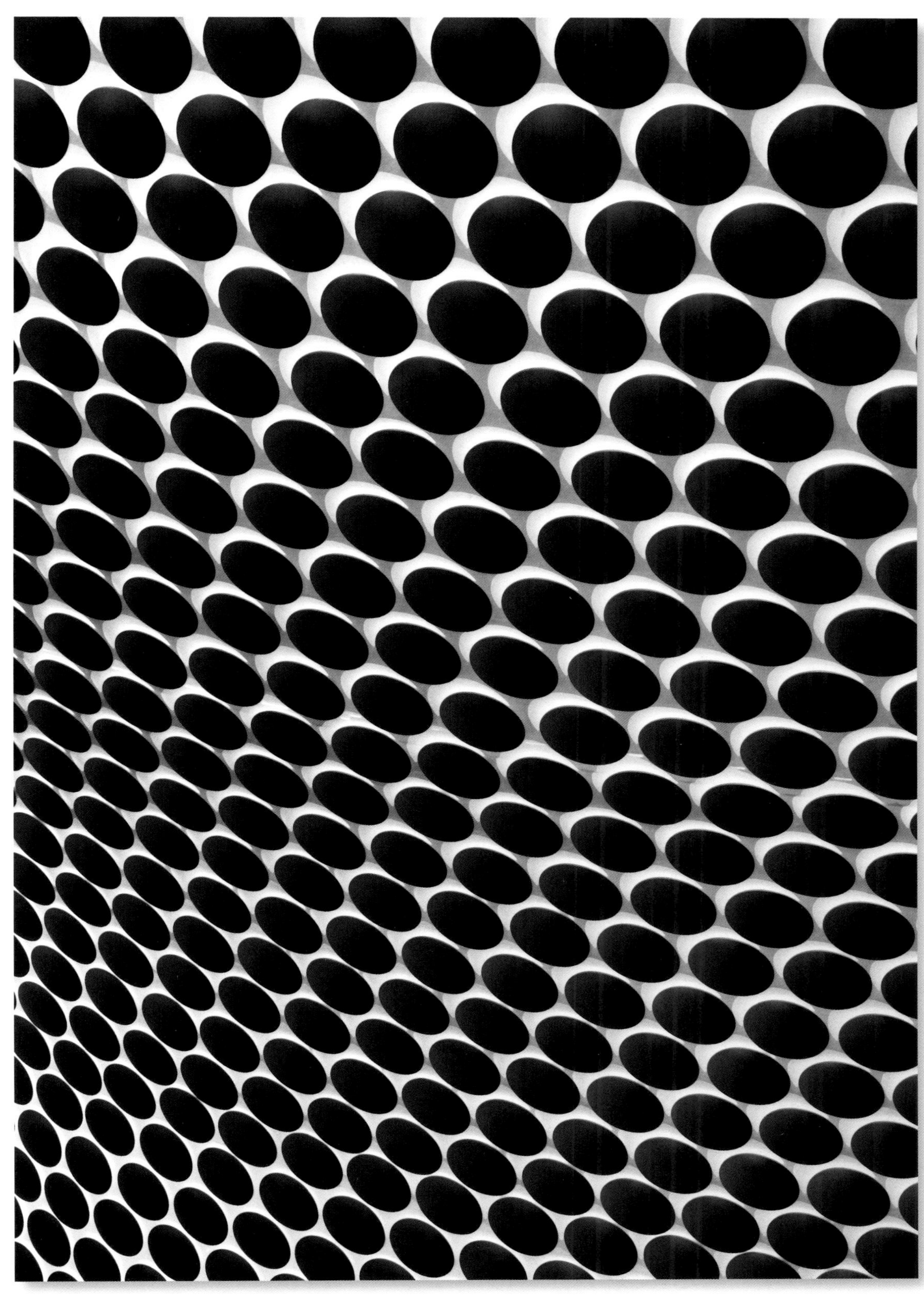

≪ BIRMINGHAM
DAY
2007

≪ BIRMINGHAM
NIGHT
2007

< ROSSLYN
WASHINGTON
2004

< MINATO-KU
TOKYO
2014

METROPOLITAN PLAZA
CHONGQING
2006

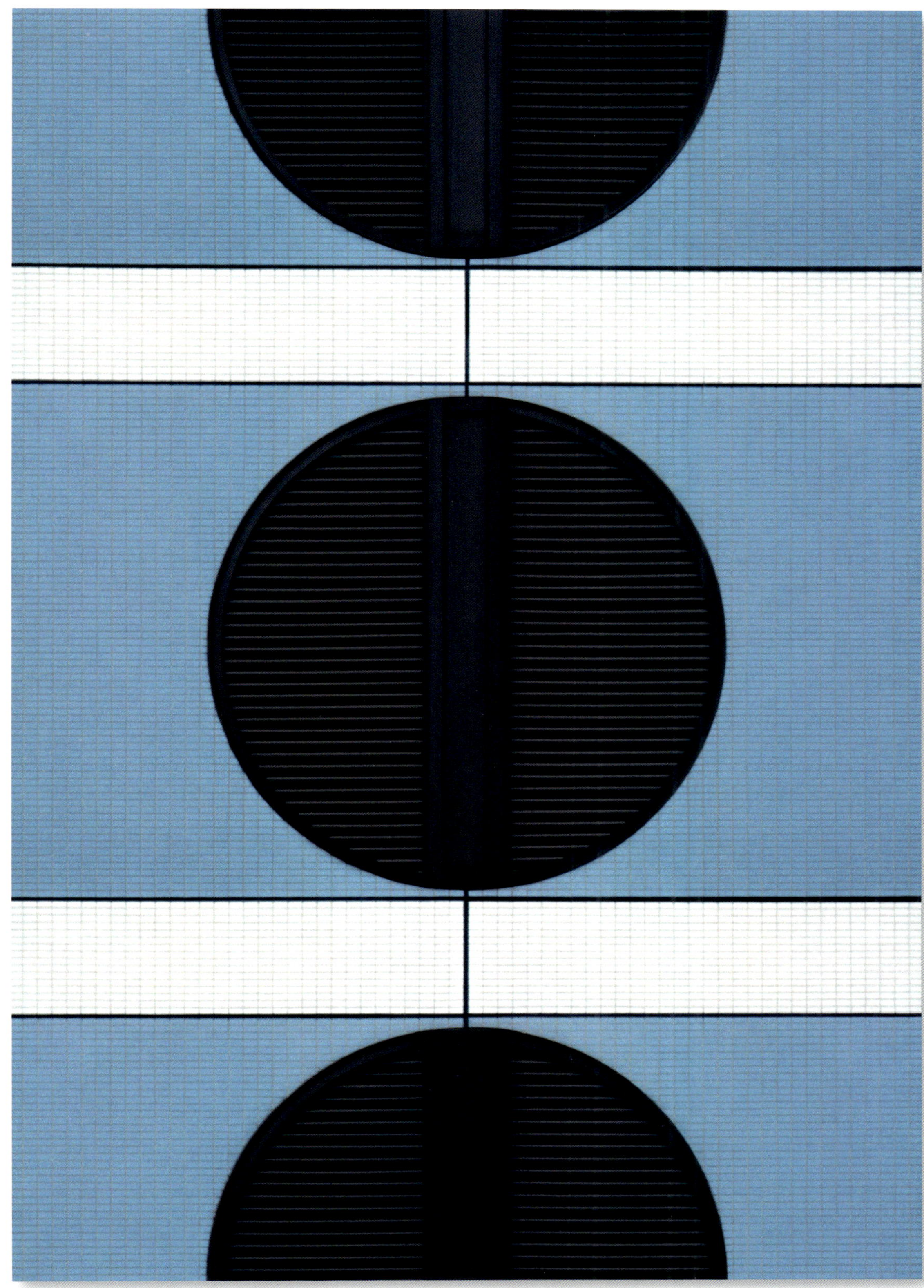

PLAZA TOWER
DALLAS
2006

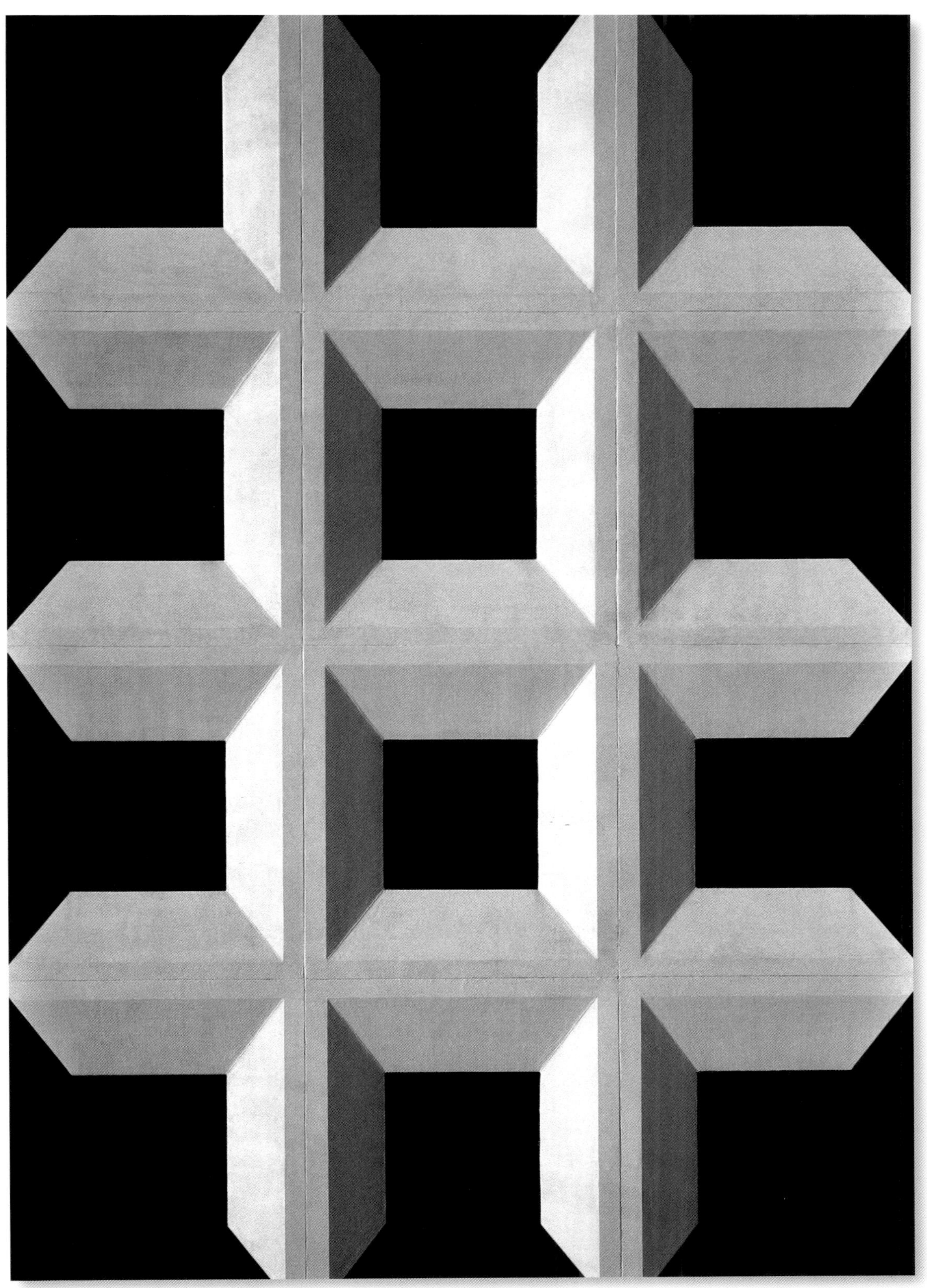

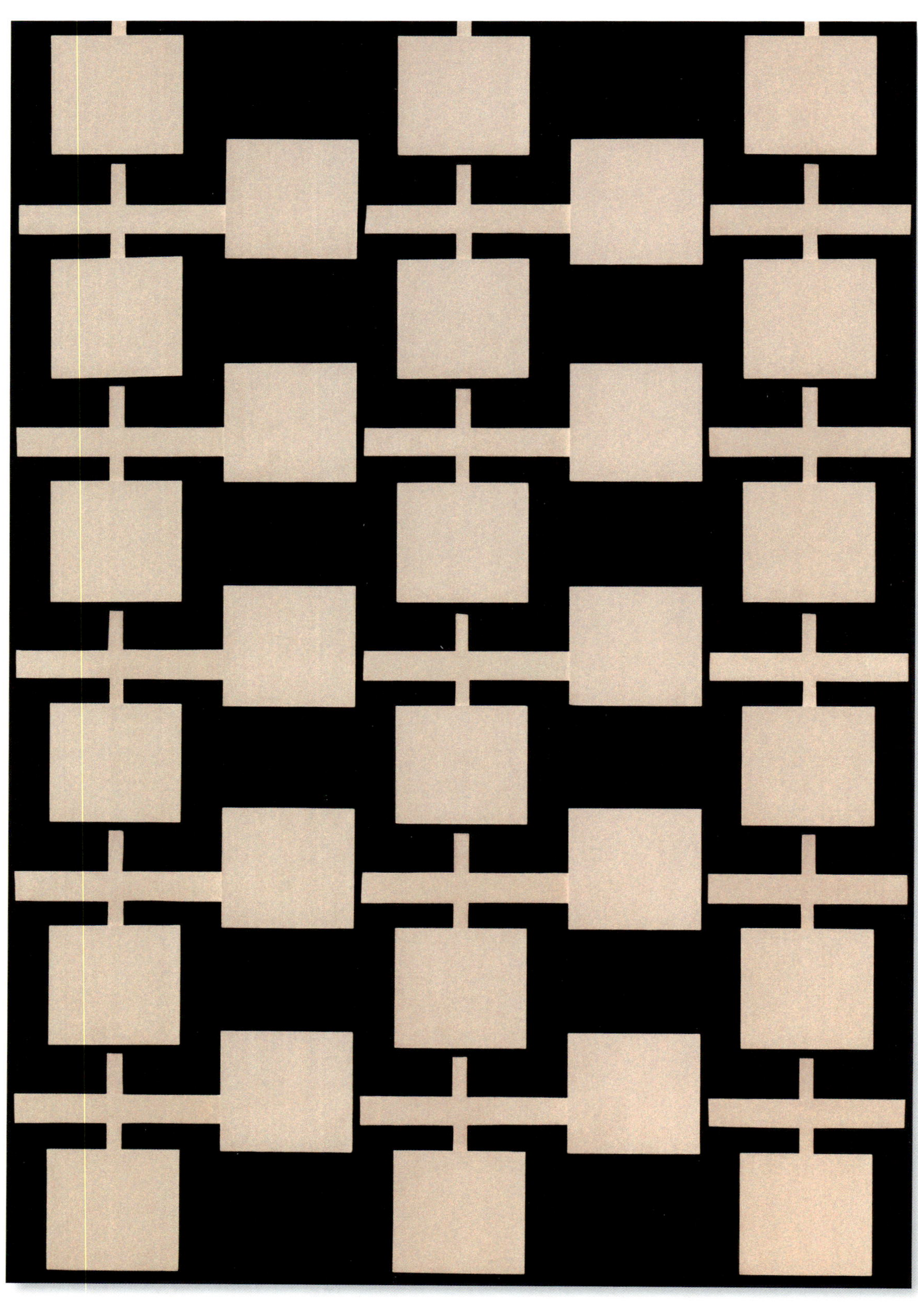

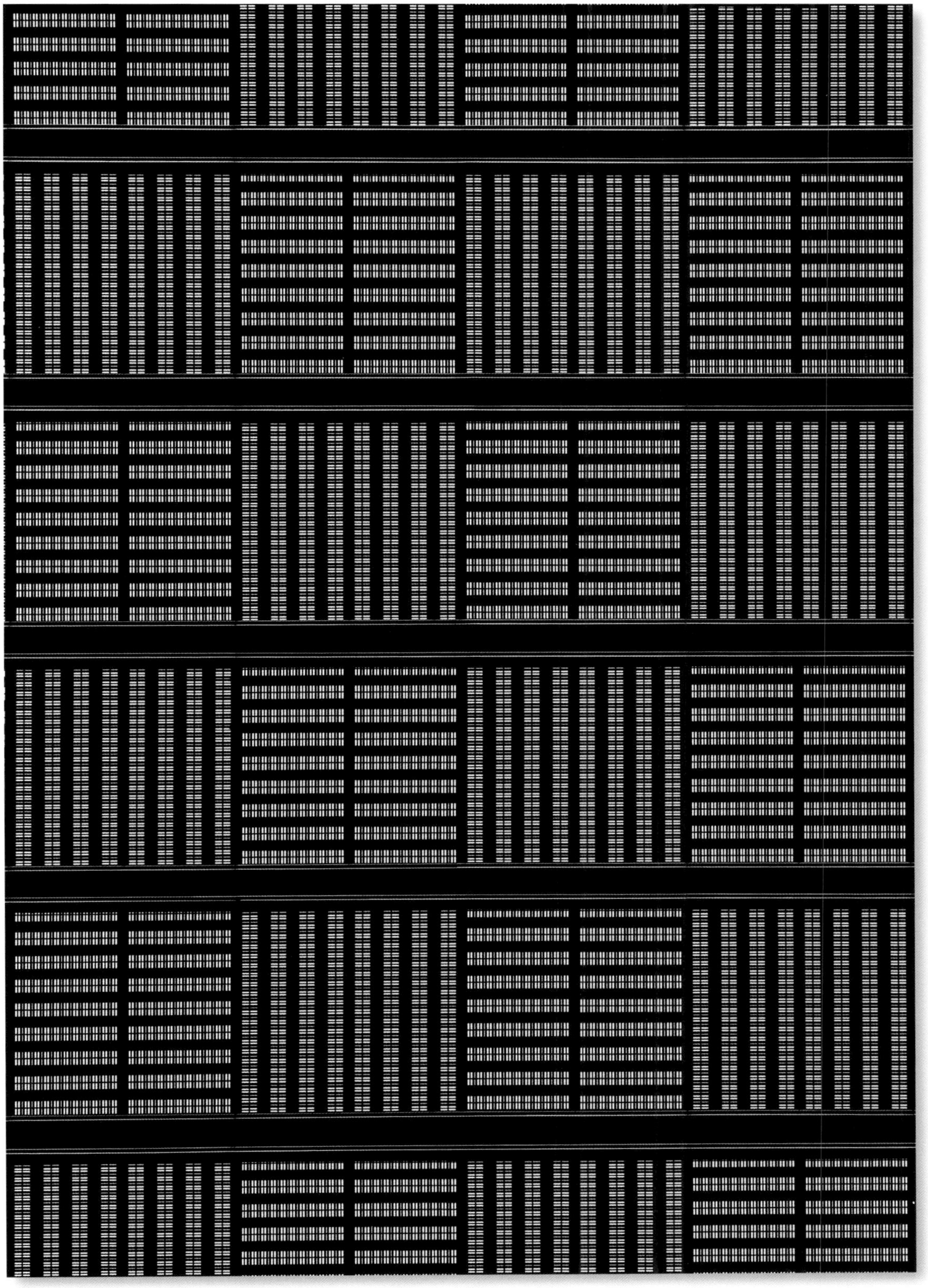

< MARRIOTT
DOHA
2011

< DUKE STREET
MONTREAL
2005

PRADA
NAGOYA
2014

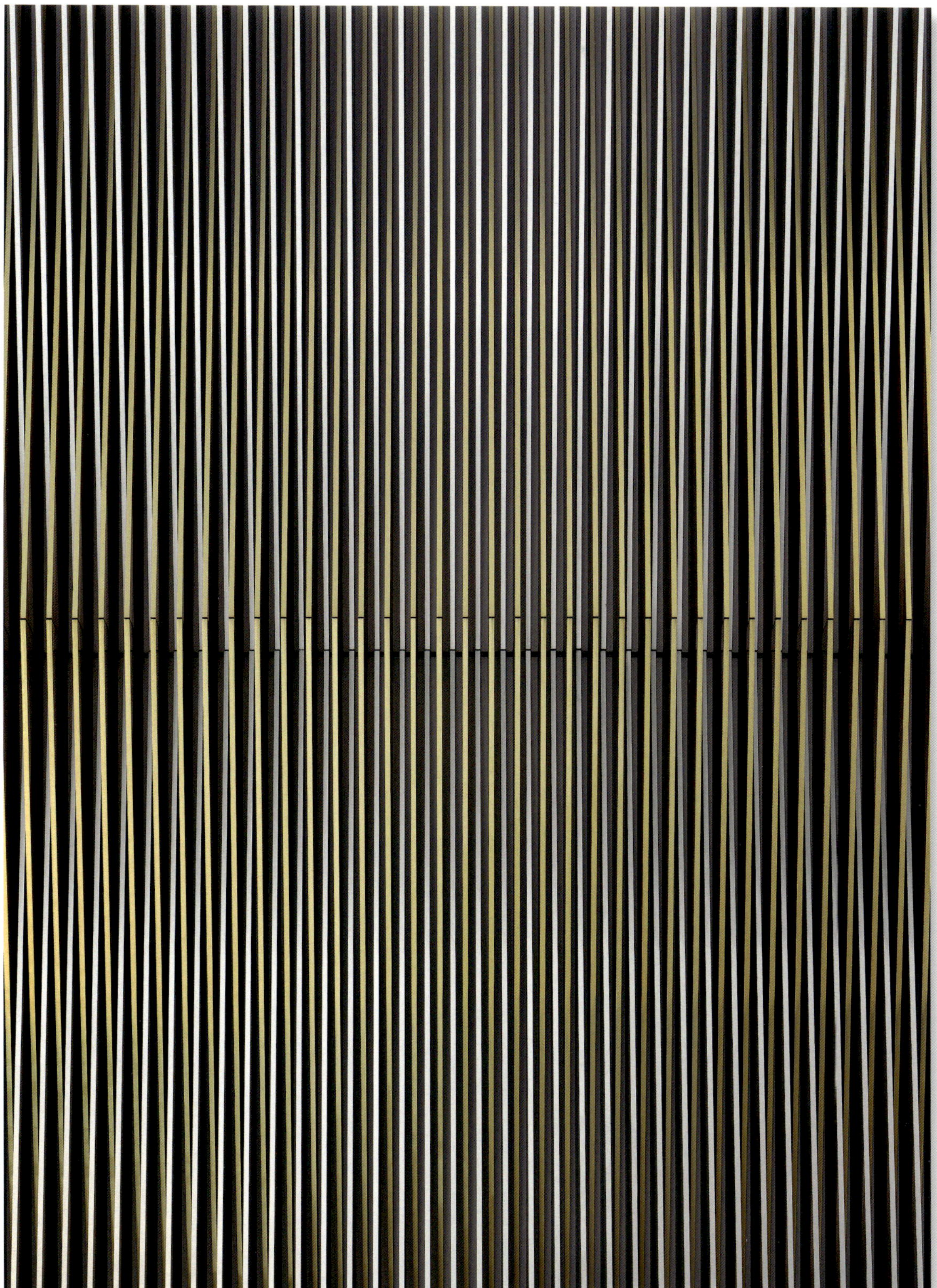

SIGNAL BOX
BASEL
2001

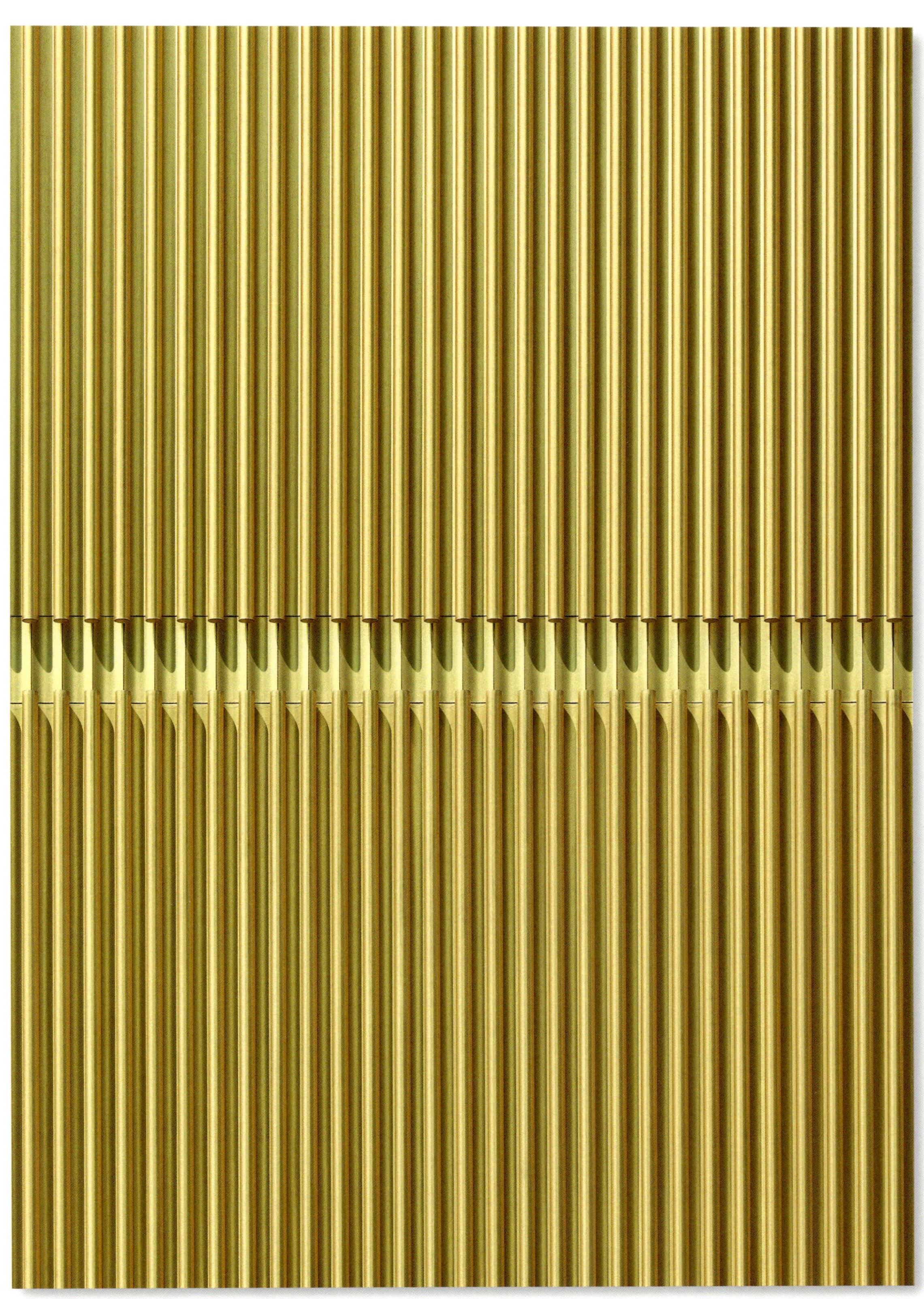

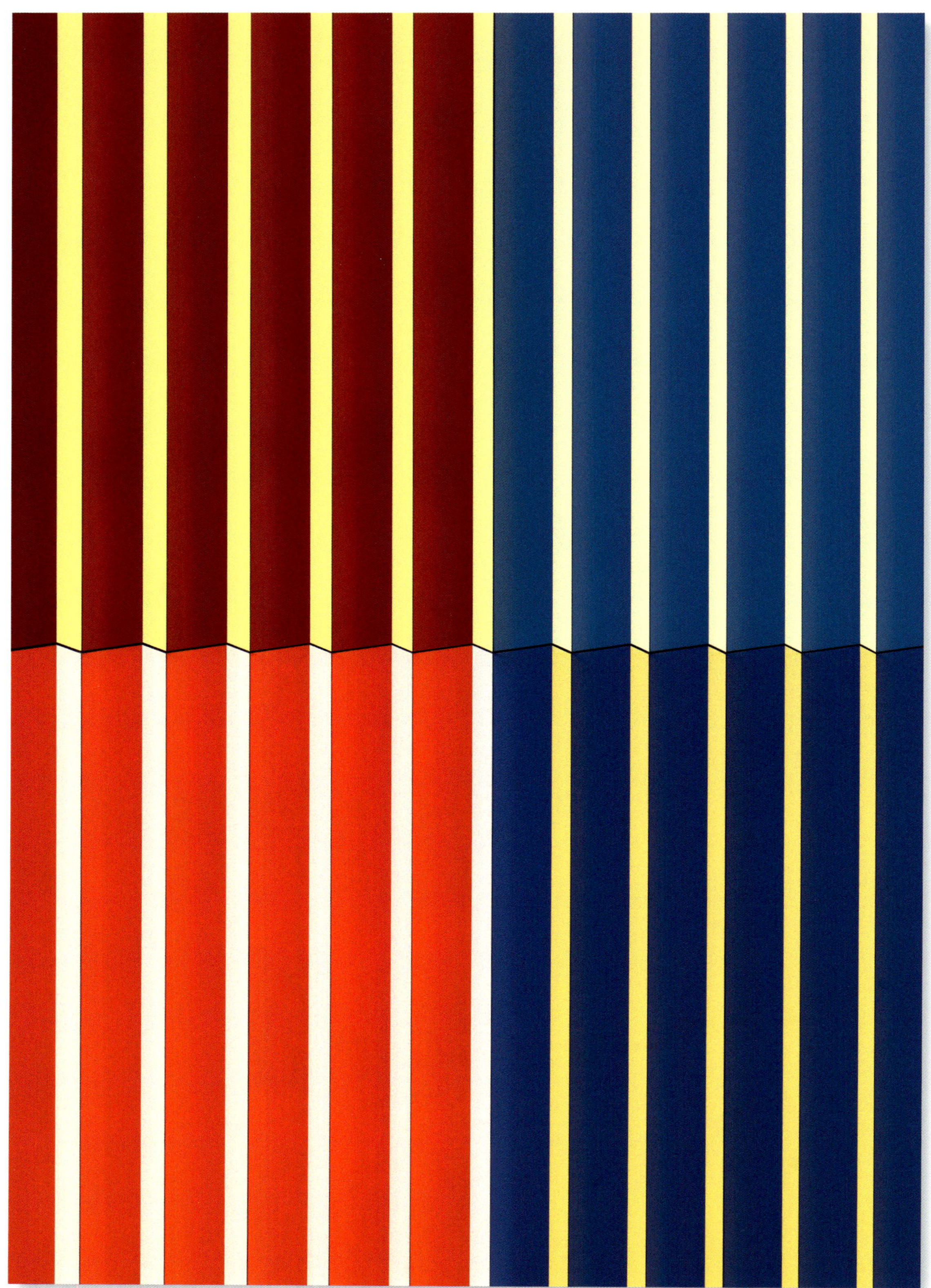

MALL
MUNICH
2013

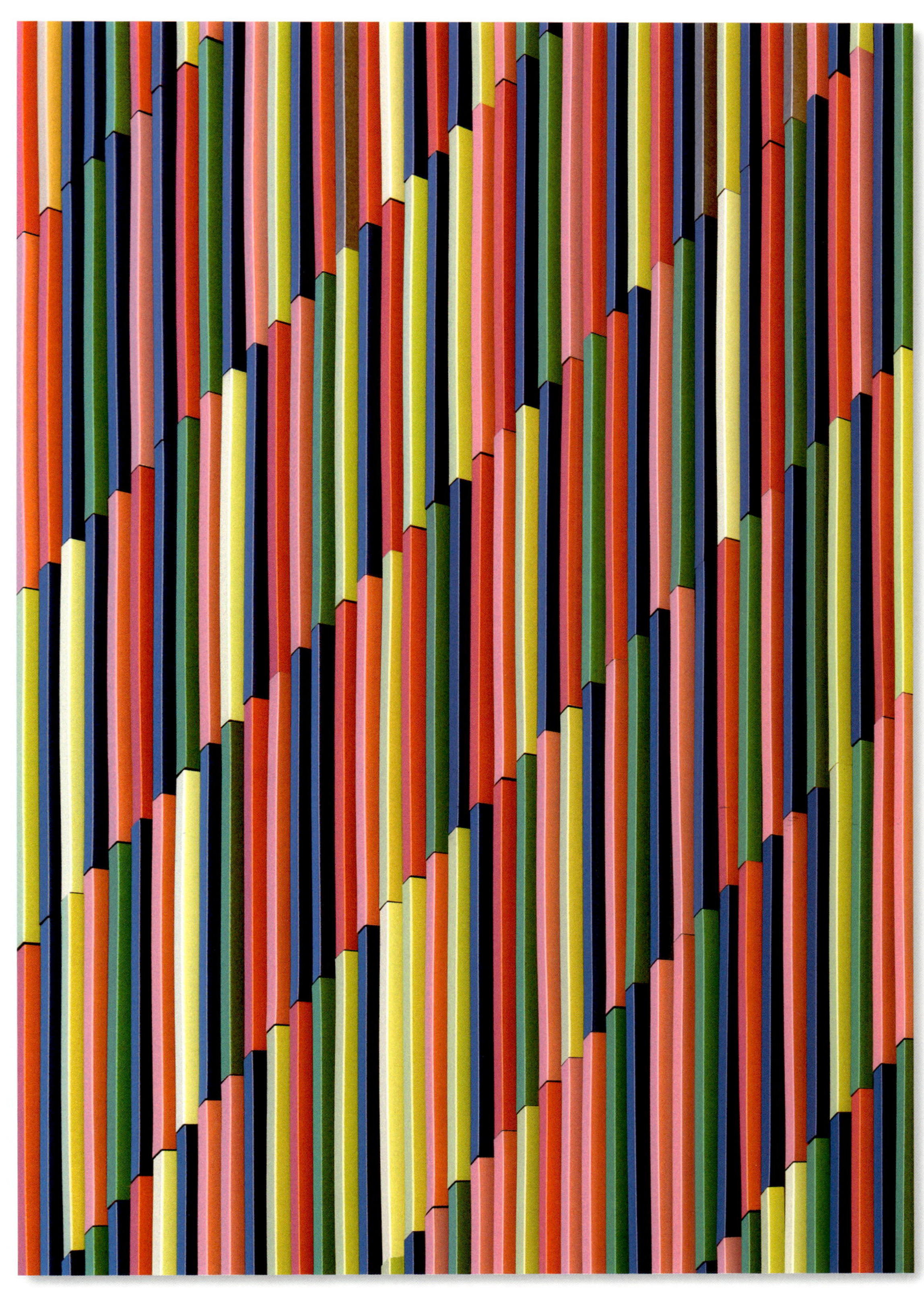

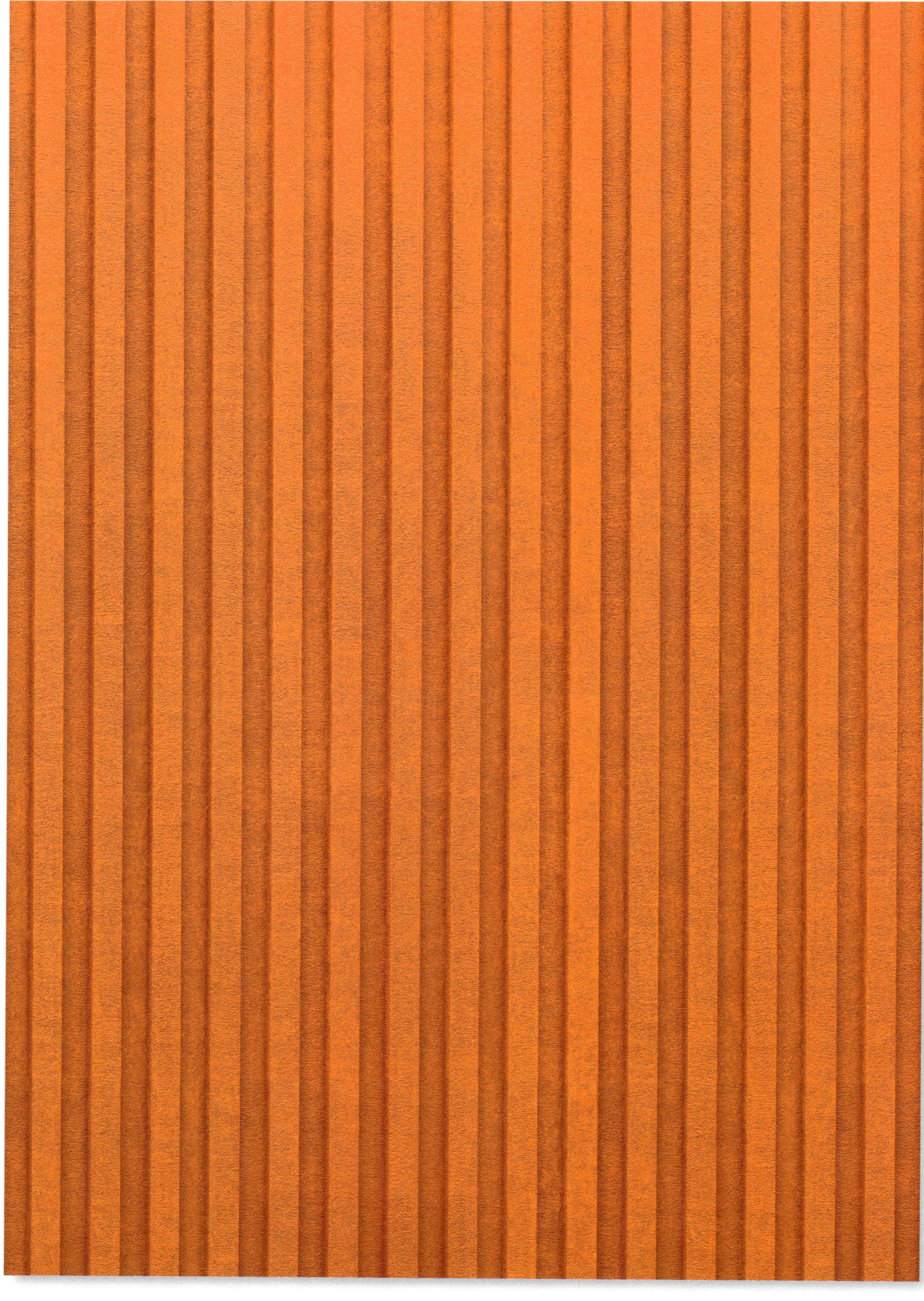

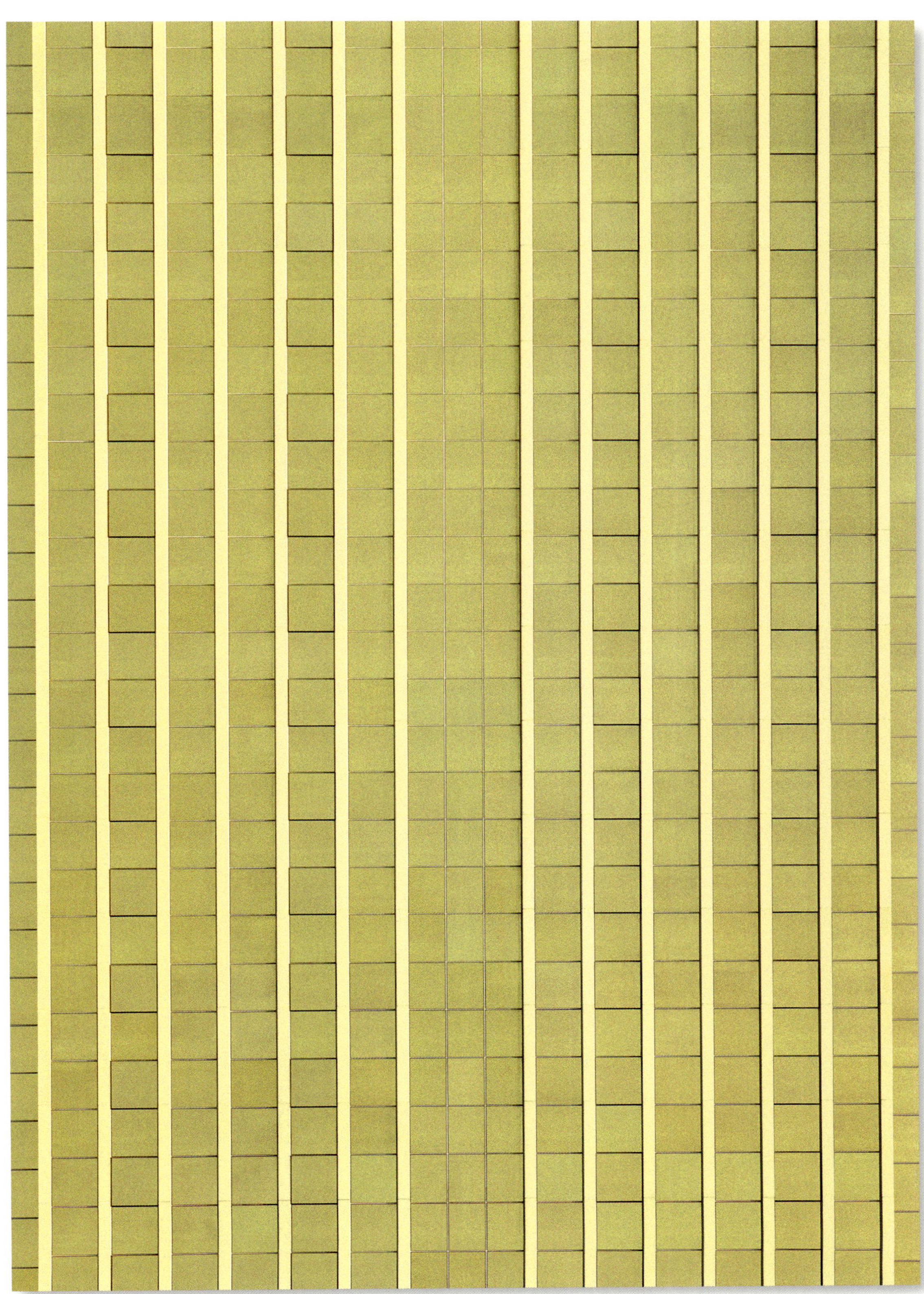

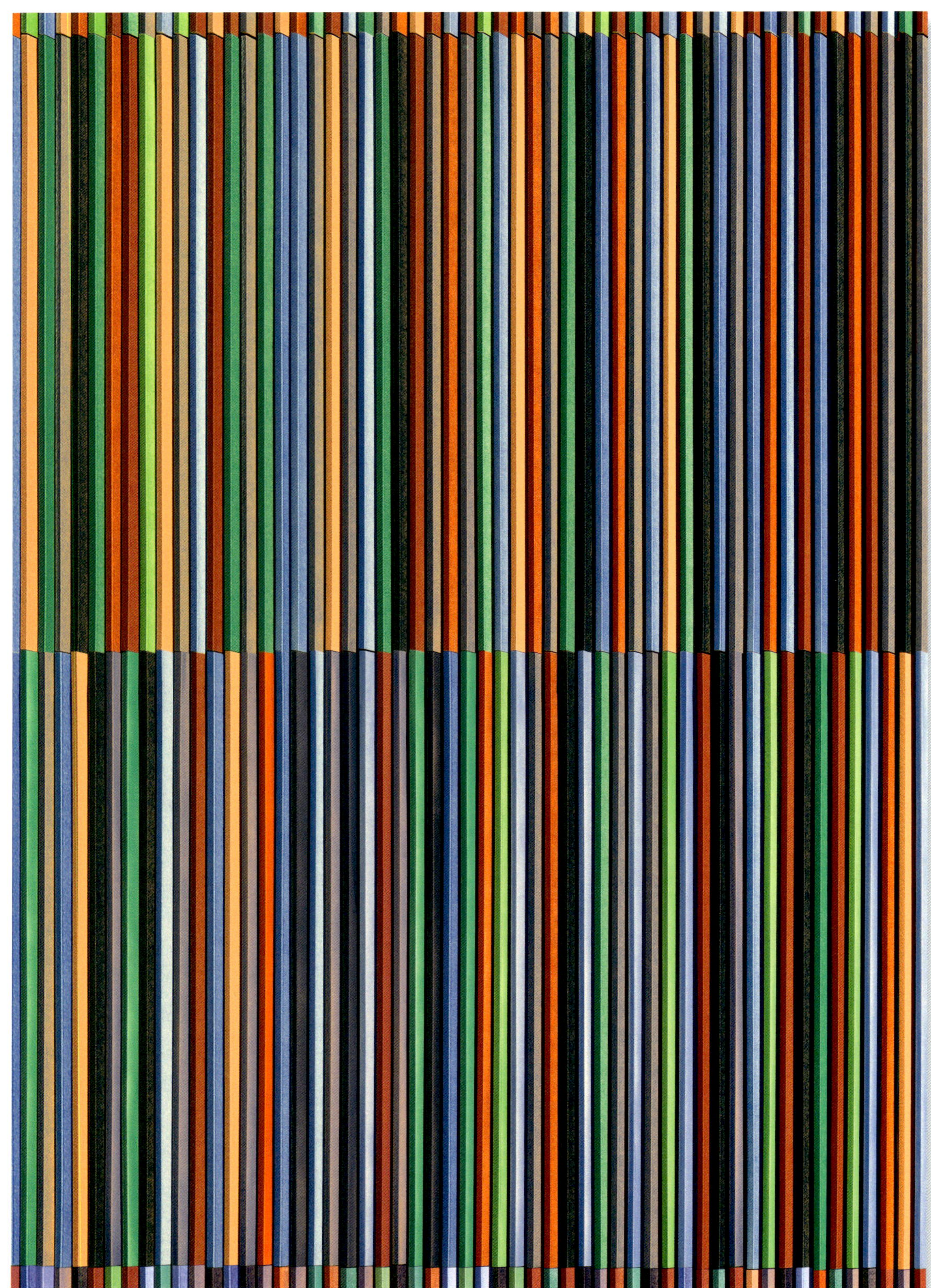

MUSEUM #2
MUNICH
2011

< LOS POETAS
MEXICO CITY
2011

< SHENNAN ROAD
SHENZHEN
1999

SOGO
KOBE
2014

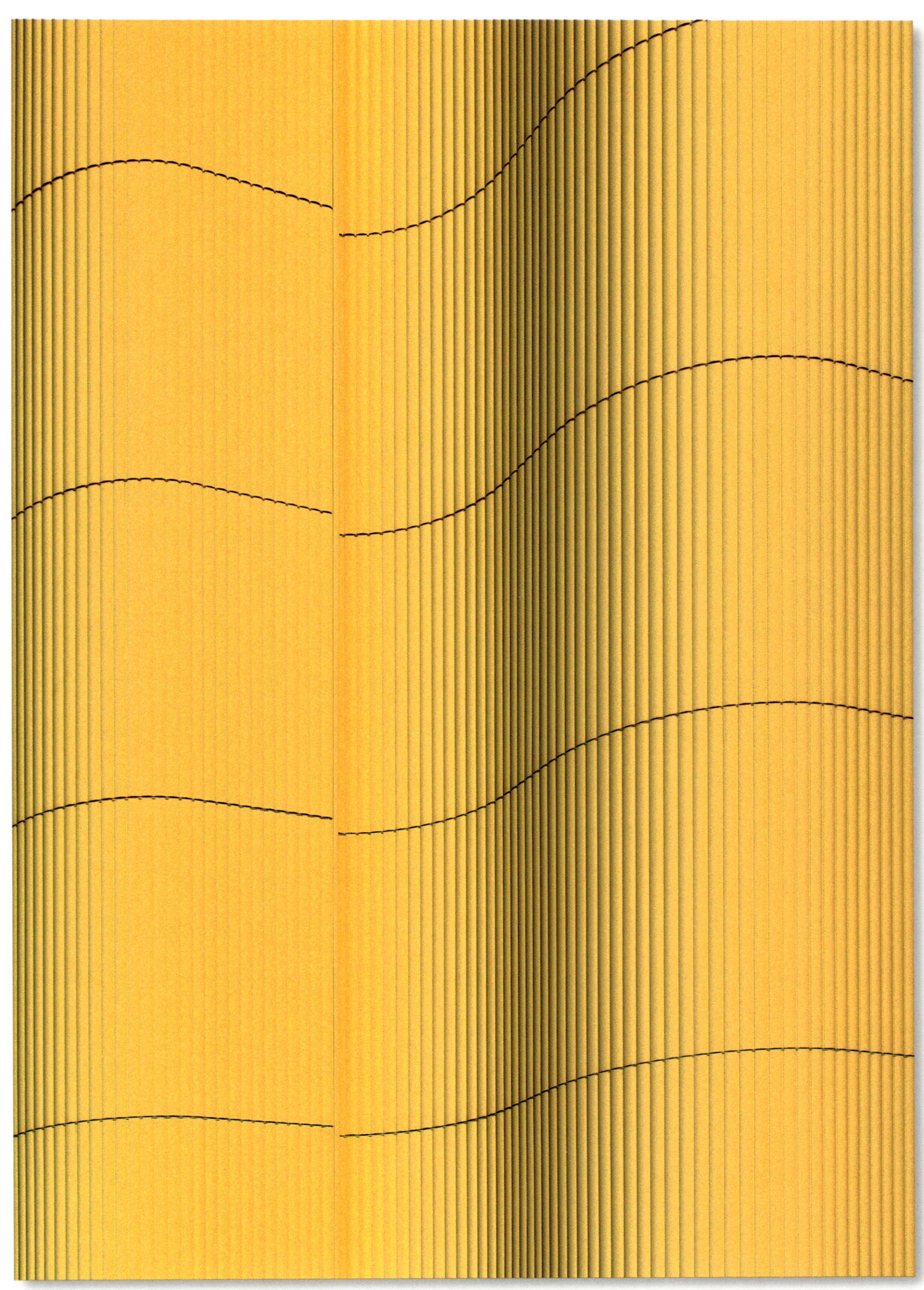

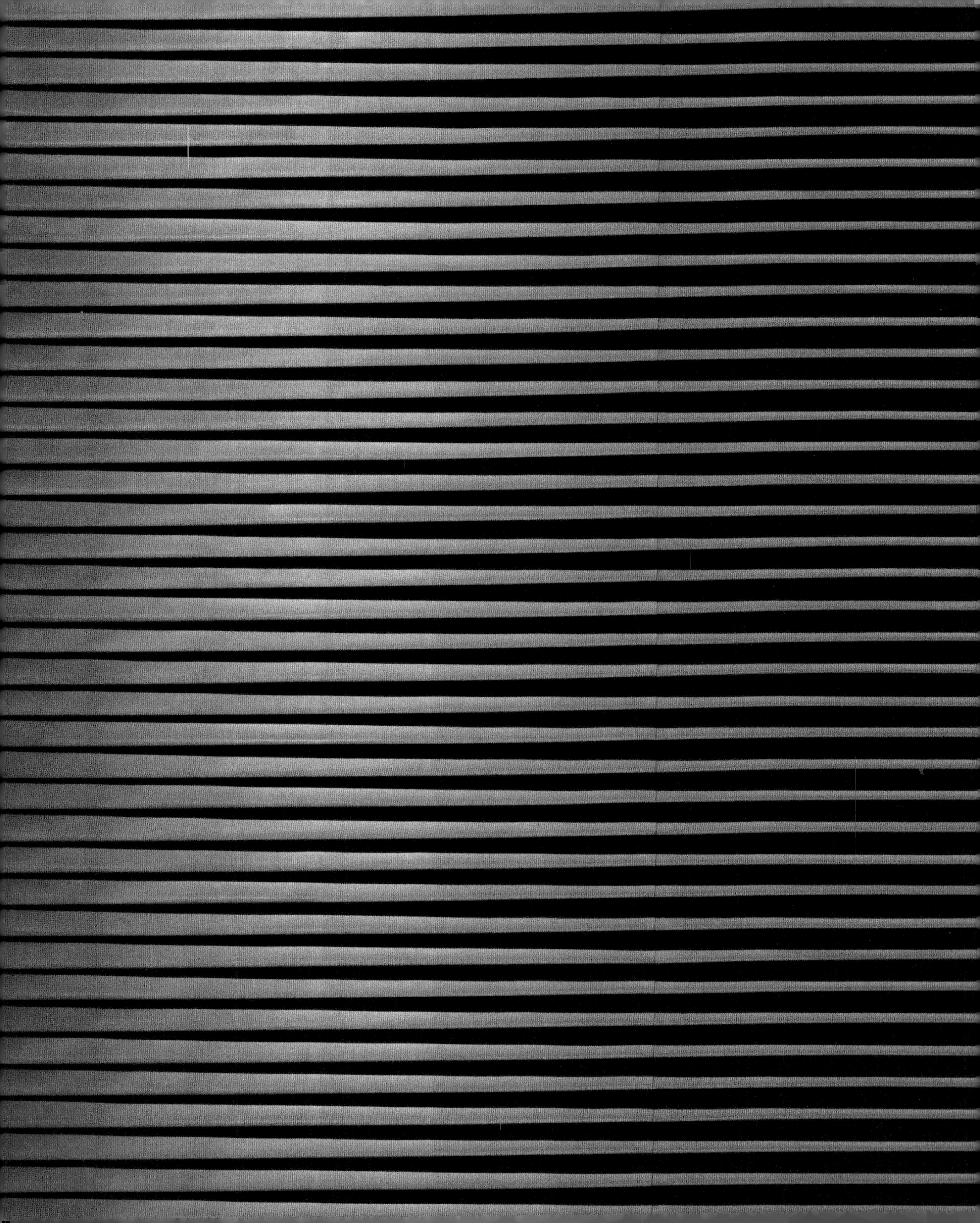

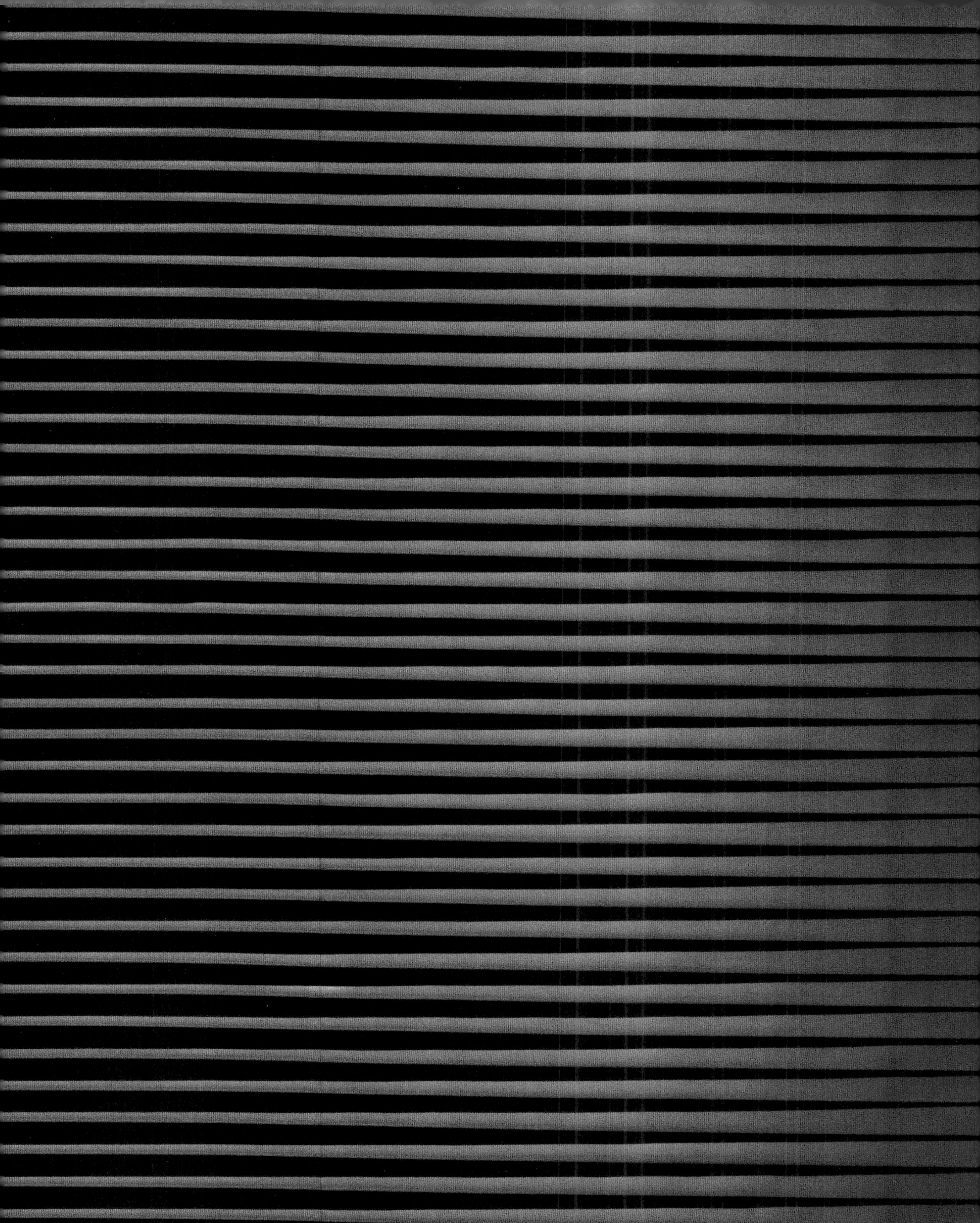

EIN VOKABULARIUM URBANER OBERFLÄCHEN

ROLAND FISCHERS UNIVERSELLE SYMBOLE EINER NEUEN ORDNUNG

Petra Giloy-Hirtz ist Kuratorin und Autorin. Zu ihren jüngsten Publikationen und Ausstellungen gehören *Julian Schnabel: Polaroids*, Fotomuseum Den Haag (2011), *David Lynch: The Factory Photographs*, The Photographers' Gallery, London (2014), *Dennis Hopper: The Lost Album*, Royal Academy of Arts, London (2014). Sie lebt in München.

PETRA GILOY-HIRTZ

IKONOGRAFIE DER METROPOLEN

Linien, Gitter, Rhomben, Kreis, Rechteck und Quadrat, Farbfelder in strenger Reduktion und hochästhetisch: ein Inventar der Formen und Strukturen. Bilder wie Malerei. Sie sind nicht erdacht und konstruiert von einem schöpferischen Geist, sondern gefunden in den Städten und festgehalten mit einer Kamera. Es sind Porträts, die Gesichter des Urbanen, die Oberflächen der Gebäude. Seit den Neunzigerjahren fotografiert Roland Fischer die Fassaden von Banken, Unternehmen und Museen in den Metropolen der Welt. Die Bilder, eine Serie von etwa hundert Fassaden, fügen sich zu einem Kompendium der zeitgenössischen Architektur, zu einer visuellen Grammatik abstrakter Formen. Die Schauseite neuer Urbanität wird in Bilder transformiert, abstrakten Gemälden ähnlich, voller kunsthistorischer Referenzen. Sie erzählen von der Veränderung der Welt, von einem neuen globalen Paradigma, wo Geld, Technologie, Menschen und Güter nationale Grenzen mühelos überwinden. Ihre ästhetische Erscheinung gründet nicht im jeweiligen soziokulturellen Kontext. Die Ikonografie der Zeichen ist unabhängig von der Geografie, ob in Peking, Tokio, Schanghai, New York, Hongkong, Melbourne, Osaka, Boston, Brasilia, Los Angeles, Paris, São Paulo, Singapur, Dallas, Madrid, Washington, Mexiko-Stadt, Chicago, Toronto, Chongqing oder Montreal, das »Bildrepertoire einer Stadt«, ihre »Repräsentationskategorien«[1] sind übernational homogenisiert.

1 Richard Sennett, Fleisch und Stein. Der Körper und die Stadt in der westlichen Zivilisation, Frankfurt a. M. 1997, S. 451.

FOTOGRAFIE NACH DEM DOKUMENTARISCHEN REALISMUS

Roland Fischers Interesse an Architektur unterscheidet sich konzeptuell nicht von seinem Interesse am menschlichen Antlitz. Wie seine *Nonnen und Mönche*, die *Los Angeles Portraits* und die *Collective Portraits* von *Soldiers, Workers, Farmers* und *Students* sowie den *Pilgrims* nicht Porträts im klassischen Sinne sind, so stehen auch die *Fassaden* nicht in der Tradition einer Dokumentarfotografie. Immer hat Fischer »mehr das Bild[,] weniger das Abbild« interessiert, die Abstraktion.[2] So überlagert er den Innenraum eines Gebäudes und dessen äußere Wände, wie in der Serie der Kathedralen, um in der Überblendung die Hülle zu durchdringen und den Blick freizugeben. Oder er verschränkt simultan in kubistischer Manier von unterschiedlichen Standpunkten aus fotografierte Ansichten von profanen modernen Räumen und Strukturen wie in der Serie *New Architectures*. Sein Tableau aus 1050 individuellen Aufnahmen von Pilgern in Santiago de Compostela wirkt aus der Ferne abstrakt wie das Muster einer Fassade.

2 Roland Fischer, Interview mit Agar Ledo, in: Roland Fischer, Camino (Ausst.-Kat. Centro Galego de Arte Contemporánea, Santiago de Compostela / Diözesanmuseum Freising), Santiago de Compostela 2003, S. 53.

Schon als er in Los Angeles lebte, hat Roland Fischer urbane Oberflächen fotografiert, aber erst in den Metropolen Chinas entstand aus dem Interesse an den Hochhausfassaden ein konzeptuelles Projekt: »Hier konnte ich zwei entscheidende Aspekte des Mediums Photographie auf den Punkt bringen: die Tatsache, dass jeder Pixel einer Photographie immer mit der Realität verbunden ist und die unabhängige Erscheinung einer Photographie als Bild ohne Referenz. Von weitem könnte man diese Photos sozusagen als ›Color Field Paintings‹ wahrnehmen, auf der anderen Seite bleiben sie ein ›klassisches‹ Photo eines Objektes, das irgendwo besichtigt werden kann. Im Bild sind beide Aspekte verwoben, jedes Detail hat eine Doppelbedeutung.«[3] Die Fotografien, alle 180 mal 125 Zentimeter, C-Prints auf Acryl in technischer Perfektion, ohne Rahmen, das Licht reflektierend, wirken an der Wand wie Objekte.

3 Ebd., S. 54f.

GLOBALE MASKEN DES URBANEN

Was kann Fotografie? Welche Geschichten erzählt sie? Wie ist ihre Metaphorik lesbar? Welche Aussagen macht sie über den Zustand der Welt? Wenn Fischers Arbeit die Fassade zeigt, dann reduziert sie das Gebäude auf seine Oberfläche, auf Design, Dekor, Ornament. Sie präsentiert die Haut, die das Innere vor dem Öffentlichen schützt und verbirgt: Technik und Funktion und den Menschen. Sie zeigt nicht Behausungen, nicht das Humane. Ihr Spezifisches liegt in der absoluten Reduktion: weder Himmel noch Erde noch eine Nachbarschaft als Begrenzung und Hintergrund, vielmehr herausgelöst aus jeglichem Kontext und zum abstrakten Bild transformiert. Ein Ausschnitt jeweils, der für das Ganze steht, pars pro toto, jeder anders und trotzdem merkwürdig standardisiert, ob Industrieunternehmen, Bank, Hotel,

Universität, Gefängnis, Gewerkschaft, Rathaus oder Luxusladen. Die jeweilige Identität, Ort und Zeit ergeben sich allein aus dem Titel der Arbeit.

Jene »Fassaden« erscheinen als Kommentare zu Macht, zu Aneignung und Assimilierung. Mit dem Prozess der globalen Verteilung von Kapital und Technologie hat sich die Architektur der Stadt verändert. Und dies nicht allein durch einen »International Style«, der sich aus dem Wunsch, das Individuelle, das Lokale, Nationale zu überwinden, herausgebildet hat. Innenräume schotten sich ab: »Festungsarchitektur«[4] – hinter undurchdringlichen Fassaden.

4 Michael Hardt und Antonio Negri, Empire. Die neue Weltordnung, Frankfurt a. M. 2002, S. 321.

GEOMETRIE UND DEUTUNGSMUSTER

Eine Fülle von Bildern entfaltet Roland Fischer in seinen *Fassaden*-Fotografien, ein Kompendium der Symmetrien, Ähnlichkeiten und Differenzen. Woher kommen diese Formen, was verbirgt sich hinter ihnen? Ihre Verwandtschaft zur Malerei ist offenkundig: Allusionen zu Mondrian, Frank Stella, Peter Halley und zu vielen anderen. Die Ursprünge gleichwohl liegen weit vor der europäischen Moderne; unter verschiedenen zivilisatorischen Bedingungen und zu unterschiedlichen Zeiten gibt es geometrische Formen, oft sind es archaische Muster anderer Kulturen, die auf Spirituelles, Magisches, Symbolhaftes verweisen.[5] »Patterns that Connect«,[6] die weltweite Verknüpfung universaler Zeichen und Symbole weist auf

5 Jürgen Adam, Magiciennes de la laine. Marokkanische Teppiche und die Malerei des 20. Jahrhunderts (Ausst.-Kat. Pinakothek der Moderne, München), Stuttgart 2013, S. 16.

6 So der Titel der Untersuchung des amerikanischen Kunsthistorikers Carl Schuster: Patterns That Connect: Social Symbolism in Ancient & Tribal Art, New York 1996.

den Bilderschatz im kollektiven Gedächtnis, aus dem Kunst und Architektur schöpfen und den sie gleichermaßen vermehren.

Ordnung, Proportion, Balance waren im 20. Jahrhundert mit transzendentaler Bedeutung aufgeladen. An die Stelle jener »geometrischen Mystifizierung« sind heute andere Assoziationen getreten, etwa die Strukturhomologie von geometrischen Formen und einer Geometrisierung des sozialen Raumes. Inspiriert von den französischen Strukturalisten, zu deren Denken auch Roland Fischers Werk eine Nähe hat,[7] beschreibt der amerikanische Maler Peter Halley in seinem Essay *The Deployment of the Geometric* die Transformation der Landschaft, der Gesellschaft und des Denkens durch die Geometrie als Reglementierung. Seine eigene Malerei versteht er als Gemälde von Gefängnissen, Zellen und Mauern.[8] Geometrie als Referenz an eine vernetzte Welt. Und das Humane? Richard Sennett deutet in seiner Studie über den Körper und die Stadt, *Fleisch und Stein*, »Ordnung als das Fehlen von Kontakt«.[9]

So lagern hinter der Oberfläche von Roland Fischers *Fassaden* tiefere Schichten von Bedeutung. »Was Bilder von uns begehren« jedenfalls, ist unsere Aufmerksamkeit, unseren »Schautrieb«.[10] So wünscht man dem Betrachter, mit ästhetischem Vergnügen und im Erstaunen über die faszinierende visuelle Vielfalt durch das Buch zu flanieren.

7 »Roland Fischers photographisches Werk und der Strukturalismus« heißt die Untersuchung von Roland Augustin, in: Roland Fischer, New Photography 1984–2012 (Ausst.-Kat. Saarland Museum, Saarbrücken), Heidelberg 2012, S. 19–23.

8 Peter Halley, The Deployment of the Geometric, in: ders., Collected Essays, 1981–1987, Zürich u. a. 1988, S. 127–130.

9 Sennett 1997 (wie Anm. 1), S. 28.

10 W. J. T. Mitchell, Das Leben der Bilder. Eine Theorie der visuellen Kultur, München 2008, S. 8, 97f.

ROLAND FISCHERS FASSADEN: DIE GESCHLOSSENE SPRACHE DER ARCHITEKTUR

Lyle Rexer ist Kritiker, Kurator und Dozent. Der Autor zahlreicher Bücher und Fachbeiträge über Fotografie ist Core Faculty Member der School of Visual Arts in New York. Er lebt und arbeitet in Brooklyn.

Um die Kluft, die zwischen dem Menschlichen und dem Göttlichen liegt, so recht zu ermessen, braucht man nur die zittrigen Zeichen, die meine hinfällige Hand auf den Einband eines Buches krakelt, mit den organischen Lettern im Inneren zu vergleichen: gestochen, feingeschwungen, tiefschwarz, unnachahmlich symmetrisch.

— Jorge Luis Borges, *Die Bibliothek von Babel*

dt. Übers. Karl August Horst

In New York gab es vor vielen Jahren ein Restaurant, dessen Wände große Schwarz-Weiß-Luftaufnahmen von wichtigen Metropolen dieser Welt bedeckten: New York, Paris, London, Buenos Aires, Rio de Janeiro, Mexiko-Stadt, Caracas, Chicago, Los Angeles. Bei jedem Besuch betrachtete ich diese Topografie urbanen Wachstums mit starker Faszination und zunehmender Hoffnungslosigkeit. Die Städte weckten in mir ein Gefühl von Pracht, doch auch die eher unangenehme Erkenntnis, dass sie einander alle ähnelten, denn die Formen der Erfahrung, die sie verkörperten, waren grundsätzlich gleichartig und gestaltet durch identische Entwicklungen. Abweichungen, die früher durch Sprache, Klima, Geschichte und physikalische Geografie befördert wurden, ließen sie nicht mehr zu. Die moderne Stadt war der Verkünder des weltweiten Kapitalismus mit vereinheitlichten Wünschen und marginalisierten Unterschieden. Dieses Phänomen hat in einer Welt, der ihr eigenes Wachstum zur Last wird, noch zugenommen. Das Überleben des Menschen ist in einem anderen

System nicht mehr vorstellbar, wahrscheinlich aber auch nicht mehr in diesem. Hongkong, Beijing, Guangzhou oder Dubai ergänzen die Weltkarte der modernen Architektur, allerdings ohne ihre Ursprungsmythen. Die heutige Stadt entwickelt sich nicht, wie die Mitglieder des Bauhauses sie sich vorstellten, als eine die soziale Erneuerung vorwegnehmende Herausforderung an die Gestaltung, sondern als der Ausdruck ökonomischer Gesetze, Verhältnisse und technologischer Anwendungen. Das Ergebnis ist an allen Orten dasselbe: anstelle einer als Gesamtheit gestalteten Stadt wie Chandigarh oder Brasilia der unternehmerische Auswuchs von Schanghai, eine ganz andere Form der Rationalisierung, das zufällige Ergebnis lokaler, aber universell einheitlicher Entscheidungen. In der Praxis hat sich die zeitgenössische Stadt wegen der für die progressive Vorstellungskraft unvorstellbaren ökonomischen Unterschiede formal als weniger einförmig erwiesen: Luanda, Mexiko-Stadt, New Orleans, die grenzüberschreitende Megalopolis der Bucht von Benin.

Die Architektur ist beim Aufbau eines globalen bildlichen Esperanto als der formgebende Prozess dieser hyperrationalisierten, aber nicht zielgerichteten Verstädterung miteinbezogen. In dieser Schilderung erscheinen die Anstrengungen einzelner Architekten, so radikal ihre Meinungsverschiedenheiten, so visionär ihre Beiträge auch sein mögen, als an den Rand gedrängte Events, die lediglich die Peripherie einer weitaus größeren Zustandsbeschreibung abstecken. Wie poetische Ausdrücke etwa die Grenze zwischen dem weitgehend funktionalen und dem eigenwilligen, nicht zweckgerichteten Sprachgebrauch markieren. Roland Fischer hat, wie schon im Genre der Porträtfotografie, die Analyse einer formalen »Sprache«, hier der modernen Architektur, zu einem Endpunkt geführt.

Geschichtlich betrachtet wuchs die Fotografie mit dem Erscheinen der modernen Architektur auf, die nichts anderes bedeutet, als herrschaftliche Stile – und einheimische Methoden – durch reproduzierbare, skalierbare, dem Zusammenhang entrissene, industrielle Formate zu ersetzen. Die anfängliche Aufgabe der Fotografie war eine doppelte und bestand darin, an die ausgemusterte Vergangenheit zu erinnern und sie zu archivieren sowie die Formen und Tätigkeiten der entstehenden großstädtischen Welt zu fördern, wenn nicht gar zu feiern. Nur die Fotografie war in der Lage, beide Aufgaben zu meistern. In erster Linie betonte die Reduktion durch Zweidimensionalität und Schwarz-Weiß-Tönung die formalen Regelmäßigkeiten und Wiederholungen der neuen Formen. Zweitens sicherte die Reproduzierbarkeit die Entstehung von Archiven zu vielfachen Verwaltungszwecken. Schließlich betonte – oder verstärkte – ihre monokulare Perspektive, wie bereits viele Kritiker hervorgehoben haben, die rationalisierte Geometrie utilitaristischer Kontrolle, die noch effizientere und produktivere städtische Umgebungen ermöglichten.

Anfang der 1970er-Jahre haben Fotografen, Künstler, Theoretiker und selbst die Architekten begonnen, diese Entwicklungen zu untersuchen und auszuwerten sowie anspruchsvoller bildlicher und sprachlicher Kritik zu unterziehen. Von Bernd und Hilla Bechers formalen Katalogen vergangener Industriearchitektur über die New Topographics der US-amerikanischen Fotografen, von der Sachlichkeit und dem großformatige Detail in der Arbeit der Düsseldorfer Kunstakademie-Absolventen bis hin zu den digitalen Dystopien von Beate Gütschow haben eine Menge zeitgenössischer Arbeiten die Verbindung zwischen formaler Sprache und Architektur als ideologisches Instrument beleuchtet. Fischer hat diese Beziehung an der Basis erforscht.

Seine Vorgehensweise ist zwar einfach, die Konsequenzen sind allerdings weitreichend. Die grundlegende Frage, die Fischer zu stellen scheint, ist: In welcher Hinsicht bilden die generalisierten Architekturformen, denen man immer wieder in städtischer Umgebung auf der ganzen Welt begegnet, eine Sprache, das heißt, ein Kommunikationssystem, das nach Regeln funktioniert, denen die Nutzer unterworfen sind, aber unbelastet von der Spezifizierung durch Inhalt oder Situation und nicht dem Eingriff einzelner Agenten ausgesetzt ist? Um diese Untersuchung auszuarbeiten, hat Fischer grundlegende Einsichten des Surrealismus – und amerikanischer Fotografen der 1920er- bis 1960er-Jahre – nachvollzogen, nämlich die Dekontextualisierung des Gegenstandes, indem der Bildausschnitt zur Betonung formaler Eigenschaften und zur Reduzierung anekdotenhafter Informationen radikal beschnitten wurde. Fotografen wie Aaron Siskind oder Minor White dürften eine solche Herangehensweise verfolgt haben, um dem Betrachter psychologische, linguistisch-dichterische und geistige Assoziationen zu eröffnen. Das Foto dürfte damit eine Brücke zwischen den Subjektivitäten bauen, eine Brücke, deren Verkehr durch den Künstler initiiert und weitgehend kontrolliert würde.

Im Gegensatz dazu verstärkt Fischer grafische Form und Muster mit dem Ziel, Assoziationen zu verringern. Allerdings versucht er nicht, ähnlich dem Werk Gottfried Jägers – und dem vieler jüngerer Fotografen –, eine zeichenlose, nichtdenotative konkrete Fotografie zu gestalten. Es interessiert ihn nicht, seine Bilder zu veredeln oder zu einem vorsprachlichen, vorreferenziellen Garten Eden zurückzukehren. Stattdessen versucht er, die ungeteilte Aufmerksamkeit auf das bildliche Sujet zu lenken. Nur unbedeutende Spuren der Zeitlichkeit erscheinen in den verräterischen Schatten, die manche Fassaden kennzeichnen, und der Hinweis auf die künstlerische Subjektivität ist auf wenige, schwach gewinkelte Standpunkte begrenzt. Ansonsten sind die Standpunkte gerade und streng flach, isoliert von jeder Hintergrundinformation. Weil Muster vorherrschen, ist es unmöglich, die Fassaden real, historisch oder geografisch zu lokalisieren. Sie haben keine

Urheber, Epochen oder Schauplätze – außer die durch Titel angezeigten. Fischers Gegenstand ist nicht das Gebäude oder die Bauweise, sondern nur die Oberfläche und auch nicht die ganze Oberfläche, sondern nur ein Teil. Genug, um ihn als ein Motiv auszuweisen. Die Bilder geben keine Hinweise auf die Größe der Fassaden, und die Fotos ihrerseits verschleiern die Originalgröße durch die Veränderlichkeit ihrer Präsentation: Sie können buchstäblich in jeder Größe abgebildet werden – wie auch für die Gebäude jede Größe möglich und denkbar ist. Von (fast) jeder Verantwortung, ihre Sujets auszuweisen, befreit, bewegen sich die Bilder nahe der reinen Abstraktion und zeigen an Phoneme erinnernde Elemente in Systemen organisierter Wiederholung.

Der Weg, den Fischer im Bereich des Porträts verfolgt hat, beleuchtet auch die Ziele bei seinen Fassaden. In diesem Genre hat er sowohl mit großformatigen Einzelbildern wie auch mit *Kollektivporträts* (*Collective Portraits*) genannten riesigen Rastern oder Gittern mit regelmäßigen Reihen experimentiert. Wichtiger allerdings war die fotografische Behandlung der Sujets selbst. Indem er für eine Serie der 1980er-Jahre Mönche und Nonnen auswählte, ließ er die Diskussion über die Idee wieder aufflammen, das fotografische Porträt könnte Zugang zum Innenleben des Modells verschaffen oder Schlussfolgerungen über die Dinge hinter der Oberfläche auf der anderen Seite des Bildes erlauben. Die Fotografien hatten, besonders auf Kritiker wie den Amerikaner Michael Fried, eine große Wirkung, gerade weil sie die Entscheidung der Frage über den einen oder den anderen Weg verweigerten. Die Gesichter der ältesten Personen in ihren religiösen Habiten zeigen Altersspuren, die Topografie unübersehbarer Erfahrung, doch kein Lebensereignis oder Geisteszustand kann von den Bildoberflächen abgeleitet werden. Die Betrachter können über die individuellen Entscheidungen, die zum Eintritt in den jeweiligen Orden geführt haben, zwar spekulieren, doch bleiben ihre Leben Rätsel, versiegelt durch die Berufungen, und verbergen sich in aller Sichtbarkeit.

Die zehn Jahre später entstandenen Pool-Porträts, aufgenommen in Los Angeles und später in China, boten noch weit weniger von ihren Sujets an, weniger noch als die ausdruckslosen Porträts von Thomas Ruff und Thomas Struth. Fischer ließ die Modelle im Wasser bis zu den Schultern untertauchen und stellte sie frei von Emotion und jeglicher identifizierender Ausstattung dar. Sofern es eine der Intentionen der Düsseldorfer Schule gewesen ist, dem Sujet Autonomie von den Projektionen des Fotografen – und des Publikums – zu gewähren, so ist Fischer über diese politische Position hinausgegangen, um ihr Aussehen von allen bereits existierenden Bedingungen der Wirklichkeit zu befreien. Besonders bei den chinesischen Pool-Porträts gibt es so wenig zu spekulieren, dass wir auf die Merkmale des Gesichts oder eher die Elemente der

Fazialität (»Gesichtlichkeit«) zurückgeworfen sind, fotografischer »Gesichtserscheinung«, bereits reduziert – zumindest für westliche Augen – durch die Auswahl junger, makelloser asiatischer Fassaden. Die geringfügigen Änderungen in der Pose scheinen so etwas wie ein Lexikon oder Inventar der Geisteshaltungen ohne entsprechende Emotionen. Fischers Porträts revidieren in ihrer Gesamtwirkung das Konzept des fotografischen Zeichens und der Wiederherstellung der Beziehung zwischen Betrachter und Bildgegenstand. Sie entwickeln einen Prozess des Bezeichnens, der die Komponenten dessen analysiert, was ursprünglich als Grundlage der Darstellung gegeben war. Julia Kristeva hat für die abstrakte Malerei ähnlich argumentiert. Anders gesagt thematisieren die Porträts Aspekte der Fotografie, die die Bildkonventionen unsichtbar gemacht hatten. Sie pflastern den Weg für die Strenge der Fassaden.

Auf Gebäude als Gegebenheiten kann man nur von ihren Fassaden her Rückschlüsse ziehen. Fassaden funktionieren wie Synekdochen, Teile, die auf das größere Ganze verweisen. Doch das größere Ganze ist jeweils nur eine Vervielfältigung von Gestaltungselementen und erfordert unsere Aufmerksamkeit nicht bloß als formales Objekt, sondern als Element der Kommunikation. Eine streng linguistische Herangehensweise ist hier weniger zielführend als eine semiotische. Was kommunizieren die Fassaden in diesen Fotografien und wie machen sie es?

Zuallererst zeigen sie einen Code, doch streng begrenzt. Sie zeigen industrielle Formen der Konstruktion, die auf präziser und konsequenter Wiederholung beruhen und diese Formen lassen sich auf viele kulturelle und geografische Schauplätze anwenden – Le Corbusiers »Modulor«. Die Muster sind individuell, doch in keinster Weise lokal oder regional bedingt oder vorgegeben. Eng mit der Idee der Wiederholung ist ihre nichtorganische, geometrische Struktur verbunden. Es gibt keine Möglichkeit, sie mithilfe von Hinweisen auf Handarbeit oder Spontaneität oder auch hier durch die Beiträge eines individuellen architektonischen Stils oder Materials (»das ist ein Gehry«, »das ist ein Hadid«) an einem menschlichen Maß zu messen. Auch erinnern sie nicht an die Elemente und Dekore eines mittelalterlich-christlichen oder muslimischen Stils, deren Ziel es war, das Auge in die Unendlichkeit zu führen. Sollten die heutigen Formen Unendlichkeit feiern, dann nur die Unendlichkeit in der heutigen Form eines sich verzweigenden Netzwerks finanzieller Institutionen, die in der Lage sind, solche Gebäude beinahe über Nacht zu errichten. Fischers Leistung ist, uns im Wesentlichen die Vorherrschaft und Kontinuität moderner Architekturpraxis zu zeigen. Gleichzeitig enthüllt die Reduktion der Fassaden auf ihre Gestaltungselemente eine Verwandtschaft mit den Methoden der konkreten Kunst diverser Positionen der letzten achtzig Jahre, vom Konstruktivismus eines Mondrian bis zu den *fisicromia* von

Carlos Cruz Diez, vom Neokonkretismus von Lygia Clark und der Op-Art von Bridget Riley bis zu den typografischen Gemälden von Tauba Auerbach. Unter anderem. Zusammengenommen scheinen sie bloße Illustrationen von Johannes Ittens Grundkurs in Design am Bauhaus. Auf sie alle findet sich in Fischers Bildern ein Widerhall.

Moderne Architektur – unternehmerisch-kommerzielle und öffentliche Architektur – hat diese Positionen absorbiert und erneuert, um ästhetische Elemente ohne geistige Ziele hervorzubringen. Sie umgrenzen einen bloß bildlichen Raum für die Ästhetik in der Architektur (und Gesellschaft). Die gemeinsame Fantasie der vorangegangenen Avantgarde-Bewegungen in der Kunst und im Design war der Glaube, dass Abstraktion, in welcher Form auch immer, ein Mittel und Maß der Befreiung ist. Der Glaube, dass ästhetische und künstlerische Bewegungen sich von ökonomischen Kräften trennen oder diese verändern und im Prozess der Bewusstseinserneuerung auch soziale Beziehungen erneuern könnten. Die Abkehr von der unerbittlichen klassengeprägten Wirklichkeit zugunsten der ästhetischen Theorie ist unaufhörlich kritisiert worden, doch Fischer betont, wie auch Gerhard Richter, wie die Welt auf der anderen Seite der Abstraktion aussieht. Mit Richters neuesten Streifen-»Gemälden« – und mit denen von Wade Guytons in den Vereinigten Staaten – kommt die ganze Geschichte der modernen Malerei und ihrer vielfältigen Ambitionen zu einem Ende in der Eliminierung jedweder Möglichkeit inhaltsverbundener Elemente. Dies sind große Designobjekte, die existieren, um eine spezifische wirtschaftliche Rolle zu übernehmen und physischen Raum inmitten von Kollektionen ähnlicher Objekte einzunehmen, ähnlich einer Währung, die in verschiedenen Farben gedruckt, aber in alten Bankgewölben gelagert und auf dieselbe alte Art ausgegeben wird.

So zeigen Fischers Fassaden auf vergleichbare Weise, dass das, was im Inneren des zeitgenössischen Bürogebäudes geschieht, keine einleuchtende Beziehung zu den an der Außenseite gezeigten Mustern hat, außer in dem Sinne, dass beide abstrakt sind. Erstere hinsichtlich der Datenverwaltung und der Kapitalströme, Letztere in Bezug auf den Design-»Fluss« durch die Kreisbahnen städtischen Wachstums und Verbrauchs. Dies hat, um es noch einmal zu betonen, nichts mit der Wahrnehmung des einzelnen Gebäudes als schön, anregend, nützlich oder in einem gewissen Sinn sogar transformativ zu tun. Die Fassaden-Serie – idealerweise sollte Fischer sie fast bis ins Unendliche fortsetzen – kommuniziert die Botschaft ihrer eigenen Ubiquität, Austauschbarkeit und Ersetzbarkeit. Sie bildet eine perfektionierte Sprache, unendlich vielfältig in ihrem Vokabular, doch in ihrer Syntax begrenzt. Sie reflektiert eine perfektionierte Gegenwart ohne Vergangenheit, das Ende von Geschichte ohne Apokalypse.

FAÇADES

Sheryl Conkelton ist Kuratorin, Autorin und Pädagogin. Sie lebt in Houston, Texas.

Roland Fischers Serie *Façades* zeigt äußerst abstrahierte Bilder von Gebäudefassaden. Sie sind auf geometrische Strukturen reduziert, von Zufallseinwirkungen wie Licht und Schatten befreit und zudem eng beschnitten, um jede genaue Bestimmung des Ortes oder anderer Verbindungen zum Gegenstand zu tilgen. So scheinen sie jeder Interpretation zu widerstehen. Die Sujets geben sich nur in den Titeln zu erkennen: *Suntory, Tokyo*; *Museum, Munich*; *nab, Melbourne*; *Uniqlo, Osaka*; *Wells Fargo, Dallas*; *Holiday Inn, São Paolo*; *Iglesias, Mexico City*; *High School, Utrecht* – eine Liste von Unternehmen und Institutionen aus allen Teilen der Welt. Auf dem vertrauten Terrain einer spezifizierbaren Sprache wird eine Landschaft globalisierter Kultur lesbar und die leeren, straffen Oberflächen erscheinen als mehrdeutige Referenzen an die abstrakte und verborgene Dynamik des Spätkapitalismus.

Der flache und sich wiederholende Charakter der *Façades*-Bilder lenkt die Aufmerksamkeit auf die »Fassaden« des Serientitels: Die Gestaltung dieser Gebäude profitiert von den heute alltäglichen Verallgemeinerungen der Abstraktion, um Modernität zu signalisieren, ohne zu provozieren und bar allen Inhalts. Sie verschleiern die Tätigkeit der dem Namen nach dahinterstehenden Institutionen. Die Fassaden erweisen sich in dieser Darstellung als glatte, undurchdringliche und nicht differenzierbare Oberflächen, die auf den Umlauf der undifferenzierten Wirtschaftsgüter des Kapitals verweisen. Als Beispiele für die neoliberale kapitalistische Produktion stehen sie für das Verdrängen des »Raums der Orte« durch den »Raum der Datenströme«.[1]

Diese Lesart ist passend und gewollt, doch das Erscheinungsbild dieser abstrakten Designs ermöglicht noch einen anderen Bezug auf frühere Abstraktionen, besonders der modernen Kunstrichtungen wie Konstruktivismus, Suprematismus und Neoplastizismus. Fischer verfolgt in diesem Projekt ein Interesse, das alle seine wichtigen fotografischen Serien beeinflusst hat: die Erkundung zu Wesen und Funktion der Kunst und – besonders in *Façades* – ihren Platz in der modernen Gesellschaft, in der sich die Wege, wie Fotografien – Bilder aller Art – entstehen, verteilt und empfangen werden, gründlich verändert haben.

Fischer nutzt eigentlich stets das großformatige Bild und typologische Gebäude, sein Werk teilt einige Merkmale mit Arbeiten von Thomas Struth, Andreas Gursky und Candida Höfer. Deren Werke verfügen über eine unübersehbar bildhafte Objektivität, die zwar zu genauer Prüfung einladen, sie zugleich aber behindern, indem sie die Betrachter an die Oberfläche binden und die Aufmerksamkeit von den vordergründigen Sujets auf die Anordnung konzeptioneller Vorgänge umlenken. In der Bewertung durch die Kritik sind diese Arbeiten schrittweise theoretisiert worden: als eine neue Art der Objektivität, antiästhetisch und desinteressiert; als medien-

1 Diese Formulierung stammt von Manuel Castells; siehe Manuel Castells, The Information Age: Economy, Society and Culture, Malden, MA 1996 (dt.: Das Informationszeitalter, 3 Bde., Opladen 2001–2003).

kritisches Spektakel; und als zum Zweck der Konfrontation entworfene *tableaux*; ihre Position wurde als ein Knotenpunkt der konzeptuellen Fotografie historisiert.

Fischers Projekte sind zwar in bildlicher wie in konzeptioneller Hinsicht durchaus ähnlich, unterscheiden sich von ihnen aber durch den Einsatz gewisser taktischer Gegensätze. In drei der Serien schuf er eine besondere und auffällige Mischung, indem er typologische Studien mit vergeistigt-entrückten Bildwelten kombinierte. Die Personen der *Nuns and Monks* (1984–1986) sind Menschen, die sich entschlossen haben, einem kontemplativen Orden beizutreten – deren strenger Glaube sich in ihrer Wahl spiegelt, einer religiösen Innerlichkeit zu folgen –, keine anonymen Einzelpersonen oder eine Auswahl von Typen. In *Los Angeles Portraits* (1989–1993) isoliert das umgebende Wasser zwar, ist aber nicht neutral oder ohne Wirkung; sein tiefes Blau und die auf Zufall beruhende Wirkung sorgen für doppelsinnige Tiefe und manchmal sanfte Bewegung, was den Bildern ein unerklärliches und ruhiges Leben verleiht. In *Chinese Pool Portraits* (2007) erscheint das blaue Wasser noch einmal, in dieser Serie aber wenden die meisten Frauen ihren Blick vom Betrachter ab, sind mit sich selbst beschäftigt oder von etwas außerhalb des Bildfeldes abgelenkt. Wenn sie hingegen gerade herausschauen, blicken sie ein wenig am Betrachter vorbei, konfrontieren ihn nicht, sondern sind einfach da. Statt der Demonstration von Desinteresse oder statt leerer Gesichter, die als Projektionsfläche dienen, zeigen sich die Bilder all dieser Serien in gewisser Weise sanft belebt, deuten auf oder verkörpern buchstäblich eine Art geisterfüllten oder metaphysischen Zustand.

Das während eines Aufenthalts in China entwickelte Projekt *Collective Portraits* (1998–2005) unterscheidet sich von diesen frühen Serien in Konzeption und Wirkung und scheint von seinem Ausgang her auf typologische und archivalische Anliegen zurückzuverweisen. Es zeigt verschiedene Typen von Menschen, kategorisiert durch ihre Arbeit oder ihre Tätigkeit: Studenten, Farmer, Soldaten, Pilger, Arbeiter. Hunderte von Einzelbildnissen sind in jeder Arbeit zu großen, in Rastern angeordneten Bildern zusammengefügt. Mit behutsamem Beschneiden, der Entfernung von Unterscheidungsmerkmalen, der strengen Anordnung und dem strengen Fokus auf Vergleichbarkeit, kommen sie am ehesten einer typologischen Manipulation gleich. Ihre schiere Zahl lässt an ein Archiv mit seinen gewaltigen Reserven für Meinungsmache und der Möglichkeit vielfacher Ausleg- und Auswertbarkeit denken. Jedoch erzeugen die *Collective Portraits* auch eine Wirkung, die über das hinausgehen, was man von einer Typologie erwartet, da Fischer sehr große Formate verwendet, um aufseiten des Betrachters eine physische Reaktion zu evozieren. Die Anordnungen mit der schlechterdings unmöglich zu quantifizierenden Menge beschwören eine erhabene Wirkung herauf, eine, die – weil sie einschüchtert – die Neutralität und das rein intellektuelle Vorgehen unterläuft.

In diesen unterschiedlichen Serien zielten Fischers Vorgehensweisen und das Arrangement von Elementen konzeptioneller Methoden darauf ab, Aspekte des Fotografischen zu erkunden – seine indexikale Stellung, seine Möglichkeit der Archivierung, seine serielle Ausdehnung. Doch er experimentierte auch mit dem Gefühl. Jede Serie enthält Elemente, die ein starkes Gefühl, wenn nicht sogar körperliche Erfahrung hervorrufen, ein Missklang also, der das ausschließlich begreifende Lesen oder Betrachten stört und die Funktion als Metapher möglicherweise auch ausschließt. Die Projekte bedienen sich der Vorstellung von Ästhetik, nicht als Ausdruck des Schönen, was die Bilder gleichwohl oft sind, sondern um ein allgemeines Konzept von der symbolischen Funktion der Kunst und dem Verleihen von Bedeutung auszuformulieren.

Die Serie *Façades* (1998–2014), mit der Fischer seine Erkundungen fortsetzt, bildet ebenfalls ein vielschichtiges Untersuchungsfeld ästhetischer Funktionen. Er nutzt den Bildgegenstand der modernen Abstraktion nicht einfach als ein erholsames Projekt, sondern als Brecht'sche Haltung, die eine produktive Wechselwirkung zwischen Vergangenheit und Zukunft eröffnet. Fischer nutzt die Abstraktion, ihr metaphorisches Potenzial und ihre historische Bedeutung, um einen vielfältigen Diskurs über die Möglichkeit der Kunstvermittlung innerhalb einer neoliberalen Kultur zu beginnen, die ihre Unabhängigkeit aufgekündigt hat. Die Abläufe dieses Kapitalismus hängen ab von der fortwährenden Abstraktion der Finanzwirtschaft, um Produkte und Arbeit durch finanzielle Spekulation zu ersetzen. *Façades* bezieht sich, wörtlich genommen, auf die Inanspruchnahme moderner Kunst als Deckmantel durch den neoliberalen Kapitalismus. Die Serie weist auch auf ihre eigene historisch komplexe Position innerhalb des Neoliberalismus hin, mit ihren vielfachen Verfahren der Abstraktion: dem formalen Rüstzeug moderner Kunst und ihrem spezifisch historischen Bezug auf transzendentale Bestrebungen; der Entfremdung durch Darstellung; der sozialen Prozedur, die Objekte umkodiert und in der die Fotografie dabei zu sehen ist, wie sie parallel zur Abstraktion des Finanzkapitals produziert.[2]

2 Eine weit nuanciertere Darstellung zur Entfaltung der Abstraktion stammt von Mark Godfrey; siehe Mark Godfrey, Response to George Baker: Photography and Abstraction, in: Alex Klein (Hg.), Words without Pictures (Ausst.-Kat. Los Angeles County Museum of Art, Los Angeles), New York 2010, S. 285–287.

Die *Façades*-Fotografien sind selbst offenkundig nicht als Abstraktionen zu bewerten. Sie sind durchaus Abbildungen von Bildgegenständen, die aber sorgfältig gerahmt und so strukturiert wurden, dass sie nicht-darstellend erscheinen. Damit verweist Fischer auf das Wesen der Fotografie als abstrakten Vorgang, die Verwandlung des dreidimensionalen Sujets in ein zweidimensionales Bild. Diesen Effekt verstärkt er durch eine nur geringe oder fast vollständige Elimination von Tiefe; das camoufliert das eigentliche Subjekt und betont seine Flächigkeit. Viele der abgebildeten Oberflächen sind nahezu identisch mit ihrer materiellen Bildfläche, was bezüglich ihrer

Beschaffenheit und Bedeutung als wirkliche Objekte Verwirrung und Furcht auslöst, eine Wirkung, die Fischer auch in der verwandten Serie *Groups of Five* (1998–2014) nutzt.[3] Das große Format der *Façades*-Bilder erlaubt der abstrakten Musterung, sich wie ein bildliches Feld zusammenzufinden und auch, ironischerweise, das Spektakuläre seiner Größe zu entschärfen. Stattdessen erzeugt der sich wiederholende Rhythmus der geometrischen Muster kompositorische Bewegung und erzeugt eher ein bildliches Spiel als Information.

Abstraktion ist eine Vorgehensweise in den *Façades*, aber auch ein Thema, das in Fischers Konstruktionen hinterfragt wird. Die verflachten und reduzierten Bilder beziehen sich auf den historischen Zeitpunkt der frühen modernen Kunst. Die Fortentwicklung der nichtgegenständlichen Kunst durch moderne Künstler stand unter dem Einfluss vieler nichtmaterialistischer und geistiger Lehren. Deren neue Bildsprache verweigerte die Nachahmung der sichtbaren Welt, sie sollte stattdessen wie ein Zeichensystem mit metaphorischen Möglichkeiten funktionieren, das Unaussprechliche erfassen und ein neues Erhabenes erzeugen. Fischers Mimikry abstrakter Motive und Kompositionen ist eine experimentelle Konstruktion der Referenz, eine die sein Projekt bewusst mit den Erfindungen früherer Künstler verbindet. Das lässt ein Interesse an ihren Beweggründen vermuten und er erinnert, indem er sie evoziert, an die Entstehung der Abstraktion.

3 Diese Serie (unvollendet, aber auf ungefähr zwanzig Werke insgesamt angelegt) besteht aus Gruppen von fünf Bildern, in der Größe kleiner als die *Façades*-Bilder. Es gibt wenig Hinweise auf Tiefe in jedem Bild und die Vergleiche, die aus ihrer seriellen Anordnung entstehen, erlauben es, dass sie leicht als geometrische Abstraktionen gelesen werden, was ferner die Verwandtschaft zu gemalter Abstraktion betont.

Fischer stellte in einem Kommentar zu *New Architectures*, ein Projekt, das ihn während der Arbeit an *Façades* beschäftigte, fest, dass seine Bilder mit Vielfachbelichtungen Transformationen von »Räumen/Gebäuden in einer Art kubistischer Tradition« seien, »das Ergebnis ist – in gewisser Weise – wie eine ›dritte‹ Realität«.[4] Als Metapher gedeutet, können die mehrfachen Ansichten im Kubismus eine unentschlossene oder unwirkliche Position bedeuten, eine entrückte, geistige Perspektive. Fischer erzielt dies in seiner Serie *New Architectures* mit übereinanderliegenden Ebenen, die eine Referenz an die multiplen Perspektiven des Kubismus bilden. In *Façades* erreicht er mit der Einbeziehung grundverschiedener historischer Momente etwas anderes: die Abbildung von Abstraktion ist ein Weg, sich auf diese frühen modernen Bewegungen zu beziehen und auf die Werte hinzuweisen, die in ihrer idealen und idealistischen Form angelegt waren. Die *Façades*-Bilder provozieren gleichsam eine Kommunikation der institutionellen Bildgegenstände und neoliberalen Bedingungen mit denen ihrer modernen Gegenbilder; verschiedene Funktionen von Abstraktion erscheinen und verschwinden, weil Subjektivität sich verändert und Bedeutungen fortwährend wechseln.

Die Anspielung auf die Erfindung der Abstraktion schließt auch den Auslöser, die historisch vorangegangene Krise der Gegenständlichkeit, die grundlegende Veränderung in den Formen und die Erwartungen an die Aufgabe

4 Roland Fischer, Artist Statement, in: new architectures,2009, URL: <http://www.rolandfischer.com/wp-content/uploads/2012/10/statement-newarchs.pdf> (gelesen am 1. Juli 2014).

des Künstlers mit ein. Die Abstraktion begründete einen radikalen Bruch mit der traditionellen Darstellungsweise und eine Abkehr vom Bildlichen. Der Vorgang der Abstraktion erweiterte das begriffliche Repertoire der ästhetischen Formen; zusätzlich zu den Schilderungen der Wirklichkeiten und der Erklärung ihrer möglichen Bedeutungen lieferte die Kunst ihre eigene besondere Erfahrung und forderte intellektuelle und körperliche Reaktionen heraus. Kunst sollte ein ideales Reich werden, unabhängig von der Welt und in der Lage, besondere Erfahrungen bereitzustellen, die die Bedingungen der sozialen Existenz berühren und überschreiten konnten.

Die *Façades*-Serie beschäftigt sich mit einem vergleichbaren Krisenmoment und reflektiert die Sorge um Funktion und Status der Kunst als eine bedeutungsvolle Produktion. Der neoliberale Kapitalismus steht unter der Vorstellung vom Austausch der Märkte als der fundamentalen gesellschaftlichen Dynamik, ein Ethos, das alle Produktion leitet.[5] Die Kunst wird im Neoliberalismus mit der Integration unter Marktbedingungen ihres unabhängigen kritischen Status und ihrer historischen Kraft beraubt; Kunst ist eine kaum mehr von anderen zu unterscheidende Ware. Die digitalen Formen, die solch ein System ermöglichen, bilden ein Mediennetz, das die Differenzen und Grenzen zwischen Kunst, Dokumentation, Text, Fotografie, Video und Animation beseitigt. Losgelöst von zugrundeliegenden anfänglichen Intentionen, ist der Wert

5 Das ist drastisch reduziert von der Beschreibung des Neoliberalismus, die David Harvey entwickelte; siehe sein A Brief History of Neoliberalism, New York 2005 (dt.: Kleine Geschichte des Neoliberalismus, Zürich 2007).

eines jeden Objekts nicht mehr bestimmt durch die Absicht oder durch die Umstände in der realen oder praktischen Herstellung, sondern durch seine Verfügbarkeit und Nutzbarkeit zu jedem beliebigen Zeitpunkt: Dann verbreitet sich Kunst wie alle Bilder dies tun. Die Ästhetik wird zu einem besonderen Instrument degradiert und die Kunst ist nicht länger ein glaubwürdiges anderes.[6]

6 Nicholas Brown, The Work of Art in the Age of Its Real Subsumption under Capital, 2012, URL: <http://nonsite.org/editorial/the-work-of-art-in-the-age-of-its-real-subsumption-under-capital> (gelesen am 14. Juni 2014).

Fischer aktiviert mehrere Strategien, um diese Bedingungen zu erfassen. In den *Façades* finden sich etliche Auslassungen und Konfrontationen von Abstraktion, Schilderung oder Darstellung, spielerisch eingesetzt, um das Material und die theoretischen Vorgänge seines Sujets und Mediums zu verkomplizieren. Als digital produzierte Werke[7] sind die Fotografien sowohl postmediale Gegenstände als auch Abbilder der sie beherbergenden neoliberalen Institutionen. Fischer hat den fotografischen Prozess von Exzerpieren und Verflachung voll ausgeschöpft, um Kompositionen zu erzeugen, die seine Bilder noch abstrakter erscheinen lassen, schon das macht die Bezüge zur modernen Kunst noch offensichtlicher. Sie sind als Bilder nicht Abstraktionen, verweisen aber auf die Abstraktion als Bildgegenstand und beziehen die metaphorische Funktion wie auch die historische Bedeutung mit ein. Diese wurde entsprechend einiger theoretischer Darstellungen ausgelöst durch die Möglichkeit der Fotografie, die Realität genauer abzubilden als die realistische Malerei. Die *Façades*-Bilder beziehen sich auf diese Situation und

7 Die *Façades*-Bilder wurden bis 2007 mit analoger Kamera gemacht, als Fischer zu digitalen Kameras wechselte. Alle Abzüge sind Digital drucke, das heißt, gedruckt von digitalen bzw. digitalisierten Dateien .

führen gleichzeitig ihre eigene Situation vor, der Wechsel zwischen Abstraktion und Darstellung wird mithilfe feiner Variationen wiederholt. In einigen Bildern ist die Bildfläche mit der fotografierten Oberfläche identisch, was den Unterschied zwischen Bildgegenstand und dem Bild als Objekt auslöscht. In anderen Fällen wurde die Kamera leicht geneigt, was Tiefe und ein Gefühl von Räumlichkeit evoziert, was die Aufmerksamkeit wieder auf den Status der Bilder als Fotografien lenkt. Fischer nutzt die Fotografie, ein abstrahierendes Medium, um die Abstraktion darzustellen, und er erreicht, durch den Vorgang des Abbildens, ironischerweise auch das genaue Gegenteil.

Fischer macht auf einem anderen Weg Gebrauch von den gegensätzlichen Vorgängen der Abstraktion und Darstellung. Bilder generieren alle Möglichkeiten: Metonymie, Metapher; einen Moment und seine unendliche Ausdehnung; die Umstände ihrer eigenen Entstehung und einer parallelen Situation in der wirklichen Welt; die Bindung an ein Sujet oder einen Referenten ebenso wie die vollständige Loslösung. Sie funktionieren wie die Fassaden der Institutionen – sie verdecken, sie verschleiern, sie leiten um – und können diese Vorgänge gleichzeitig hinterfragen. Fotografien können dies als Bilder und stellen wohl auch eine materielle Verschiedenheit dar, als Objekte mit einer sich von anderen Medien unterscheidenden Oberflächenqualität sowie mit einer Aufnahmefähigkeit, materiell und konzeptionell, um andere

Sinneseindrücke als Malerei oder Sprache zu erzeugen. Fischer interessiert das Problem der Verschiedenheit von Fotografie, ihr »Entweder-und«-Potenzial; in jedes seiner Projekte hat er Widersprüche eingebaut, die diesen Gesichtspunkt von wahrem bzw. nacktem Leben nahelegen: der beständige Austausch von Gegensätzen, die »Kaskade von Antinomien«, die im Alltagsleben aufgelöst werden müssen oder denen zumindest Rechnung getragen werden muss.[8] Fischer erstellt einen greifbaren Sinn von Irreduzibilität und Zweideutigkeit und erweitert ihn durch die Komposition von *Façades* als einen steten Wechsel zwischen Darstellung und Abstraktion.

Diese Dynamiken und ihr Hin- und Herschieben zwischen vielen verschiedenen Deutungsmöglichkeiten flößen den *Façades* so etwas wie Lebendigkeit oder sogar Tätigkeit ein. Im Unterschied zu Fischers frühen Serien mit ihren Gegensatzschauern zwischen anscheinender Objektivität und den feinen Gesten in Richtung einer Symbolik, ist diese nun eine, die vielfältige Emotionen auslöst. *Façades* reicht über den eingebetteten Widerstand einer zur Schau gestellten neoliberalen Strategie hinaus und die Nutzung vielfältiger Nachforschungen legt eine dynamische Subjektivität nahe, eine, auf die in Bezügen zu moderner Abstraktion angespielt wird und die in ihrem Trend noch durch die Vielfalt von Bedeutungen verstärkt wird, die das *Façades*-Projekt vorschlägt.

8 Fischer zitierte diesen Satz des Filmkritikers Peter Wollen, der sich mit der besonderen Ästhetik des Films und seiner Möglichkeit, als Zeichensystem zu funktionieren, beschäftigt, in einem Interview mit der Autorin, 2. August 2014.

Eine Reihe von Theoretikern hat jüngst vorgeschlagen, dass die geeigneten Aktivitäten, die in der neoliberalen Herrschaft von affektiven Ökonomien »Bedeutung machen« erzeugen, eine neue Art von Subjektivität und individueller Kraft konstituieren. Fischers *Façades* beschäftigt diese theoretischen Positionen mit der Wiedereinführung der modernen Abstraktion und ihren Positionen, sie in das einfügend, was Frederic Jameson »die weniger greifbaren Abstraktionen des Bildes oder des Logos, die mit etwas von der Werte-Autonomie des heutigen Finanzkapitals arbeiten«, genannt hat.[9] Darunter sind die Möglichkeiten der Fotografie mitumschrieben, nicht nur auf der Ebene der Darstellung oder Information, sondern in der kritischen Position, die durch die wechselnden Vorgänge von symbolischer Bedeutung und wirklichem Affekt entstehen. Fischer konstruiert in den *Façades* eine produktive Unterhaltung zwischen historischen Momenten und eröffnet eine lebhafte und aktivierende Wechselwirkung zwischen Positionen und Subjektivitäten.

9 Frederic Jameson, The End of Temporality, in: Critical Inquiry 29, Nr. 4 (2003), S. 703.

ROLAND FISCHER

For more information see:
www.rolandfischer.com
—
Für weitere Informationen:
www.rolandfischer.com

BIOGRAPHY

Roland Fischer (b. 1958) lives in Munich and Beijing. His work has been shown in more than forty solo exhibitions at museums and other institutional venues throughout the world, such as the Musée d'Art Moderne de la Ville de Paris, the Pinakothek der Moderne in Munich, Centro Galego de Arte Contemporaneo (CGAC) in Santiago de Compostela, Saarlandmuseum in Saarbrücken, Museo Casal Solleric in Palma, The Photographers' Gallery in London, Kunstmuseum Nijmegen, Kunsthalle Bielefeld, the Goethe-Institut in Hong Kong, and many others. His works are included in major private and public collections.

BIOGRAFIE

Roland Fischer, geboren 1958, lebt in München und Peking. Sein Werk ist weltweit in über 40 Einzelausstellungen in Museen und Institutionen gezeigt worden, wie Musée d'Art Moderne de la Ville de Paris, Pinakothek der Moderne in München, Centro Galego de Arte Contemporaneo (CGAC) in Santiago de Compostela, Saarlandmuseum in Saarbrücken, Museo Casal Solleric in Palma, The Photographers' Gallery in London, Kunstmuseum Nijmegen, Kunsthalle Bielefeld, Goethe-Institut in Hongkong, und vielen anderen mehr. Seine Arbeiten sind in bedeutenden privaten und öffentlichen Sammlungen vertreten.

INDEX

Roland Fischer, *Façades*, 1998-2014
C-Print-Diasec, 180 × 125 cm
(71 × 49¼ inches)

Published by
Erschienen im
Hirmer Verlag GmbH
Nymphenburger Straße 84
80636 München
Germany

Editor
Herausgeber
Petra Giloy-Hirtz

German translation
Deutsche Übersetzung
Katrin Boskamp-Priever

English translation
Englische Übersetzung
Bram Opstelten

German copyediting / proofreading
Deutsches Lektorat / Korrektorat
Stefanie Adam

English copyediting / proofreading
Englisches Lektorat / Korrektorat
Philippa Hurd

Picture credits
Bildnachweis
Alle Werke von
All works by
Roland Fischer
© VG Bild-Kunst,
Bonn 2015

Hirmer project management
Projektmanagement Hirmer
Rainer Arnold

Design / typesetting
Gestaltung / Satz
Philippe Loup
www.loup.ch

Pre-press / repro
Lithografie
Reproline Mediateam GmbH

Printing / binding
Druck / Bindung
Printer Trento
Paper
Papier
GardaMatt Art
150 g/qm

Printed in Italy

Bibliographic information published by the Deutsche Nationalbibliothek. The Deutsche Nationalbibliothek lists this publication in the Deutsche Nationalbibliografie; detailed bibliographic data is available on the Internet at http://www.dnb.de.

Bibliografische Information der Deutschen Nationalbibliothek. Die Deutsche Nationalbibliothek verzeichnet diese Publikation in der Deutschen Nationalbibliografie; detaillierte bibliografische Daten sind im Internet über http://www.dnb.de abrufbar.

www.hirmerverlag.de
www.hirmerpublishers.com

ISBN 978-3-7774-2559-7